$4.50

P9-DGX-968

It took Enrico Caruso fifteen years

3

4

8

9

10

13

14

Enrico Caruso
Feb 27, 1873 - Birth

PHOTOGRAPHS IN THE ENDPAPERS

CARUSO

CARUSO

*The Man of Naples
and the Voice of Gold*

BY T. R. YBARRA

HARCOURT, BRACE AND COMPANY

NEW YORK

COPYRIGHT, 1953, BY T. R. YBARRA

first edition

23489

Library of Congress Catalog Card Number: 53-11458

DESIGNED BY ROBERT JOSEPHY

PRINTED IN THE UNITED STATES OF AMERICA

to *Penny*

CONTENTS

CARICATURES

ACKNOWLEDGMENTS

The author is indebted to Simon and Schuster, Inc. for permission to quote from *Enrico Caruso, His Life and Death* by Dorothy Caruso, copyright 1945. This book is invaluable for the light it throws on Caruso's private life, and no biography of Caruso can be complete without taking account of the colorful and intimate view it gives of the tenor.

The author and publishers are also grateful to Marziale Sisca for his kind permission to use ten caricatures from *Caricatures by Enrico Caruso*, published by *La Follia di New York*, 1951, copyright by Marziale Sisca. Mr. Sisca has also kindly granted permission for the use of the photograph of Caruso and his two sons. His assistance in the preparation of this volume is here gratefully acknowledged.

The author is further indebted to the following copyright holders: to Harper and Brothers for permission to quote from *My Thirty Years of Friendships* by Salvatore Cortesi (copyright 1927); to Bruno Zirato for permission to quote from *Enrico Caruso* by Pierre van Renssalaer Key and Bruno Zirato (copyright 1922); to George Allen and Unwin Ltd. for permission to quote from *Nights in London* by Thomas Burke (copyright 1918); to Houghton Mifflin Company for permission to quote from *Men, Women, and Tenors* by Frances Alda (copyright 1937).

Material from *How to Sing* by Enrico Caruso is used by permission of the copyright owner, John Church Company, Bryn Mawr, Pennsylvania; excerpts from "An Interview with Caruso" are reprinted by special permission of the

Etude music magazine, from January 1912 issue; the material reprinted from *Midway in My Song* by Lotte Lehmann (copyright 1938) is used by special permission of the publishers, the Bobbs-Merrill Company, Inc.; the material reprinted from *Memories of the Opera* by Giulio Gatti-Casazza (copyright 1941 by Leon Schaeffler) is used by special permission of the publishers, Charles Scribner's Sons.

All photographs, with the exception of that lent by Mr. Sisca, are included by courtesy of the Culver Service.

CARUSO

CHAPTER 1

UNHAILED, THE
CONQUERING HERO COMES

Half a century ago this year—on November 23, 1903, to be exact—Heinrich Conried, German-American manager of the Metropolitan Opera House in New York, was feeling some alarm. He was elated because, on that night, a new Italian tenor, engaged by him shortly before, was to sing at the Metropolitan for the first time; but he was alarmed by the thought that, after the manner of tenors, his new acquisition might suddenly develop stage fright at his debut, sing a lot of sour notes, and return to Italy with his tail between his legs.

There is a story in connection with the reason for that tenor's presence in New York in November 1903, which is vouched for as true by the late Gustav Kobbé, a noted musical pundit of the New York of the beginning of this century.

When Heinrich Conried was made ruler of the Met, he knew practically nothing about managing grand opera. His previous theatrical experience had been gained as manager of a well-known stock company which gave plays in German at New York's Irving Place Theater. As the story goes, one day he had said to himself: "Now, if I wanted to achieve a big success by importing a German actor into the United States, what would I do? I would ask Germans of assorted kinds who they considered the best actor in Germany. Well, now that I need an Italian tenor . . ."

The Met manager left his office in the opera house, walked to a bootblack stand run by an Italian, climbed into the bootblack chair, and, while the Italian was busily polishing his shoes, inquired: "Who is the best tenor in Italy?"

"Enrico Caruso," replied the bootblack.

Deciding that one bootblack's unsupported opinion could hardly be considered a sufficient reason for spending many thousands of dollars, Herr Conried resolved to try the other end of the local Italian social scale. So he got himself down to the region of Broadway and Spring Street, near the Bowery, had himself ushered into the office of the president of an Italian-American bank, and asked the bank's president: "Who is the best tenor in Italy?"

"Enrico Caruso."

Returning to the Metropolitan Opera House, Herr Conried instructed an assistant to find out whether there was anything in the files about one Enrico Caruso. The assistant discovered a contract, signed by Maurice Grau, Conried's predecessor, with a person of that name. Since Grau's death several years before, this contract had been completely forgotten by the Metropolitan management. It must be reinstated, decided Conried, remembering what the bootblack and bank president had said. So he returned to the Italian bank for further information concerning this Caruso person.

"You have come to the right place," said its president. "Our vice-president, Mr. Simonelli, knows Enrico Caruso well." So Conried was introduced to Simonelli, Simonelli cabled to Caruso, Caruso signed a new contract with the Met. And, early in November 1903, he landed in New York, installed himself in one of its big hotels, and got ready for his debut toward the end of the month with, no doubt, the same mixture of elation and alarm being felt by Herr Heinrich Conried.

Enrico Caruso made his debut on the evening of November 23, 1903, the opening night of the opera season. The opera was Verdi's *Rigoletto,* in which the new tenor played the profligate Duke of Mantua—a part in which many hundreds of thousands of Americans were to acclaim him in after years. With him in the cast that night were Marcella Sembrich as Gilda and Antonio Scotti as the Jester.

He did not succumb to stage fright. He disgorged no sour notes. On the contrary, he was a success. But the heavens did not fall. It was just a success. Possibly, says that veteran commentator on grand opera, Irving Kolodin, it was the least effective of Caruso's 607 appearances on the stage of the Metropolitan.

Perhaps a few people in the audience sat up, electrified, conscious that the sound of Caruso's voice in *"Questa o quella"* and *"La donna è mobile,"* carrying its golden part in the *"Bella figlia dell' amore"* quartet in the last act, was the sound of operatic history being made right there on the spot—the shape of operatic history coming into being before their eyes—the presage of an unborn future ringing in their ears. Perhaps.

But for almost everybody else at the Met that night it was just another brilliant opening of another season. As usual, the stars of the evening were not Caruso or any of his warbling comrades. They were the bosom-showing, bejeweled ladies of the Diamond and Golden Horseshoes, the white-shirt-fronted, black-tail-coated gentlemen sitting in their boxes, bored with everything except themselves—New York's social empresses and emperors, gazing in languid interest (that is, when they weren't talking animatedly with one another) at Enrico Caruso and the other figures on the stage. At the Metropolitan Opera House, on the night of November 23, 1903, a future-revealing gadget would have been a rewarding thing to have had about one.

But a look into the past would have been even more rewarding. Where had this new tenor come from? Through what highways or byways had he made the journey to the stage of the Metropolitan?

CHAPTER **2**

BELLA NAPOLI

There is a city in Italy better fitted than any other anywhere for being the birthplace of a singer. The blue waters fringing it, the blue skies which are its canopy, the magnificent volcano, plumed with smoke, rising over it, are song made visible, imperiously demanding songs in their honor; and its people, laughing, impudent, and carefree, are the living embodiment of song. That city is Naples. There—most appropriately—on the 27th of February 1873, occurred the birth of the most successful singer who ever sang. His parents, Marcellino and Anna Caruso, named him Enrico.

"We know which were the last notes sung by Enrico Caruso," says an Italian who wrote about him. "They were the notes at the end of the *romanza* from the opera *Martha*, sung by him to his wife and a visitor in Sorrento, a few days before his death. But what were his first notes? I know. They came at the beginning of his first wailing song as a newborn baby, and were uttered on the day of his birth on the second floor of the house where he was born."

That house was at No. 7 Via San Giovannello agli Otto Calli, in Naples, a rather imposing label for a street in a far from imposing quarter of that city of beauty and want, rags and sunshine. But Naples runs to names like that. Enrico's father was a mechanic employed at the factory (or, rather,

machine shop) of Signor Meuricoffre, a Swiss. When
Enrico was still a little boy, the elder Caruso was promoted
to the post of superintendent of the factory and his boss
turned over to the Caruso family a house which he owned
in the Sant' Anna alle Paludi section of the city. That
second house was Enrico's home for the rest of his boyhood and early youth.

Enrico was the eighteenth child of Marcellino and Anna.
Seventeen brothers and sisters, born before him, died in
infancy. After his birth, another little brother arrived, only
to die in babyhood, because—whispered the friends of
Marcellino and Anna, as they stood sadly around the little
coffin, "he lacked the strength to live." After that, another
sister, Assunta, and another brother, Giovanni, were born.
These last two, with Enrico, were the only ones, among
their parents' many children, who lived to maturity.
Twenty-odd years, twenty-one children, eighteen coffins.
That sums up the married life of Marcellino and Anna
Caruso.

Enrico adored his mother. With her he refrained from
the willfulness which soon began to be characteristic of
him when he was with others. Once this willfulness so
exasperated Marcellino, his father, who was much severer
with him than was Anna Caruso, that he ordered little
Enrico to go down on his knees and apologize to a singing
teacher to whom he had been disrespectful.

For his mother he was always ready to run errands, to do
chores around the house. One day, when he was old enough
to start thinking about clothes (in maturer years he was
to become a fastidious, though rather flamboyant, dresser),
he put on a shirt, fashioned by him out of paper, and
strutted peacock-like before her, just to see her smile.

When she died, he was brokenhearted; and, until his
own death more than thirty years afterward, he kept by

his bedside, wherever he happened to be—in de luxe steamship cabins, sumptuous hotel suites, magnificently furnished and decorated country villas or city residences—a
photograph of his mother. So clear did he make his un-
dying love for her, so frequently did he speak of it, that,
after his death, his American wife wrote for her book about
her married life with him this dedication:

"Because Enrico so deeply loved her I dedicate this book
to the memory of his mother."

Enrico had the sketchiest sort of schooling. His mother
did what she could to teach him; and a goodhearted
neighbor, Rosa Baretti, gave the boy lessons when Anna
Caruso was ill—which was often. From his earliest years
his voice attracted attention; and, while still a little boy,
he picked up singing lessons where and when he could.
His first regular singing was done at the little church of
San Giovannello, from which the street on which he was
born got its name. After a while, another neighbor, a
woman who was a friend of his mother, took a hand in
Enrico's musical education. Years later, when he was famous, says Eugenio Gara in his biography of Caruso,*
the great singer used to tell friends this story of how that
woman happened to become his singing teacher:

"At that time a doctor used to come often to see my
poor sick mother; and, as there was no money in the house,
she used to send him some mozzarella, fresh from the
country, as payment for his visits, which I used to take
to his house.

"As soon as I had left the stuff in the kitchen there,
I used to stop and listen outside the door of a room, from
which came the sounds of scales and trills, produced by a
sister of the doctor, who was a singing teacher. I liked very

---

* Eugenio Gara, *Caruso, Storia di un Emigrante*, Ruzzoli, Milan, 1947.

much to stand there as long as I dared; and, just as soon as I got home, I started to imitate her exercises.

"After a while the lady found me out and began to take an interest in me. She heard my voice and liked it. But, as she was very much shocked by my fiery gesticulation and my hundred per cent Neapolitan accent, she offered to give me singing lessons free of charge on condition that I would tone down my extravagant gestures and never utter in her hearing a single word of Neapolitan dialect.

"Well, I can't deny that it was easier for me to learn some dozens of songs than to drop my Neapolitan lingo. However, so strong was my desire to learn to sing that for a whole month I did my best to do as she wished. But, one morning, when she asked me suddenly what I had eaten for supper the evening before I was caught off my guard and blurted out—not only in the broadest Neapolitan accent but with inelegant, far too graphic gestures—*'Pasta e fasule'* (macaroni and beans). For this I got as a reward such a stinging box on the ear that I vowed never to enter that house again."

Whether he kept his vow is not on record—but it is a known fact that, to the end of his life, Enrico Caruso, though he sang in orthodox Italian throughout his operatic career, often lapsed into Neapolitan dialect when he was among friends, especially Neapolitan friends, and reveled in doing so.

His real school was Naples. He roamed her streets as soon as he could propel himself unaided; and the bluest of bays and the brightest of sunlight and the most pervasive of volcanoes became his substitutes for books and slates and blackboards. In her sunlit streets he sang as soon as he talked, pocketing occasional soldi from those who stopped to listen. "I began singing," he said afterward, "when I was ten. Some of it I did in churches. There I gave the faithful worshipers much joy—at least, I think I did. Anyhow, they never showed the least dissatisfaction with my efforts."

With his early attempts at song he combined active swimming in the waters of the Bay of Naples, into which he plunged from the city's water front. He became quite an adept at it. This, beyond doubt, was responsible for some of that robust physique, which, in the years of his glory, contributed magnificently to the phenomenal power behind his voice.

For a few years more Enrico's study of singing continued to be rather haphazard. But he stuck to it all through boyhood and early manhood. Among his earliest regular teachers were Domenico Amitrano and Signor Gatti, both of whom tried valiantly to pound musical lore into him. With the daughter of the latter he is said to have had an affair of calf-love, but nothing came of it.

Meanwhile, his father, not taking Enrico's singing seriously as yet, tried to make a mechanic out of him by putting him to work regularly at the Meuricoffre factory, where he himself was employed. But he soon gave up the idea of turning his son completely away from song; he realized that, in attempting to do so, he had attempted the impossible. So Enrico continued on his melodious way.

Marcellino Caruso ("a good mechanic and a better drinker," as someone said of him), though thwarted, was not resentful. He allowed Enrico to keep some of the coins earned by his singing, and drank up the rest.

At this time Enrico's voice was wavering between baritone and tenor. It finally resolved itself as a tenor voice. Always, however, it retained a certain baritone quality. This may account in part for the robustness of the Voice of Gold all through his career, which enabled him to tackle dramatic tenor roles beyond the capacities of singers whose voices were entirely lyric. But some admirers in later years deplored these excursions of Enrico Caruso into the domain of *tenore robusto*; they believed that, having a most beautiful lyric tenor voice, he always should have stuck to purely lyrical operatic parts.

Perhaps the credit for "discovering" Enrico Caruso belongs to his early friend, the baritone Eduardo Messiano. Caruso always spoke of him in after years with the deepest gratitude; and, when Messiano died, he cried bitterly, like the little Neapolitan boy he always remained at heart. "Always," said Enrico, "he was my best friend."

The two used to sing in summer at resorts around Naples. On one of their excursions, Messiano said: "Enrico, your voice is unique in the world." Caruso laughed heartily. What nonsense!

Undeterred, Messiano scolded him for not studying harder, and he scolded to such good effect and was so persistent in telling Enrico that it was up to him to do something toward improving his voice that his friend finally consented to call upon Giuseppe Vergine, a prominent singing teacher, who gave regular lessons to youths inclined to become professional singers (among them was Antonio Scotti, the famous baritone).

Accompanied by Messiano, Caruso sang before Vergine. After listening for a bit, the singing teacher said: "Caruso, my friend, your voice sounds like the whistling of the wind through a window."

So the two lads slunk away from the abode of Giuseppe Vergine. Enrico thought that there would be no more nagging from his friend. He was mistaken.

"Enrico," insisted Eduardo Messiano, "I repeat what I told you before. Your voice is miraculous. Vergine must be crazy." And he nagged away until Caruso, to stop his scolding, returned to Giuseppe Vergine. This time, Vergine (though still without a sign that he had changed his mind about Enrico's voice) agreed to give him singing lessons —to the great joy of faithful Eduardo Messiano.

Under the guidance of Vergine, Caruso began to study singing seriously. At that time Vergine favored his "holding back" his voice, instead of "letting it out." He thought that this would conserve its strength for maturer years, enabling Enrico's voice to reach more easily those high notes so dear to operatic audiences, and to keep it from "breaking" when it reached them.

In talking about his early singing lessons after he had become famous, Caruso was not complimentary sometimes to Vergine's methods of teaching. "He restrained all my inclinations to color a note," said the tenor, "and deprived me of all power of emphasis. For three years I studied, as it were, against the grain, repressing nature in order to become a Vergine product."

He continued to combine more regularly paid work with his street singing. For some time, off and on, he stuck to his job with Signor Meuricoffre—and he worked desultorily on other jobs. The thrifty Swiss paid him at the rate of two cents per hour. In another direction, though, he showed more generosity; he saw to it that Enrico's job at his factory did not interfere too much with the boy's singing. This, by now, included regular engagements, obtained through individuals bearing a faint resemblance to theatrical agents, for evenings of singing at special church festivals, mostly in nearby villages.

After a considerable spell at the Meuricoffre factory, Enrico asked for a raise. It was refused. So he turned to other jobs. One was at another small factory; and, after that, at a third, run by Signor Palmieri, whence issued

various iron products. In later years, when he was celebrated, Enrico used to take friends along a certain street
in Naples, stop suddenly, and say to them: "See that drinking fountain?"

"Yes. What about it?"

"I made it."

"Some day," remarks a biographer of Caruso hopefully,
"there may be an inscription on that fountain."

Some time later he was back again at the Meuricoffre
factory, where he worked with such an increase of industry
that he was promoted by being put in charge of the ware-
house of his employer; and he also became a bookkeeper
of sorts. With him, however, singing always came first.

His street concerts began gradually to take on the aspect
—in comparison with his earlier open air performances—
of big business. For instance, he added to his other musical
activities a new line—serenading. He hired himself out to
sing serenades to young Neapolitan damsels, to further the
loves of maturer swains. While one of the latter would lurk
in the shadows outside the window of a local Juliet, Enrico
Caruso, as a deputy Romeo, would open his mouth in
sweet caroling; and, when the hidden lover concluded
that the lady was sufficiently melted, he would emerge
from the shadows to do his own lovemaking, leaving Enrico
to fade away, the richer by perhaps one lira (about twenty
cents, at the rate of exchange prevailing that romantic
evening).

Assisted by a musical confederate (sometimes a pianist,
sometimes a violinist or mandolinist or guitarist), Enrico
Caruso also master-minded a series of musicales outside
a big Naples public bath establishment. The proprietor
allowed him and his companion to perform for would-be
bathers, who often had to wait a long time before they
could be accommodated in the crowded bathhouse, so

great was its popularity. While his confederate pounded or strummed popular songs to grownups about to wash (or already washed), Caruso would raise his voice in song. And, since the youth's voice was growing more and more melodious every day, the crowd of auditors sometimes swelled to a really remarkable size—as did also the "take" of Enrico and his fellow performer, compared with earlier earnings.

Receipts from church singing also showed a gratifying upward trend. Sometimes, for an evening's performance at village church festivals, Enrico earned as much as ten lire ($2.00)—which, in view of the fact that, a little later, for enacting roles in bona fide grand opera performances, he sometimes received exactly the same amount, was good pay for a boy-singer.

Once, long afterwards, when he was putting his signature on a contract for singing in opera at 10,000 lire ($2,000) per appearance, he remarked to the impresario who was signing him up: "Do you know what I like best about that figure 10,000? *The* 10. That's what I earned for my first regular evening performance."

The trouble with those village evenings of song was their duration. On one occasion, Caruso, having sung for several hours in a village church, was preparing to return, very tired indeed, to Naples, fifteen miles away.

"Hey, you!" shouted the manager. "Come back here! Your work isn't finished yet. You must sing for Baron Zezza."

Baron Zezza, it turned out, was the local equivalent of mayor. He liked young Caruso's voice so much that he kept the poor young man singing in his house *all night*. When the exhausted singer finally seated himself wearily at dawn in a Naples-bound conveyance, the only singing came not from him but from birds. All the way to Naples,

Enrico alternately denounced the baron-mayor and wrapped around himself more closely an old coat which that exacting individual had lent him to guard that precious voice of his against the chill morning air—perhaps the baron was looking forward to listening to another "evening" of Caruso song—free of charge.

Long afterward, Enrico Caruso, triumphant in a brilliant season at one of the world's leading opera houses, received a letter from Baron Zezza, running somewhat as follows: "If you are the Enrico Caruso who sang to me twenty years ago, what about that coat of mine?"

"I am that Enrico Caruso," answered the tenor, "but I haven't the remotest idea what became of your damned old coat. Of course, I can send you a new one to replace it, but, before I do, you must pay me for eight hours of free singing at your house. I sang there with the same voice which now earns me $2,000 per evening. So I will send you a coat if you will send me $2,000—*plus 20 years' interest.*"

Baron Zezza wrote back: "Let's compromise. Instead of a coat, send me an autographed photograph of yourself." Which Caruso did.

He continued to take lessons from Giuseppe Vergine for some time. And his teacher still continued to act and talk as if he saw nothing remarkable about his pupil's voice. Once, doubtless in reply to someone who had spoken of the golden quality in it, Vergine sneered: "Pooh! It's like the gold at the bottom of the Tiber in Rome—not worth going after."

However, Vergine proved that his often-expressed contempt was by no means as deep as he pretended by wheedling young Caruso into signing a contract obligating him to pay to his teacher over a period of years a considerable chunk of his future earnings. And whenever and wherever

Enrico sang Vergine invariably appeared to pocket his 25 per cent commission.

One day, years later, after Enrico had already climbed high, Vergine bobbed up before him, waved the contract in his face, and demanded a large sum of money, which, he said, was due him. There was an awful row. It culminated in acrimonious legal proceedings. Eventually Caruso agreed to pay his ex-teacher a lump sum of 20,000 lire ($4,000, very much scaled down by the court from Vergine's original demand). Vergine tore up the contract, and there was peace between them.

Enrico's mother died early in 1888 when he was fifteen years old. She never really had been well since the birth of her twentieth child in 1876, three years after Enrico was born. The morning of her death she persuaded him against his own will (for he realized that her condition was serious) not to give up singing at a church festival for which he had been engaged. "If you don't sing," she told him, "you will bring us all bad luck."

He reluctantly obeyed. When he returned to his home she was dead.

For months he was inconsolable. Constantly, in later times, no matter where he was or how famous, he loved to talk about her. "She used to go barefoot," he would tell friends, "so that I might have singing lessons."

Fate had been cruel to Anna Caruso by bringing her little happiness; crueler by stabbing her with much pain; cruelest by denying her the joy of knowing that she had borne a son who was to bring joy to millions of people. I have seen a picture of her—a woman simple and stoical, plainly dressed, with goodness and suffering etched on her face.

Marcellino Caruso did not long remain a widower. Having been assigned by Signor Meuricoffre, his boss at the factory, to install some machinery which had been bought from him by a fellow manufacturer, Baron Ricciardi, who had a factory at Aversa, near Naples, the elder Caruso took lodgings at the home of a widow, Maria Castaldi, in Aversa. He was able to assuage his grief with surprising promptness. In November 1888—the year of Anna Caruso's death—he and Maria were married.

Enrico, his sister Assunta, and his brother Giovanni, were spared that affliction so common in the lives of step-children—an unloved and unloving stepmother. Maria proved a real mother to the bereaved trio. Enrico was her favorite. His younger brother, Giovanni, said, after Enrico had become famous: "Whatever Enrico did was always right, but I was forever getting into trouble." "Of my own making," he had the grace to add.

To the day of his death Enrico Caruso never wavered in his affection for Maria Castaldi. Repeatedly he urged her to change her simple and frugal life—at his expense. But she invariably refused.

As young Caruso roamed through Naples, with melody on his lips—not knowing, perhaps, where his next meal was coming from, but singing just the same—the songs which he sang were often those which had been submitted by their composers at the famous Neapolitan song contests, which, held annually, again and again inspired popular songs played and hummed and whistled all over the world. These contests were looked upon by the city's local musical enthusiasts with an interest similar to our American attitude toward baseball; and the winning composers (as well as some of the also-rans) often achieved a celebrity akin to that of Joe DiMaggio.

For weeks before the contests, the partisans of the various local ditty-manufacturers worked themselves up into a high state of Mediterranean excitement. And, while they awaited the decision of the judges with measureless impatience, Enrico Caruso would be caroling the tunes which had won (or almost won) the prizes of other years—Luigi Denza's *"Funiculí, Funiculá,"* for instance (Is there anybody anywhere who doesn't know that one?); or some insidious little melody by Tosti (he of "Good-by Forever," later a close friend of Enrico's); or Rotoli or Tirindelli. Or, maybe, Enrico Caruso was warbling that popular song which he loved to the end of his life—which the renown and riches of his most glorious years never made him forget or despise—that *"Torna a Surriento,"* which vied, and still vies, on Caruso records with *"Vesti la giubba"* and *"Celeste Aïda."*

After more study with Giuseppe Vergine, young Caruso enrolled himself at a small singing school in Naples run by a Signor Bronzetti. Soon after his admission, Bronzetti, hampered in his voice-fostering work by a badly unstuffed pocketbook, decided to give a benefit performance for the school.

The piece chosen was an operatic hodgepodge with the charming title of *I Briganti nell' Giardino di Don Raffaele* (The Brigands in the Garden of Don Raffaele). One of its two composers was Maestro Fasanaro, who had tried his hand some time before at giving lessons to Enrico and refused payment for them when he realized the impecuniosity of the Caruso family.

Enrico played the leading comic part. One of his fellow performers was Peppino Villani, who grew up to become a famous comedian in Italy. There was something ironic about the apportionment of the parts in the Bronzetti opera: Caruso, renowned later in serious operatic roles, got the job of keeping the auditors amused by his stage antics; and Villani, who later set audiences roaring with laughter, was cast as a sentimental young girl. Since the piece about the doings of the brigands in the garden was given as a benefit, Caruso doubtless was paid nothing for his singing and acting—which, after all, was not so very much below his customary rate of emolument in those beginner's days.

Despite an undeniable haphazardness in his progress, Enrico Caruso was getting ahead. But, at this point in his career, the time came for him to do his three years' military service in the regular army of Italy.

Young Caruso was enrolled as a raw recruit in the barracks at the town of Rieti. However, he made the best of it. And he soon made a great impression on his comrades-in-arms by his singing. Sometimes, when some crony or other was put under arrest for a petty misdemeanor, officers of the regiment would tell the tenor-recruit that they would release the culprit if Caruso would sing to them. This he would do with his customary good humor—and out pranced the prisoner from his cell.

After a while he attracted the attention of an angel in disguise, whose terrestrial appellation was Major Nagliati. Having on several occasions heard Enrico warbling lustily to his comrades, the major walked up to him and curtly told him to report to him at his quarters.

"He does not like your singing," said his comrades, sagely shaking their heads. "He is going to lock you up."

Caruso presented himself before Major Nagliati.

"Ha, the singer, eh?" growled that officer. "What did you do in civil life?"

"I was studying to go on the operatic stage."

"How long are you supposed to serve in the army?"

"Three years."

"Too bad," muttered the major. "Three years a soldier, and then—no voice."

"Yes, sir."

The major signed to him to go away. Enrico saluted —and went.

Some days later Enrico was again summoned to Major Nagliati's presence. In tones as curt as before, the officer snapped out: "You are now coming with me to the house of a nobleman, a friend of mine, who loves music."

"Yes, sir."

That was the first of many visits by Caruso to the home of the major's noble friend. The latter, an excellent musician, proceeded to take his place with alacrity on the growing list of Enrico's singing teachers.

He spent hours listening to the young soldier's singing. He pointed out his mistakes. He told him how to do better. At times, he was ruthless in criticism—which, undoubtedly, was a very good thing for his pupil. Once, in exasperation, he exclaimed: "Your notes are clamped down in your throat like rats in a trap!" But, in general, he thought so well of Caruso's warblings that he actually taught him, besides regular singing exercises, the entire tenor part (that of Turiddu) in *Cavalleria Rusticana*, the opera by Pietro Mascagni, which a short time before had blazed across the operatic heavens and was still a sensational novelty in opera houses all over the world.

Soon after he had introduced Caruso to the musical nobleman, Major Nagliati summoned the young singer once more.

"Soldier and singer too!" he grunted. "Ridiculous! Impossible! I've arranged to have a substitute do the rest of your military service for you."

Enrico Caruso was overwhelmed with joy and gratitude. A few weeks of soldiering instead of three years! When he found out where he had put his tongue, he

gasped: "Thank you, major. Thank you very much. I—
I—"

Impatiently, the major waved him away.

Enrico Caruso rushed happily back to Naples. I do
not know what happened afterward to Major Nagliati,
angel in disguise. I hope that it was something nice.

Released from military life, back again in his adored
native city, Caruso fell in again with his teacher Vergine.
By this time Vergine was really interested in the young
man's voice. (And, besides, it must be remembered, he
had in his pocket that mortgage on Enrico's future, the
contract signed by the tenor.)

Vergine was acquainted with Nicola Daspuro, a regular Neapolitan-about-town, typical of his epoch. Daspuro led a dual life. First (or, sometimes, second, de-
pending on financial conditions at the moment), he was
a producer of grand opera; second (or, sometimes, first),
he was the representative in Southern Italy of the famous
Sonzogno music-publishing house of Milan.

In those days Sonzogno was engaged in violent rivalry
with the mighty Milan firm of Ricordi, which, ever since
it had signed up Giuseppe Verdi many years before—after
the famous composer's first sweeping success with *Nabucco*—had been publishing all the subsequent Verdi
operas (including some of the most successful works ever
composed)—and, in addition, works by other composers,
which had placed the firm at the top of the music-publishing business. In combating Ricordi, Sonzogno was
leaning heavily on the composers of the young Italian
operatic school, including Mascagni, of *Cavalleria Rusticana* renown—and also on the output of several French
composers favored by Italian operagoers. When Vergine
cast his eye in the direction of Daspuro, the latter was

getting together a company for a season of opera at the Teatro Mercadante in Naples.

Vergine painted for Impresario Daspuro a picture of Enrico Caruso's merits which (in glaring contrast to what he usually told the young singer to his face) fairly sizzled with Neapolitan exuberance.

"Bring him around," commanded Daspuro. It was arranged that Caruso should sing before Daspuro and other experts.

For this ordeal Caruso chose to sing for his judges excerpts from the tenor part in Ambroise Thomas's *Mignon* —the Italian rights for which had been snapped up by Sonzogno in conjunction with the rights for the output of two other more famous French composers, whose music Caruso in future years was destined to sing with triumphant effect—Gounod (*Faust*) and Bizet (*Carmen*).

In a highly nervous state, like the policemen in *The Pirates of Penzance,* Caruso stood before the Daspuro tribunal and started singing.

He made a mess of it. He could not get hold of himself. He squawked unmelodiously. His high notes failed to gain altitude. Ominously Daspuro shook his head. So did the other judges convened for the audition. Like whipped puppy dogs Caruso and Vergine stole away— to the nearest café probably, to trot out all the might-have-beens appropriate to the crisis. The vision of the Teatro Mercadante faded away.

But Neapolitan clouds are equipped with silver linings of peculiar brightness. The silver lining of Caruso's Teatro Mercadante cloud revealed itself in the form of his official debut in opera—at another theater.

Perhaps "official" is too high-flown a word, for there was about that debut a strong amateurish touch. It happened that, around that time, there was a young and affluent native of Naples, Signor Morelli, who fancied himself as a composer. Morelli had composed an opera— a feat as unworthy of remark in Naples as blowing your nose elsewhere. So, blithely shouldering the financial responsibility of a production, he set about recruiting a company. In it he included Enrico Caruso, who had celebrated his twenty-first birthday some months before. Morelli hired Caruso at fifteen lire ($3.00) a night per performance; and he munificently slipped him an advance of eighty lire ($16.00).

When Caruso appeared some days later for the first rehearsal of Morelli's opera (it was called *L'Amico Francesco*), he was wearing a pair of ordinary street shoes. Morelli's stage manager was shocked.

"Why are you wearing those things?" he asked angrily. "You received an advance for buying a proper outfit for your role. What did you do with the money?"

"Spent it for meals," replied Caruso. "I had to keep alive until the rehearsal, didn't I?"

L'Amico Francesco was produced at the Teatro Nuovo in Naples on the evening of November 16, 1894, nine years and one week before Enrico Caruso's debut at the Metropolitan Opera House in New York. It ran two nights. It has not been revived. Only those very close to the composer ever heard of it or him again. But Signor Morelli's opera has one unique distinction. In it Enrico Caruso made his first appearance in a professional operatic production. No other opera can take that honor away from *L'Amico Francesco*.

That is, it can't do so if we ignore what Nicola Daspuro, Caruso's close associate in the days of the tenor's youth, had to say on the subject in later years.

Writing long afterward, when he was an old man, Daspuro declared that Caruso's professional debut was at the Teatro Cimarosa in Caserta, on December 24, 1895. And he takes issue with those who got up a grand gala performance in New York's Metropolitan Opera House in 1919 in honor of the twenty-fifth anniversary of Caruso's professional debut, the date of which they considered to be 1894, and the place Naples, instead of, respectively, 1895 and Caserta.

Perhaps Daspuro thought Caruso's 1894 performance rather more amateur than professional; or perhaps, in his old age, his memory played him tricks. Anyhow, I, for one, prefer to line up with those who staged the Met gala night in 1919. After all, if they got off on the wrong foot, why did not Caruso, the central attraction at that twenty-fifth anniversary celebration, who was on the spot throughout the preparations for it, not put them on the right one?

To return to *L'Amico Francesco:* Caruso's singing of the tenor part in it did not set the Bay of Naples on fire. But Morelli, the composer, was so pleased with him that he promised the young singer a part in his next opera— the dismal fate of the first-born had not crushed the youthful musician's hopes. What is more, he gave the tenor a bonus. Fifty lire. Ten dollars. Enrico Caruso was on the march.

Undoubtedly, that bonus was soon swallowed up— literally. But what of it? Who cared? Was not the sun of Naples shining and the Bay of Naples sparkling and old Vesuvius puffing forth his vaporous wreath of smoke? Tomorrow would bring another job in another opera, full of paid songs. And, meanwhile, there was macaroni to be eaten at places where credit, though strained, was still good; and, failing that, there were shellfish to be had on the water front, and glasses of heady wine, and water-melons, appetizingly sliced, all at infinitesimal prices. "A slice of watermelon," Enrico Caruso used to say in later years of wealth and fame, "was a most useful thing in those days. If you had one, you could eat, drink and wash your face."

CHAPTER **3**

POVERTY AND GAIETY

Luckily for Caruso the audience at the second (and last) performance of *L'Amico Francesco* included an impresario named Ferrara. Ferrara buttonholed the young tenor on the street a few days after the lamentable demise of Signor Morelli's opera and signed him up for a series of performances which he was planning for Caserta, a town not far from Naples.

Caruso got himself from Naples to Caserta with the rest of Ferrara's company, which included a young and agreeable prima donna called Emma Carelli, with whom he became good friends. On December 24, 1895, they opened in *Cavalleria Rusticana*, in which the noble friend of Major Nagliati had drilled Caruso with such praiseworthy persistence.

Many years later, I saw Caruso as Turiddu in *Cavalleria* several times, in the days of his prime, and it seemed to me that the part fitted him perfectly. But it did not fit him at all that night in Caserta. He should have been excellent in it, considering how hard that nobleman of Rieti had coached him in the part at the time when Enrico was a soldier. But he was not excellent. He was very bad indeed.

Cavalleria was followed by *Faust*, with Caruso in the title role and La Carelli as Marguerite. Neither he nor she nor anybody else in his vicinity that night thought much of his performance. He confessed years later that he went sour on no less than six notes in *"Salve, dimora"* and he described his acting to friends in New York, in after years, as "awful."

Then came an opera called *Camoëns*, by the composer-conductor Mugnone, which has perished without leaving a trace. Caserta—en masse—did not like it. After that third flop Impresario Ferrara called it a day. And Enrico Caruso climbed into a third-class carriage on the train for Naples and arrived in the city of his birth with twelve cents in his pocket. Back to the life of strained credit and cheap wine and cheaper watermelon! He was disappointed, of course; but the buoyant Neapolitan in him asserted itself again (after reinforcements had been found for the twelve cents). And once more his cloud had a silver lining à la Napoletano. He met Francesco Zucchi.

Zucchi was a Sicilian who, at first, had been an actor, but he had given up acting in favor of the career of a theatrical agent. He had an "office"—a table at the ramshackle Caffé dei Fiori—and there he gathered around himself a raffish assemblage of actors and singers out of jobs, over whom he ruled autocratically and paternally. Zucchi promptly took young Caruso, temporarily among the unemployed, under his august protection—concerning the value of which to youths in Caruso's circumstances he had inflated and volubly expressed opinions.

Zucchi was a character typical of Caruso's Neapolitan milieu. Tall and thin, he had a fierce, bristling mustache, which he had dyed to a deep henna color. He added to the ferocity of his appearance by letting his hair run wild all over his skull without benefit of comb or brush.

Zucchi had quite a system as a theatrical agent. Say, for example, that an impresario from some small place in the vicinity of Naples wanted to recruit a company to give a

series of operatic performances. Could Zucchi supply him
with what was wanted? *Could he? Dio mio!* "My boy, you
have come to the right shop." Was a tenor sought? Why,
Zucchi had one who could hit high C's with the non-
chalance of Tamagno himself. Or would the out-of-town
impresario prefer one who sang just like Gayarre (another
famous tenor of long ago)? Was a prima donna needed?
Why, Zucchi had one who (except that she bore another
name) was exactly like Adelina Patti. Was a basso required? "What an extraordinary piece of luck! I have a
basso who can go 'воом!' like the cannon on the walls
of the Castle of Sant' Elmo."

At this point, the impresario would probably remark,
somewhat frightened by Zucchi's boasts, that all he wanted
was a second-rate tenor—even a third-rate one—and that
he wanted this tenor at a low price.

"Ah!" Zucchi would exclaim, unabashed. "I have no
second-rate or third-rate singers. But I'll tell you what I'll
do. I like you, my friend. So, for you—*only for you*—I'll get
one of my first-string tenors—whose usual charge is 1,000
lire a night—to sing in your company at your price. By
the way, what is your price, Signore?"

"Ten lire."

"Excellent! Simply to oblige you—and I would not, I
assure you, do this for anybody else—my 1,000 lire tenor
will sing for you at ten lire." And the deal would be closed
and Zucchi would pull his fierce mustaches and flash his
bright eyes and rumple his dyed hair and one of his tenors
would be sure of square meals for a while.

One day an emissary of Zucchi's, all out of breath, rushed
up to Caruso as he sat enjoying a life of leisure outside a
café and told him that he was wanted in a terrific hurry
at the Teatro Bellini, one of the leading playhouses of
Naples. There they were preparing to produce *Faust,* but

the man cast for the tenor part had suddenly become hoarse, and unless a substitute capable of replacing him could be found immediately there would be a crisis when the time came for that evening's performance. While the management wrung its hands and tore its hair with true Neapolitan abandon the baritone of the company, one Pignataro, who had sung with Caruso in Caserta of un-happy memory, told the agitated management that, if Caruso could be found, he was just the man for the role— which, on the basis of Enrico's Caserta performance, left something to be desired as a sample of the truth. Zucchi, added Pignataro, was Caruso's agent.

So the management stopped its hand-wringing and hair-tearing, a messenger found Zucchi, a henchman of the latter discovered Caruso sunning himself at his café table, and the tenor was duly delivered at the stage door of the Teatro Bellini.

The critical situation there was agitatedly explained to him. Would he sing *Faust* that night?

"How much do I get?" inquired Caruso.

"Twenty-five lire."

"Done."

So he duly strutted and fretted on the Bellini stage, in the plumed hat and nobby outfit of the Goethe-Gounod operatic hero, and there is no record that he emitted sour notes in "*Salve, dimora*" or anywhere else.

When the final curtain came down the erstwhile hand-wringers and hair-tearers, now with broad grins, asked him deferentially to sing in *Rigoletto* for them and their public.

"How much do I get?" asked the tenor.

A figure was named—low, but not without lure.

"Done."

Enrico sang not only in *Rigoletto* but in other operas at the Bellini. He was forging forward. His success attracted

marked attention among members of the raffish entourage
of Francesco Zucchi, gathered around the latter at his
"office"—the sole furnishings of which were bowls of spaghetti and wine bottles and glasses—at the ramshackle
Caffé dei Fiori. There was much talk among them about
this young Enrico Caruso. Some of the talk was unfavor-
able. "Which," observes Eugenio Gara, in his book about
Caruso, "was a good sign."

When the Teatro Bellini season ended Caruso got employment at the rival Teatro Mercadante of Naples, the
scene of his catastrophic audition before the Daspuro tribunal. But this time there was no hitch for him at the
Mercadante. He sang there in *Traviata, Capuletti e Mon-
tecchi* (Bellini's operatic version of *Romeo and Juliet*), and
other stock pieces. Sometimes he sang with (and at) Emma
Carelli, the agreeable young soprano with whom he had
appeared in Impresario Ferrara's ill-starred Caserta venture.
His pay still bore no resemblance whatsoever to what Heinrich Conried and Giulio Gatti-Casazza, within a few years,
were to press earnestly upon him at the Metropolitan in
New York. But why worry? Did not the money in his
pocket suffice for macaroni and shellfish, wine and watermelon? All was well with Enrico Caruso.

Around this time, in 1896, he made his first trip abroad.
Zucchi, buzzing around Naples on behalf of his seedy followers, got him a job with a company being formed to
give operas at the Ezbekieh Theater in Cairo, Egypt—in
which Caruso's friend, Emma Carelli, was to sing the leading prima donna roles. The impresario agreed (via Zucchi)
to pay Caruso six hundred lire ($120) for a month of work
—and work, at that stage in his career sometimes meant
singing seven nights a week, with occasional matinees.
There were even times when singers taking part in an

afternoon and evening performance on the same day had only fifteen minutes for rest. Rest!

On one occasion, while under Zucchi's wing, Enrico sang *Rigoletto* three times in two days. Zucchi was delighted with this triple feat. "I tell you, my friends," he announced to the assembled company at the Caffé dei Fiori, "in a little while *u nicu* [Neapolitan for "the lad"] will be this world's greatest tenor!"

On the steamer carrying him from Italy to Alexandria, Caruso had a financial windfall which dwarfed the pay promised him by the impresario who had signed him up for Egypt. Among the passengers were several lively young Englishmen, who, having heard that there was a tenor lurking on board, collared Caruso, hauled him into the bar, and demanded that he sing for them. Caruso refused. Maybe visions of two-a-day opera in Cairo were making him nurse his voice. The young Englishmen—not entirely sober—insisted. "If you don't," they said, "we will throw you overboard."

Caruso decided to sing. He was a great success. The Englishmen—and other frequenters of the bar—called for more. Next day and the next the young Britishers again got on the singer's trail and set him to warbling again. As the ship neared Alexandria, one of the Englishmen, having passed around the hat, turned over to Caruso *one hundred pounds sterling* (about $500)! "Never," said the tenor, years later, "had I seen such a sum of money."

Caruso's Egyptian season did not last long (his seasons in those days seldom did). Soon he was back in Naples, jobless. He sat among the glasses and bottles at Zucchi's headquarters, while that great personage gave profound thought to the tenor's predicament.

Thanks to Zucchi Caruso journeyed to Caserta, valiantly resolved to face again the carping operagoers of that scene of his earlier discomfiture. But Caserta remained Caserta. For Enrico Caruso it was a fatal community.

While Caruso sang *again* in *Faust* before an audience largely made up of unsophisticated country folk to whom the opera was a complete novelty, the spectators were so shocked at seeing Mephistopheles, who was, to them, the devil in person, brazenly come to earth to play his wicked tricks, that they rose in a body, surged toward the stage with wild howls, and caused the curtain to come down with a bang. Apparently the Mephistopheles escaped in one piece. Next morning, Caruso and (let us hope) Mephistopheles, together with the rest of the company, were in a third-class carriage on a Caserta-Naples train. They were in that carriage because there was no fourth class.

Then came a spell of opera for Caruso at the town of Salerno, south of Naples, later to become famous in United States history. Among the operas in which he sang there was Bellini's *Puritani*, that favorite of our grandparents.

In the Salerno theater the conductor was Vincenzo Lombardi, who was also a singing teacher. He promptly took an interest in Enrico Caruso. And that was a piece of excellent luck for Enrico, since Lombardi, a man of discernment and vision, was to help him enormously in preparing for the career of a professional singer.

The tenor part in *Puritani* is shockingly difficult—in their day great tenors like Rubini and Gayarre had moaned about it. Lombardi lost no time in telling Caruso that his singing of it was dreadful, perfectly dreadful; but, being a believer in mixing constructive with destructive criticism, he set about correcting the young Neapolitan's errors in song.

Enrico was still holding back his voice. As a result of this, it still tended to break on high notes, because the young singer did not attack them strongly enough.

Lombardi made him prop himself against a wall, throw his head back as far as he could, and then shoot out the notes from that highly uncomfortable position to the utmost of his power. This did wonders at that early stage of his career for the youthful tenor—combined with the fact that Caruso himself was already using a method of breathing which his native intelligence had told him was the one best adapted to his voice production. By the time his Salerno season was over he was almost cured of holding back his voice—and his high notes came out clear and ringing.

When Caruso first turned up in Salerno he was known as "the broken tenor," also as *"il tenore vento,"* the windy tenor, another malicious epithet which he owed to his Naples teacher, Giuseppe Vergine.

Many years later, Caruso used to say of Lombardi's teachings: "A great light shone upon me. Never again did I sing against nature. Thereafter I sang with all the voice I had when the right moment came and always with the color which my heart told me should envelop the poet's words. After that night when I sang in *Puritani* in Salerno I was never again called a 'broken tenor.' " To the last days of his life he spoke with gratitude and affection of Vincenzo Lombardi.

But Caruso's Salerno warblings were still not all that they should be. The manager who was running the Salerno theater where he was working was a Signor Grassi. Whenever Caruso rehearsed the part of Don José in *Carmen,* Grassi suffered much pain. The celebrated "Flower Song" was a pet stumbling block for the tenor; every time he sang that tricky aria, Grassi (according to Caruso's later reconstruction of the scene) "would pull wildly at the hairs on his head—which weren't many."

"If you hang around while I'm rehearsing," threatened

the tenor, "I won't sing any more!" So Grassi was elim-
inated from rehearsals of *Carmen.* "But, while I went on
with my rehearsing," said Caruso, "I knew he was hiding
in some corner of the theater, groaning every time I went
after the high notes in the 'Flower Song,' and putting the
jettatura [evil eye] on me!"

At Salerno they decided to produce *Pagliacci;* not, however, with Caruso in the tenor role. But Pagani, the tenor
chosen to sing the part of Canio (with its *"Vesti la giubba"*
aria destined afterward to be considered by operagoers all
over the world as Enrico Caruso's exclusive property), was
suddenly taken ill soon after the beginning of the performance. Again emissaries went out in search of Caruso. They
found him—and told him that he must go on in the second
act of *Pagliacci,* which, in point of time, was alarmingly
near at hand.

"But I haven't had any supper!" wailed the tenor.

"No matter," said the emissaries soothingly. "You will
be served a full evening meal in your dressing room."

So Caruso—in after years a frugal eater and a teetotaler—
devoured an enormous spaghetti dinner, helped downward
by much wine. Square meals were not an everyday hap-
pening with him at that time. None the worse for his
gastronomic feat, he took up the performance of *Pagliacci*
where Pagani had left it and acquitted himself without
mishap.

At Salerno, Vincenzo Lombardi continued as Caruso's
persistent and severe mentor. Constantly he impressed on
the youth the necessity for study, tireless study, unceasing
study. He quoted to him the dictum of a well-known Italian authority on operatic singing: "The human voice
should have two lives: one for studying singing, one for
singing." Never since the era of that nobleman-teacher at
Rieti had Caruso had such rigorous lessons.

Meanwhile, in Naples, Zucchi, Caruso's agent, had got in touch again with Nicola Daspuro, who just then was rather more interested in producing opera on his own than in furthering the interests of the great firm of Sonzogno. Zucchi informed Daspuro with much enthusiasm that he simply must hear Caruso sing. Daspuro, recalling the time when Enrico had made a botch of the tenor part of *Mignon* at the Teatro Mercadante in Naples, gloomily shook his head.

"I have already heard him," he objected. "Once is enough." And he rudely added: "If you mention Enrico Caruso to me again I'll throw you not out the door but out the window."

Zucchi, however, persisted. Finally, to keep him quiet, Daspuro took the train to Salerno. With much misgiving he listened again to Caruso—and was delighted. He met Lombardi, who was getting himself into such frenzies of gesticulation and gyration in trying to make Caruso into a real singer that he had become more a gymnastics teacher than a teacher of singing.

"How much are you earning?" Daspuro asked Enrico.

"Twenty lire for each appearance."

"How do you eat?"

"Oh, that's easy. I have made many friends in Salerno. Salernians are very hospitable. They invite me to break-fast—lunch—dinner. I eat free."

"Well, don't abuse your voice," was Daspuro's parting advice.

And Caruso, with the arrogance of youth, exclaimed: "Oh, I have enough voice for the whole world!"

While singing in Salerno, Enrico Caruso fell in love with Giuseppina Grassi, the daughter of his manager. Defying the evil eye allegedly wielded by her father, he spent much time at the Grassi residence. Soon he became engaged to Giuseppina. To show that he was really in earnest, Enrico, when he went to ask her father to allow her to become his wife, took along with him the mayor of Salerno.

But, shortly after the engagement was formally announced, Caruso went to a performance of *Gioconda*, the opera that includes the celebrated "Dance of the Hours." Each of the hours in that ballet, those who have seen it will recall, is represented by a dancer. One of the young houris captured the heart of Enrico Caruso. He met her after the end of the ballet, she listened attentively to his expressions of volcanic affection, and—they eloped. Salerno knew Enrico no more. He showed up with the bewitching ballerina at Naples.

Having been engaged to sing in the Sicilian city of Trapani, Caruso, on arriving there, was welcomed with much fervor and wine by the baritone Pignataro, a native of the place, he who had sung with Enrico in Caserta and recommended him for employment at the Teatro Bellini in Naples. Then the tenor's Sicilian manager, one Cavallaro, gave him another welcome—and more wine. The Pignataro-Cavallaro welcome continued unabated for days, while preparations were being made for a production of *Lucia*, Donizetti's operatic version of Sir Walter Scott's *Bride of Lammermoor*, the scene of which, it will be remembered, was laid by Sir Walter, in accordance with his usual custom, in Scotland. Caruso was to sing the part of Edgardo.

When the time came for ringing up the curtain on the dress rehearsal the much-welcomed Enrico Caruso was nowhere to be found.

Now, Enrico was never a drinker. Marcellino, his father, did the drinking for the whole Caruso family. But that

plentiful Sicilian wine, fiery and heady, with which he had
been so copiously welcomed to Trapani, had floored him.
When he was finally located he was in a deep sleep—"a
sleep of stone," as the Italians say. Roused at last, he
lurched mistily toward the theater.

The dress rehearsal was an exceedingly formal affair. The
members of the Board of Directors of the opera house
were present, also high officials of the Trapani municipal
government—all waiting for Caruso.

The tenor finally arrived. He was not quite sure where
he was—or who. He came out on the stage. He negotiated
the music of his role passably, but the words gave him a
great deal of trouble. When he came to a line mentioning
the "fate of Scotland" he transformed it, through some
perverse, unexplainable slip of the tongue, into the "foxes
of Scotland."

There was a loud murmur of disapproval from the Board
of Directors and the municipal authorities of Trapani.
Caruso left the stage in a hurry. The rehearsal continued
without a tenor.

Next day all Trapani had heard the story. Wherever
Caruso showed himself there were shouts of "the foxes of
Scotland." "He needed a bodyguard," said an eyewitness.
Worst of all, the Board of Directors of the theater fired
him. As he was without funds for getting back to Naples,
friends arranged with shady characters of the Trapani
water front to smuggle him aboard a Naples-bound coast-
ing vessel as a stowaway.

But he was saved by one of those sudden upheavals
which at that time occurred with remarkable frequency
in the careers of opera singers in Southern Italy. Signor
Oddo, the tenor who had replaced Caruso in the performance of *Lucia*, made no allusion in his singing to the foxes
of Scotland but there was something about him which dis-

pleased the audience to an astonishing degree. So, in the
course of the first act, they howled him off the stage.

Caruso, down by the docks, preparing for his debut as a
stowaway, was rushed to the theater. There was a hasty
transfer of plumed hat and doublet and hose from one
Edgardo to another, and, when the curtain rose on Act II,
it was Caruso, not Oddo, who appeared in the tenor part.
The audience was so relieved at not seeing Oddo that they
forgot their grievances against Caruso. But, years later,
when he went through Trapani, he was greeted with cries
of "the foxes of Scotland!"

Back in Naples again, he was suddenly confronted with
a major crisis.

He had been engaged for another Sicilian season—at the
Teatro Massimo in Palermo. The director-conductor there
was that Signor Mugnone whose opera, *Camoëns*, had been
Impresario Ferrara's third flop at Caserta. And—alas!—
Caruso knew perfectly well that Mugnone also was a lover
of the ballerina of Salerno with whom he, Caruso, had
eloped!

Now, Mugnone was an important individual. Also, he
was hot-tempered. And, at the moment, he was situated
at a highly strategic point in Caruso's career. Would Mugnone, on sight of Caruso, tear up the latter's Palermo contract and chase him out of town?

Caruso arrived in Palermo. The first meeting of the two
men lacked warmth. Enrico started to rehearse with Mugnone the tenor part in *Gioconda*—the very opera in which
the ballerina who had ensnared Enrico's heart had danced
in Salerno! Might not that fact start a perilous train of
thought in Mugnone?

As Caruso began to sing, Mugnone conducted frigidly.
But when the tenor, in the renowned aria *"Cielo e mar,"*

confided to the night his personal opinions concerning sky and sea, Mugnone proved himself an artist first and a lover second.

"Bravo!" he shouted. "Bravissimo!" From then on Enrico had a really powerful ally in the Italian world of opera —for Mugnone's stature was far above that of Grassi and Daspuro, Zucchi and Vergine and Ferrara.

After a while Enrico went warbling out of his little ballerina's life and she took her unhallowed pirouettings out of his, and no more did she poke her pert little nose into our hero's affairs.

Caruso used to say afterward that his season of singing in Palermo marked the end of the first epoch in his career.

Now he was to leave behind the gay, heedless life of Naples. He was to meet more individuals of high importance and wide influence. Instead of haphazard flirtations he was to go through the first of his two great loves.

The Caruso Voice of Gold which was to conquer the world was now ringing forth in growing assurance, volume and beauty. Only occasionally did he now hold it back; and rarely did it break on his high notes.

One year more, and he was to win his first real stage success; and, after that, for years and years, in dozens of cities on two continents, he was to dwell in glory on the topmost heights of vocal achievement. Meanwhile, he continued to hit it off pleasantly with Leopoldo Mugnone and the Palermo audiences.

CHAPTER 4

BRIGHTENING SKIES

After Palermo, the sky of Caruso's life took on unprecedented brightness. From the days of his engagement there onward, no clouds—though he came under some dark ones—entirely robbed it of its radiance.

Things were coming his way. Friends were bestirring themselves in his behalf. The next meal was becoming less and less of a problem. The first signs of the fame that was to overwhelm him, of the tidal wave of glory that was to sweep him out of reality, were already becoming faintly apparent behind the screen of the future.

When the term of validity of Caruso's Palermo contract with Leopoldo Mugnone was nearing its end, the tenor's faithful friend Nicola Daspuro wrote from Naples to his Milan boss, the great publisher, Sonzogno, regarding the terms of another contract, already half-promised to Caruso, covering a series of operatic performances during the coming opera season in Rome.

Caruso, it was stipulated, was to sing in three operas—*Il Voto*, by Giordano; *L'Arlésiana*, by Cilèa; and *Bohème*, by Leoncavallo. Enrico's former teacher, Vergine, who was co-operating with Daspuro in the interests of the tenor, promptly objected to the inclusion of the last-named work. It was too heavy, said Vergine, for Caruso's voice. In all probability, however, that was not Vergine's real reason for objecting to the Leoncavallo work. He knew perfectly well that it had not achieved success either at its *première* or subsequently, whereas Puccini's opera on the same subject was already launched on the triumphant career which now, over half a century later, continues unchecked. Why waste time on Leoncavallo's "dead duck" when an opportunity might turn up for Caruso's appearance in Puccini's very much alive rival *Bohème?* So, doubtless, ran Vergine's reasoning; and he must have felt satisfaction at the course soon to be followed by Caruso with regard to Puccini and Puccini's *Bohème.*

While the faithful (and not entirely disinterested) Daspuro and the faithful (and not at all disinterested) Vergine (who still had his contract with Caruso locked up where he could get at it easily should occasion arise for brandishing it in the tenor's face) were zealously conducting their pro-Caruso campaign for the coming Rome opera season, another friend—newer, but more influential than Daspuro and Vergine—was also doing his bit for Enrico. This friend was Leopoldo Mugnone, Caruso's fellow ballerina-fancier.

From Palermo, Mugnone had written to an impresario, Lisciarelli, who was planning to launch an opera season at Livorno, to include performances of Puccini's *Bohème.* The man, wrote Mugnone, to sing Rodolfo in that opera was Enrico Caruso.

Lisciarelli was in a quandary. He had a Mimi for his *Bohème* production—Ada Giachetti, a competent, good-looking, and intelligent prima donna. For his Marcello he placed firm reliance on the baritone Pini Corsi (whom New York was to know later). But what about Rodolfo? So much depends on the tenor in an opera! Was his friend Mugnone right about Enrico Caruso? Should he hire him? If he did, what would the Ricordis think of the choice?

For the powerful Ricordi publishing firm, who controlled Puccini's output, constantly put in their oar regarding singers chosen by managers for singing assignments in Ricordi-published operas, and sometimes met managerial suggestions regarding such singers with a flat veto.

Finally, the impresario got tired of tearing his hair and corrugating his brow. He would summon Caruso to Livorno and make his selection for the role of Rodolfo conditional on the approval of the great Puccini himself, who was staying at his country place at Torre del Lago, not far from Livorno.

So Caruso journeyed to Livorno, presented himself before Lisciarelli, and made a counter-proposal: If Puccini disapproved of him for the part, and Lisciarelli, nevertheless, decided to sign him up as Rodolfo, he was to get fifteen lire ($3.00) for each performance; but, should the great man approve him, he was to receive 1,000 lire ($200) for each *Bohème*. Lisciarelli refused to agree. And, for a short time, nothing more was heard either of the Lisciarelli proposal or the Caruso counter-proposal.

But one day Caruso was out hunting with a friend near Torre del Lago, and the friend, who was acquainted with Puccini, took Caruso to the composer's villa.

Soon Puccini seated himself at the piano, with Caruso standing beside him. To the great man's accompaniment, the tenor began to sing *"Che gelida manina,"* from the first act of the Puccini *Bohème*.

After the first few phrases, Puccini suddenly stopped playing, swung around on the piano stool to face Caruso, and said to him, in an awed voice: "Who sent you to me? God?"

Then and there the great question was settled as to who was to sing Rodolfo for Lisciarelli at Livorno. The com-

Puccini at rehearsal

poser wholeheartedly approved the candidacy of Enrico Caruso for the role.

Caruso, of course, was overjoyed; but certain misgivings, based on his awareness of still unconquered defects in his singing, returned to plague him. He informed the composer diffidently that he still had difficulty in negotiating high notes—that one of the notes which caused him most trouble was the high C at the end of *"Che gelida manina."*

"Oh, don't let that worry you," counseled Puccini. "Remember: it's not obligatory." And he pointed out that it might be sung, if need be, half a tone lower.

"But no matter what you do with that note," he went on, "just go ahead and *sing the entire aria well.* Don't be like many tenors who, because they concentrate their thoughts entirely on that final high note, sing the whole aria badly."

Caruso returned to Livorno walking on air. Filled with gusty Neapolitan elation he rushed into the presence of Lisciarelli. And Lisciarelli proceeded, figuratively speaking, to douse him with a large bucketful of ice water.

He informed the tenor that, since he had gone to see Puccini on his own initiative, without consultation with his manager, he, Lisciarelli, was not obligated to pay 1,000 lire for each Caruso performance of Rodolfo—no, not even with the great Puccini's accolade—but only the fifteen lire which Caruso was earning for singing other tenor roles under the Lisciarelli banner.

It took all the insouciant Neapolitan in Caruso to stand up to this blow. But stand up he did. Never a worrier, he was soon his carefree self again—even though his pay was only 1½ per cent of the fee which had shimmered before him in his short post-Puccini dream.

Having been chided by Vergine for dallying in Livorno

instead of co-operating more zealously with Vergine's and Daspuro's efforts to get Caruso roles in Rome, Enrico wrote a letter of exculpation to his former teacher, which included the following—showing how high he rated the importance of his meeting with Puccini and the praise which he had received from that great personage:

"I have not stayed here without good reason. What you say about my conduct has displeased me so much that I cannot sleep at night. If I return now to Naples my pockets will be almost empty. I have been pushed ahead two years in my career by having been chosen by Puccini and by having learned the part [Rodolfo] from him. That, it seems to me, is a satisfaction for which anybody would be willing to pay a high price.

"I have been in Puccini's house. I have sat down to eat with him at his table. He treats me like a brother. I see him here every two or three days. So please don't hold your grudge against me. A kiss from

Your

Enrico."

His success with Puccini was not the only reason for his wishing to stay in Lisciarelli's opera company; he had become very much interested indeed in Ada Giachetti, the soprano who was to sing Mimi in Lisciarelli's forthcoming production of *Bohème*. When Enrico finally appeared (at $3.00) in the *Bohème première* in Livorno it was to Ada Giachetti that he sang *"Che gelida manina"*; and, before long, she was his inamorata off the stage as well as on.

Enrico now found himself embarked upon the first of the two great loves of his life. Ada Giachetti was a singer and actress of merit, a handsome woman some years older than Enrico Caruso. This true romance was to last eleven years. During the first part of that period, wherever Caruso went, Ada went with him. Ada already had a husband; divorce in Italy was difficult. They never married. But, when she arrived with Enrico in New York just before the tenor's Met debut, American prejudices of the day were respected. She was introduced as Mrs. Caruso—and nobody was the wiser.

In due course Ada and Enrico had a son, who was named Rodolfo, for it was as Puccini's Rodolfo and Mimi that his father and mother first trod the stage together. This son was known always—from childhood to maturity—by the rather less poetical appellation of Fofò. And the brother who came later to the Caruso-Giachetti household, though christened Enrico, Jr., was invariably called Mimmi. There were two other sons; both died in infancy.

Once the first raptures had died away a little, Enrico and Ada got down to serious planning. Livorno had served its turn, they thought as they looked into the future; but Livorno was only a stepping-stone. The name of Caruso was growing in Italy. Puccini had praised him, and Mugnone's enthusiasm counted for more than a little. Caruso was no longer merely another Neapolitan tenor. He must now gain national recognition. He must go to Milan.

Milan. That was the next goal. Milan, the operatic capital of Italy. Milan, that prosperous and cultured community, whose citizens loved opera and were willing to pay handsomely for the privilege of enjoying it at its best. Milan, home of music publishers, impresarios, conductors, theatrical agents, and powerful music critics, who could do so much to open doors for aspiring singers—or to slam doors shut in their faces.

Yes, Milan next for Enrico, they decided. He must be resolute and constructive in his thinking.

For him to go to Milan will cost fifty lire. No matter. He is resolute. He looks up a friend. He is constructive. He borrows fifty lire. At the Livorno station, Ada kisses him and puts him on the train. Then she returns, pensive, to their lodgings, to pray for the success of Caruso's venture.

CHAPTER **5**

FEDORA AND FAME

"It is uncertain," remarks Eugenio Gara, one of Enrico Caruso's biographers, and a most amusing individual, "whether the Galleria in Milan was built on a spot which was already the market-place of operatic folk, so that they might have a roof over them, or whether it was built first and the opera people flocked to it, as soon as it was finished, as an ideal place for gossiping and bargaining."

Every American who has ever been to Milan knows the Galleria—that glass-covered congeries of offices, shops, and restaurants, the architectural wonder of its day, leading from the square in front of La Scala to the square dominated by Milan's superb cathedral. But how many of them, watching, in the years of Caruso's youth, the Galleria's ebbing, flowing, animated, gesticulating, loquacious crowds, ever knew that there, in front of Biffi's and Campari's— packed full of Milanese munching their traditional 11:00 A.M. snack and washing it down with that bitter concoction known for some mysterious reason as an Americano— operatic luck, good and bad, was being bought and sold; operatic futures fettered and freed; operatic contracts planned; operatic tours blueprinted.

How many Americans, strolling through the Galleria, just before the twentieth century took over from the nineteenth, were aware that one of those gesticulators was Giulio Gatti-Casazza, manager of Milan's famous La Scala, another, Arturo Toscanini, young but already celebrated, the perfectionist commander of La Scala's orchestra; another, Arrigo Boïto, well known as a composer and better still as an operatic librettist; another Giulio Ricordi, Italy's most prominent music publisher; another Eduardo Sonzogno, Ricordi's leading publishing rival; and still another the Grand Old Man himself, the creator of *Rigoletto* and *Aïda* and *Traviata,* of *Otello* and *Falstaff*—Giuseppe Verdi? How many of them knew that, in those autumn days of 1898, a rather nervous youth with a big black mustache, trying hard not to look too attentively at snacks and Americanos and other alluring articles beyond his means at the moment, was Enrico Caruso?

On arrival in Milan he had taken a room at the Pensione Gasperini. Price per week, meals included, thirty-five lire ($7.00). Cheap enough. That is, if you had the seven dollars. Enrico Caruso had not. Besides, he owed fifty lire to the friend in Livorno who had staked him to the train fare to Milan.

He did not want presents of money. Just a loan. In the Galleria he met obliging individuals quite willing to accommodate him with small sums—always ready to help a deserving young man—at 50 per cent interest. Enrico drew back from them in alarm; he decided, after some hesitation, to apply to the great publisher-impresario Eduardo Sonzogno, with whom his Neapolitan allies, Daspuro and Vergine, were negotiating for his next contract.

Diffidently he asked the great Sonzogno for a small advance payment. With the munificence of the well-to-do, Sonzogno advanced him a sum considerably larger than the one he had asked for. There was something of the grand seigneur about Signor Eduardo. Also, as a generous

gesture, he engaged Enrico for some performances of Puccini's *Bohème* in Fiume, across the Adriatic, then under
the Austrian flag.

That sufficed to loosen tongues in the Galleria. Who
was this upstart from Naples? How dared he try to push
himself into the sacred realm of the great tenors, presided
over by De Lucia, lord of the high C's; by Tamagno and
Stagno and Masini; by Alessandro Borgatti and Alessandro
Bonci? When Caruso returned from Fiume, where he had
done well, false rumors were whispered in the Galleria
that he had failed. Again they dragged out the old specter
of baritonism. Even Sonzogno complained to Daspuro, his
representative, down in Naples: "I ask you to send me a
tenor and you send me a baritone!" To which Daspuro,
never at a loss in bandying repartee, retorted: "If Caruso
is a baritone, De Lucia is a basso profundo." He added:
"Patience, Signor Eduardo. Listen more to Caruso's voice
and less to Galleria gossip."

A few days later Sonzogno summoned Enrico to his
presence and inquired: "Are you ready to sing the three
operas for me?"

"Two," corrected Caruso. After having been patted on
the back by Puccini, composer of the successful *Bohème*,
he was less attracted than ever to Leoncavallo's unsuccess-
ful opera on the same subject, at which audiences were
sniffing—and which was the third item on his semi-contract
with Sonzogno. He added: "My teacher [Vergine], as you
know, finds Leoncavallo's score too exacting for my voice."
Sonzogno was unconvinced.

"I'll send you an accompanist," he told the tenor, "to
help you with the Leoncavallo *Bohème*." Caruso subsided.
He knew that Sonzogno was still free to cease dealing with
him without further ado should his preliminary work prove
unsatisfactory.

That accompanist proved an angel in disguise—like Major Nagliati in the days of Caruso's short military service. After Enrico and he had gone over their music, he rushed off to Sonzogno to tell him, in enthusiastic language, about the excellence of the young tenor. Without waiting to listen himself to Enrico's voice, Sonzogno, who was partial to spur-of-the-moment decisions, sent Caruso a letter definitely confirming the contract concerning which he had been negotiating with Daspuro and Vergine.

And now Caruso was ordered—with the abruptness characteristic of opera management in Italy at that time—to forget the three operas mentioned in his contract and to prepare instead to sing in Massenet's *La Navarraise*—at five days' notice!

Caruso was so weary when he appeared for the dress rehearsal (at the Teatro Lirico in Milan) that, when he was introduced to the prima donna, an irascible female called De Nuovina, he forgot to remove his hat, whereupon she knocked it off his head. After that the dress rehearsal proceeded in an atmosphere of restraint and uncertainty.

But fate will have its fun: Signora de Nuovina made a botch of her part at the opening performance and Enrico did not. In fact, he had success that night pretty much to himself, for the critics shot their shafts not only at De Nuovina but at Massenet, the composer of the opera. "This tenor," wrote one newspaper critic about Enrico, "has a really beautiful, spontaneous voice. He is on the high road to a brilliant career."

The fruits of his success soon showed themselves. The composer Cilèa wanted him (and got him) for his new opera, *L'Arlésiana*. Again there were eulogistic adjectives in the powerful Milanese press—especially unusual because music commentators in Milan in those days were said to "distribute praise with closed fists." Much of the newspaper praise went to young Caruso's singing of the "lament" in Cilèa's opera. Indeed, some students of his career insist that, in that aria, he showed for the first time the boundless possibilities of his voice of gold. And his rendering of the drinking song (has anybody ever tried to add up all the drinking songs in grand opera?) brought him rousing calls for an encore from the audience. All this good news was duly transmitted to Ada Giachetti in Livorno—and soon she also was brought to the musical capital of Italy and installed in an apartment. There, on July 2, 1899, their first son, Rodolfo (Fofò) was born.

Sonzogno rewarded Enrico for his good work in the Cilèa opera by sending him to Genoa, where he sang with a singer destined to become well known and popular in New York, the baritone Giuseppe di Luca. As neither was making enough money to write home about, they lodged in a modest boardinghouse, where (as at Milan's Pensione Gasperini) meals were included in the price of a room. But both the singers were young, though financially embarrassed, and boardinghouse fare was not for them if there happened to be coins in their pockets. So they roamed among the city's restaurants, of which, as I remember, there are 250—249 serve fish soup, Genoese style, and the 250th has just run out of it.

They particularly liked the Righi restaurant. There, one evening, they were recognized by patrons who had been to the theater where they sang. The proprietor of the restaurant, scenting a good thing for the house, requested them to sing for the assembled diners. Caruso and Di Luca consented—indeed, they were most generous, for, after the tenor had sung the "Flower Song" from *Carmen* (the one in which the high note had bothered him so much in his novitiate), he and Di Luca obliged with the duet from Bizet's *Pêcheurs de Perles*.

There was much applause, many expressions of good will, bows from the other diners, bows from Caruso and Di Luca, wine and more wine and still more wine, toasts and more toasts. And then the proprietor, after executing a solo bow, laid on the singers' table a bill for 180 lire ($36.00).

They found it outrageous—particularly in view of the generosity which they had shown in the matter of free songs. After contemplating the bill for a while in a cold and disparaging manner, Caruso remarked to the restaurateur: "You charge us 180 lire for what we have eaten and drunk. Our usual charge for an evening of song such as we have just provided is 300 lire. So you owe us 120 lire."

It is not on record whether the proprietor saw the force of the tenor's surprising mathematical demonstration, nor whether Caruso and Di Luca paid 180 lire—or anything like it—for their food and wine.

After Genoa, an astounding piece of good fortune came to Enrico Caruso.

While he had been singing for Manager Lisciarelli at Livorno, the well-known prima donna, Gemma Bellincioni, had been favorably impressed by his performance in one of the operas of his repertoire. At that time preparations were well advanced at Milan's Teatro Lirico for the impatiently awaited *première* of Umberto Giordano's *Fedora*, in which the tenor part was to be sung by the celebrated Stagno, who, in addition to being one of the foremost tenors in Europe, was Gemma Bellincioni's lover. Giordano, a rollicking Bohemian, was living at the apartment of Stagno and Bellincioni, putting the finishing touches to his score; and Stagno, knowing the composer's irresponsibility, often locked him up in his room and refused to let

him out until he had produced another batch of music for
Fedora.

All was going beautifully, publishers and everybody else
concerned were agreeing like birds in their little nests, the
operatic public, duly excited by the condiment of newspaper gossip, was in a high state of delicious expectancy,
when suddenly—Stagno died.

Crisis. The date of the *première* was at hand. And *Fedora*
was without a tenor! At this point Gemma Bellincioni
thought of the impression made on her by Caruso in
Livorno. She suggested him as a substitute for Stagno.
She was taking a chance, of course, and so were Giordano
and Eduardo Sonzogno, the producer. But time was pressing. And when Sonzogno boldly decided to stake all on
Caruso, the stage was set for the biggest opportunity so
far in the tenor's career.

Fedora was given for the first time at the Teatro Lirico
on November 17, 1898, five years before Caruso's New York
debut. The tenor, not yet twenty-six years old, had an
electrifying success, far and away the most sensational that
had ever come to him.

His hearers went into frenzies. They roared with delight.
Their applause was terrific. Wild demands for encores
shook the theater. Next morning, the Milanese critics were
delirious. "One of the most beautiful tenor voices ever
heard." "Caruso was acclaimed." "All through the opera
he was admirable." "Each time he started a phrase, a
rustle of approval ran through the audience." "At every bit
of song by him enthusiastic applause burst forth."

Caruso had arrived. These were no part-time music
critics in Caserta, no aspiring amateur columnists in
Palermo or Livorno. These were the arbiters of the entire
Italian musical world. From now on there would be no

problem of hunting for engagements. Enrico and Ada were ecstatic.

The furor would not stop. For days all Milan talked about the new singer's victory. The columnist of a popular weekly magazine wrote, beside himself, "Caruso sang in *Fedora* and turned it into gold." The mail brought Enrico one contract form after another. Agents hinted at hitherto unapproached rates of pay. No more two-dollar indignities at suburban opera houses! There was a new light in his skies.

CHAPTER 6

CUFF LINKS
AND A SECRETARY

Caruso had ascended into international prominence overnight, for a success in Milan was tantamount to a European success. The musical world is small. Word spread quickly from Milan to Paris and London that an amazing new tenor had done marvels in Giordano's *Fedora*—it spread from Milan to Barcelona and Madrid; from Milan to Vienna and Berlin, and to St. Petersburg in Imperial Russia. The stone of success had been cast, and the ripples of fame were spreading outward and outward.

And now began the era of Caruso the Globe-Trotter. Until his smashing success in *Fedora* he had never been out of his native Italy except for that one trip to Egypt. Now he could choose from among a number of tempting offers. He accepted one for the 1898-1899 opera season in St. Petersburg.

Quite a number of Italian singers and composers of that period and earlier knew Russia as a land of rubles, zero weather, sleighs, and furs; of Grand Dukes dotted all over a snowy landscape; of a Czar living in a magnificent palace who graciously received singers of both sexes amid semi-oriental pageantry and handed out jewels of assorted kinds to all. Mario, that aristocratic Italian warbler of an earlier generation, had received in Russia a cordial welcome not only from the Czar but from the great Russian writer

Turgenev, who had kissed him. And Grand Old Man Verdi, who hated travel, had ventured some years before to the Russian capital to preside over a production of his *La Forza del Destino*, and—being distrustful of Russian cuisine— had taken along with him, mixed in with tail-coats and high hats and fur-lined gloves, a large stock of spaghetti.

Enrico Caruso made the trip to St. Petersburg in exalted company—with Luisa Tetrazzini, the soprano whose high notes were before long to arouse New York to enthusiasm; Sigrid Arnoldson, also to become well known at the Met; and the gigantic basso, Vittorio Arimondi, later, likewise, a New York favorite, who, amid Russian snow and ice, became Caruso's inseparable companion.

Enrico sang with success in the Russian capital. He explored that great city with Arimondi. And, after a grand concert at the Imperial Palace, he met the Romanoff family. "The Czar [Nicholas II]," he said later, "was a little, almost insignificant, man, with an uneasy expression on his face. Royalty, I decided, was something which, so far as I was concerned, was to be viewed at a distance. The scene in the palace was brilliant. All those beautiful ladies and imposing gentlemen, gathered in those splendid rooms! It was an entirely new experience for me."

Caruso was duly presented to the Czar, who muttered: "Thank you very much" and passed him on to the Grand Russian Imperial Distributor of Gewgaws, who gave him a pair of gold cuff links.

When he returned from Russia to Milan with his links and his laurels, he remembered that, just before his engagement to sing in *Fedora*, he had agreed with Signora Ferrari, an Italian impresario (or rather impresaria), who was recruiting an opera company for Buenos Aires, to sing for her there. Friends in Milan's Galleria now advised him to throw his contract with Signora Ferrari into the waste-

basket. After *Fedora*, after Russia, he could do better. But
one participant in Galleria confabulations, the agent Carlo
d'Ormeville, was of a different mind.

"Look here, Enrico," he said, "who ever showed any
real confidence in you *before Fedora?* Only Signora Ferrari.
When she asked you to sign up with her, you were not
famous, as you are now. I am sure you will keep your word
with her."

"I would rather die than break a contract," said Caruso.
Which was no empty rhetoric. He had always been like
that and remained so for the rest of his life.

So Caruso informed Impresaria Ferrari that his Buenos
Aires contract was sacred to him. Meanwhile, he had hard
work killing malicious rumors that the freezing weather of
Russia had impaired his voice. The impresaria herself was
worried by this tittle-tattle. But Grand Seigneur Sonzogno
rose splendidly to the occasion. "They say you have left
your voice in Russia," he said to Caruso. "Let them. Just
remember that my theaters are always open to you." And
he signed up the tenor for more performances of *Fedora*
at Milan's Teatro Lirico.

Then—off across the Atlantic to Buenos Aires. His first
appearance there was not auspicious. Even Caruso could
not sing life into Massenet's *Sappho*. But he scored in
Goldmark's *Regina di Saba*, of which one Buenos Aires
critic remarked, "Praise for the evening must certainly go
to Caruso, certainly not to Goldmark." On another evening
in the South American metropolis he repeated the drinking
song in *Cavalleria Rusticana* three times.

On his return to Europe he landed at Naples, and that
hitherto indifferent city went wild. Exuberant greetings
sounded in his ears. Crowds followed him on the streets.
Scores of persons whom he had never seen in his life
pressed around him, reminding him of how they had

given him wise counsel, helped him over early hurdles, dandled him in their arms when he was a baby. The absentee King of Naples had come into his kingdom.

His next engagement was in Rome, at the Teatro Costanzi. When he arrived there, he found that the conductor was to be Leopoldo Mugnone, his former rival for the love of the Salerno ballerina.

That individual had fallen in a short time before with Lombardi, Caruso's old teacher and fervent admirer, who had informed Mugnone confidently that before long Enrico would be earning 1,000 lire a night in Italian opera houses.

"Nonsense!" scoffed Mugnone. "When Enrico Caruso is paid 1,000 lire a night, I'll be the Pope!"

Soon after, came the news that Caruso had been engaged somewhere in Italy at 1,000 lire a night. Lombardi rushed off to Mugnone, prostrated himself before him, bowed his head to the ground, and made as if to kiss the conductor's feet.

"What the hell?" queried Mugnone.

"Haven't you heard? Caruso is making 1,000 lire a night. You're the Pope."

Life was certainly a different affair for Caruso these days. He was traveling all over the world, from the snowy elegance of St. Petersburg to the Latin ebullience of Buenos Aires. And this new success and affluence brought about great changes in his personal life. As his American biographer, Pierre van Renssalaer Key, remarks: "He had won the public. . . . He could look ahead. . . . Visible signs of this material and mental prosperity were beginning to appear. His former slenderness of figure had given way to one manifestly stocky. . . . Never given to bodily exercise and able at this time to eat whatever and as much as he pleased, Caruso was entering willingly on a period of self-indulgence. He smoked cigarettes, he laughed when asked if he were not afraid they might affect his voice. . . ." * Caruso embarked on a life of luxury and good living and good clothes. He was becoming quite a dandy. And he acquired a secretary.

Some time before, at Salerno, one of the tenor's most ardent partisans was a man called Lorello, who went around town proclaiming Caruso to be the "greatest singer in the world." To reward these eulogies, the tenor, who at that time was rather less interested in getting a secretary than in getting the price of a square meal, had jokingly promised: "When I am as successful as you say I'm going to be, I'll hire you." He kept his word. He wrote to Lorello in Salerno, reminding him of their talk. And Lorello packed up his belongings and joined Caruso in Rome as his secretary—the first in a long line.

But, into the midst of all the good things which life was now showering on Enrico came a disappointment— handed to him by that very Giacomo Puccini who had been so entranced with Caruso's singing at his Torre del Lago villa that he had hinted that God might have had something to do with bringing the two of them together.

Puccini was now the composer of the hour. His *Bohème* had firmly intrenched him in the favor of the operatic public. His next opera, *Tosca*, was being awaited with an impatience of which there had been no equal since the days when people all over the world were expecting another opera from Verdi.

Enrico had high hopes of being the first Mario Cavaradossi in Puccini's *Tosca*. After his reception at Torre del Lago he felt that Puccini would favor his candidacy for the part—one which, as everyone knows,

* P. v. R. Key and Bruno Zirato, *Enrico Caruso*, Little, Brown, 1922.

he later made almost as much his own as Canio in
Pagliacci.

But, to his chagrin, Puccini came out in favor of a
rival tenor, De Marchi. And De Marchi it was who sang
Mario Cavaradossi at the *Tosca première.* Disappointment was all the bitterer because Caruso, then as always,
delighted in singing something new. Unlike many of his
colleagues, he refused to cling blindly to old traditions
and old methods and old operas. To him the theater
was a living thing, not a museum of old relics. And yet
Puccini had given Cavaradossi to somebody else! Enrico,
in his disillusionment, was inclined to agree wholly with
the famous Spanish tenor Gayarre, who, in a somber
moment, had exclaimed, "The singer is the slave of the
composer."

But there were compensations, too. During his season
under Mugnone at Rome, Caruso sang in *Mefistofele.* His
performance was a great success. Furthermore, Arrigo
Boïto (not Puccini, but a good second best), the composer
and librettist of *Mefistofele,* approached him and said, "I
came to Rome especially to hear you. Your voice has a
something which touches my heart. In your singing there
is an instinctive quality which I cannot describe. I con-
gratulate myself on having heard you. And my heart
and soul thank you for the joy you have given to both."

In 1900, Caruso returned to Russia. He opened at
St. Petersburg in *Aïda.* In the company with him were
the famous diva Kruscheniski and the great Battistini.
Later on, he attributed much of the improvement in his
voice and acting to his having taken part more and more
in *Aïda.* It brought out dramatic qualities in his singing
and acting which no other role had accentuated so much.
"Rhadamès," said Caruso, "developed and consolidated

my voice." And Rhadamès was always one of his finest, best-rounded, most thrilling parts.

While in St. Petersburg, Caruso was awaiting one day the arrival of Ada Giachetti, who was coming to join him with the wife of the basso, Arimondi. Secretary Lorello went to the railroad station to receive them—Caruso himself could not do so, nor could Arimondi, because they were up to their ears in rehearsal work. The train failed to arrive. After trying in vain to get definite news about it from railroad officials Lorello returned to his employer and reported his failure.

Caruso flew into a rage. *"Dio mio!* What sort of a secretary have I wished on myself? Lorello, go at once to higher officials, to the highest, to the Czar, if need be, and find out exactly why the train does not arrive!" That, remarks Biographer Gara, was a large order, since poor Lorello spoke no tongue fluently "except the dialect of his native Salerno, little known among the bureaucrats of Imperial Russia."

More time passed. More fuming from the tenor. Then a telegram came. But—it was in Russian. In a fury, Caruso dashed out, hatless, his throat almost unprotected, in icy cold, to find somebody to elucidate the telegram; and, finally, he learned that the train had run off the rails, that both Ada and Signora Arimondi were all right, but that they would have to wait where they were until a relief train appeared.

They arrived after more waiting and all was well with everybody—except Enrico Caruso.

He came down with pneumonia. For a whole month he was out of the running. All engagements had to be canceled. But that illness was, in a way, a blessing. It taught him that henceforth he must take better care of himself. He was only twenty-seven years old, he felt as young as ever, but—no longer could he act the carefree Neapolitan of yesterday. His voice would not stand it. Besides, he must think of Ada, of Fofò.

Also, he said to himself as he was convalescing, it behooved him to study harder. Opera was a cruelly competitive game—so many rivals!—so many ill-wishers on the lookout for signs of a singer's slipping! As a first step, he reverted to an old Naples occupation of his, copying notes. As a youth, he had often pocketed a few soldi by copying music for others—sometimes, at night, by the light of a street lamp. Now, he discovered, putting the notes of a role on paper helped him to remember the role. To the end of his life he continued to use this method— many who knew him in New York remember him hard at work at it. On the way back from Russia to Italy, one of his companions on the train, catching him busy with his system of memorizing, thus admonished Enrico: "Be sure to copy every note correctly. If you don't, you'll be a composer!"

After his recovery he sang in Moscow. Thanks to his preliminary bout of hard study he now found *Faust*, that dreadful landmark of his past, astonishingly easy. Henceforth he looked upon it as a sort of primer of opera. *Aïda* and pneumonia had done a good job for him. Whenever, in later days, he got into difficulties in trying to master roles in more modern, more complicated operas, he went back to *Faust* to clear his mind.

Back in Milan, the malicious tongue-wagging of the Galleria again worried him. Never had he been so sensitive to gossip—which, remarks Eugenio Gara, was just too bad, because "too much sensitiveness, like too much drink, makes people see double."

Even after he arrived again in Buenos Aires (he had signed up for another season there), he was not yet himself. He sang unsatisfactorily in *Mefistofele*. He was in despair. He thought gloomily of throwing up his contract, departing for home in disgrace. But soon his voice came back to him in full, glorious volume. The operagoers of Buenos Aires roared their approval of him, and all was as gay and bright again for Enrico Caruso as if the River Plate were the Bay of Naples and Buenos Aires the enchanting city where he had been born to laughter and happiness and sunshine.

On returning to Italy he sang in Bologna, where a War of Tenors was in full cry. The local partisans of Alessandro Borgatti were arrayed in furious, voluble opposition against those of Alessandro Bonci, who was before long to sing in New York, first as Caruso's rival at Hammerstein's Manhattan Opera House, later as his fellow member of the Metropolitan Opera House forces. It looked as if Bologna were no place for Caruso. But he sang in *Iris*. He sang in *Tosca*. The Borgatti faction forgot Borgatti. The Bonci faction forgot Bonci. United Bologna acclaimed Caruso.

CHAPTER 7

"*QUESTO NAPOLETANO*"

The Opera House of La Scala, in Milan, was in 1900, as it is today, the most important musical center in Italy. It had been founded in 1778 on the site of the Church of Santa Maria della Scala (from which the opera house drew its name) by a group known as the Associated Cavaliers. In its early days the Cavaliers were granted the ownership of La Scala's boxes, each of which displayed, in colorful panoply, its noble owner's coat of arms. During its beginnings, La Scala was a place of general resort, a combination of theater, club, dance hall, and gambling joint. The spectators, in the uninhibited Italian fashion, engaged freely in give-and-take badinage with the actors.

Over the years, La Scala had established itself as the shrine of Italian music. The great tradition of nineteenth-century Italian opera had unfolded within its walls. It had seen the supreme performances of Rossini, Bellini, Donizetti, Verdi, and Boïto. Always hospitable to non-Italian composers, La Scala had echoed to the operas of Mozart, Berlioz, Wagner, Bizet, Massenet, Gounod, and the Brazilian Gomes. And it had welcomed Italian composers of the new school who were fighting upward in Caruso's early days: Mascagni, Leoncavallo, Giordano, Cilèa. Its conductors, who had included Caruso's friend and rival, Mugnone, had been the finest. And now the finest of the finest, the young Arturo Toscanini, friend of Puccini and Verdi, was its musical director. The best of the world's singers had added year after year to the glory of La Scala: Malibran, Grisi, Pasta, Jenny Lind; Rubini, Tamberlik, Gayarre, Tamagno; Streppone (Verdi's great love), Schroeder-Devrient, Sontag, Mario, Chaliapin, Maurel—this list only scratches the surface!

Not only in art did La Scala shine. Under Austrian domination, it had become revered in Italy as a symbol of Italian patriotism. Standing before the box of the Austrian military governor, a Milanese youth in mid-nineteenth century brazenly kept his high hat on during the playing of the Austrian national anthem until the governor, a peppery Austrian general, jumped up and knocked it off his head. In 1859, when the La Scala chorus in Bellini's *Norma* sang the great ensemble beginning "*Guerra! Guerra!*" ("War! War!"), every Italian in the theater leaped to his feet, crazed with patriotic ardor, to join in the singing. The performance broke down in chaos. To La Scala's audiences, the "Lament of the Jewish Captives" in Verdi's *Nabucco—premièred* there many years before Enrico Caruso was born—had embodied not the woes of alien prisoners thousands of years ago in an alien land, but cries from the hearts of fellow Italians thirsting for freedom.

Caruso could not truly feel that Italy was at his feet until he had sung at La Scala. The Teatro Lirico in Milan had been a triumph; but the real Milanese public, without whose approval no singer could say that he had conquered Italy—*that* public he had not conquered. If only Caruso could leap this most formidable among all the hurdles so far in his career! If only he could force the audience of La Scala to listen, applaud, acclaim. If only . . .

After the usual scurrying to and fro of agents and semi-agents, friends and semi-friends, Caruso was summoned before the great duumvirate of La Scala, Giulio Gatti-Casazza, manager, and Arturo Toscanini, musical director.

Both, still young, were already celebrities. Gatti-Casazza had made such a fine record managing the opera house in Ferrara that the directors of La Scala had made up their minds that they simply must have him. Toscanini was known already to the *cognoscenti* as the rising star in the orchestral heavens. Already they were peering into the future and prophesying for him that astounding career which, in New York, was to reach its zenith—and which, with the twenieth century more than half over, still flourishes.

Some idea of the extraordinary durability of Toscanini's fame may be gained by reflecting on the fact that, to conduct the *première* of Puccini's *Bohème* in Turin in 1897, it was young Toscanini who was picked from among all available candidates—*fifty-six years ago!* Throughout Italy, before and after that *Bohème* first night, Toscanini had been asserting himself inflexibly as the most relentless of disciplinarians; the most selfless and conscientious interpreter of composers (not for him the doctrine of the singer first, the composer nowhere!); the hardest worker; the leading hater of encores; the most ruthless curber of vanity and excessive temperament; the leader, the king, the emperor of perfectionists. "He used to drive us unmercifully," said one opera singer who sang under his direction in those early days. "He kept stopping rehearsals to object to what we often considered a triviality. Sometimes he made us angry. Always, however, we realized, when we cooled off, that he had a good reason for every objection that he made; that everything he demanded of us helped toward the success of the opera which he was rehearsing."

In thinking of Gatti-Casazza, Toscanini, and Caruso, Americans who knew them first on American soil, when all three were getting along in years, are inclined unconsciously to assume that they were born mature men. Yet, when the nineteenth century was giving way to the twentieth, Gatti-Casazza was under thirty. That Assyrian beard of his was not the impressive hedge which it later became while he was manager of New York's Metropolitan. Toscanini was just entering his thirties. He was not so very far removed from the days when, a musical beginner, he had played the cello in the orchestra rehearsing for the world *première* at La Scala of Verdi's *Otello*, under the baton of the Grand Old Man himself. Caruso was still in his twenties. He was full of the zest and fire of his years—with a slender figure, flashing black Neapolitan eyes and a big curling mustache. And when he twirled the mustache to attract Milanese damsels tripping through the Galleria it helped to give him the look of a young pirate on shore leave.

Such were the Gatti-Casazza, Toscanini, and Caruso of the turn of the century. All three were to go far—sensationally far—in their respective careers. Yet, for all three, probably nothing lavished on them by fame equaled the flavor of those early days in Milan.

Caruso stood before Gatti-Casazza and Toscanini. They knew his singing record. They knew all about *Fedora* at Milan's Lirico, about St. Petersburg and Buenos Aires.

After looking him over at the Scala offices, they doubtless continued at the Galleria their discussion of his merits—over two Americanos. The upshot was that Manager Gatti-Casazza, with the invaluable backing of Conductor Toscanini, had the prescience to sign up Enrico for the 1900-1901 season at La Scala. Probably a third expert had something to do with Caruso's engagement—Arrigo Boïto.

For the opening production of that season at La Scala, Wagner's *Tristan und Isolde* had been selected, with Borgatti, veteran of the Bologna War of the Tenors, in the leading male role. The second production was to be Puccini's *Bohème*, with Caruso as Rodolfo, and, as Mimi, his good friend, Emma Carelli.

The rehearsals of *Bohème* commenced, with Toscanini conducting. At the first one, Caruso sang away admirably. But when the "*Che gelida manina*" aria came in the first act, he suddenly reverted to a falsetto for the high C at the end. Why he did so, what demon of tenorial perversity possessed him, is a mystery. Ever since Lombardi, back in Salerno, had reproved him for "holding back," he had been letting himself go on high notes and eschewing voice-saving trickery. Perhaps Enrico, nervous at the prospect of La Scala, was trying to make it known that he could be as temperamental as any other musical grandee.

Toscanini asked him for a stronger high C. Caruso nodded pleasantly. However, at the end of "*Che gelida manina*" there came no strong C from Caruso.

"How about that stronger high note I asked you for?" inquired the conductor ominously.

And the tenor, in his current enslavement to temperament, answered with a touch of petulance: "I don't feel like singing it just now."

Toscanini bristled. All through the next two rehearsals the atmosphere was uneasy. Caruso maintained that he ought to husband his voice for the actual production and that it was folly to waste voice on a mere rehearsal. The only flaw in his thinking—a very serious flaw—was that Toscanini thought otherwise.

After the third rehearsal, the conductor told Caruso that he might lower the final note of the troublesome aria by half a tone if he wished—but *he must give it full voice.* Enrico sang it in half-voice once more.

The tenor was informed coldly that there would be a special rehearsal at five o'clock the next afternoon. At this rehearsal, Toscanini made the singers read through *Bohème* backward, as it were: Act III first, Act II next, Act I last of all. Caruso now sang all his music full voice, including the high C in the Act I aria. Toscanini's brow cleared. But —perfectionist then and now—he called another rehearsal for nine o'clock *that same evening.*

The singers, amazed, looked at one another in despair. Caruso, feeling tricked, was about to explode into Neapolitan violence. But Emma Carelli laid a quieting hand on his sleeve. "Never mind," she whispered. "Tonight we'll all sing half-voice."

But when the evening rehearsal opened, Emma saw before her an audience including some of the foremost Milanese musical and social leaders and all the first-string critics of the big newspapers. She completely forgot her plan and shot out her voice in full volume. Caruso, however, dog-tired and feeling completely betrayed by all the world, stubbornly sang half-voice again. Eyebrows were raised. Toscanini was fuming. The duet between Caruso and Emma was completely out of balance.

The curtain fell on Act I. Gatti-Casazza, who knew his Toscanini, hurried back to Caruso's dressing room.

"A bit more voice. Please," he begged.

Toscanini conducting a rehearsal

"I can't sing full voice," growled Caruso. "I've just eaten dinner." In the next act he continued falsetto.

That was enough for Toscanini. He stopped the orchestra. He glared at the tenor. A silence fell. He lifted his baton and pointed it at Caruso. Icily, he delivered his ultimatum.

"If you won't sing in full voice, I can't go on."

Only excuses and arm-waving from Enrico. Toscanini threw down his baton and stalked out of the orchestra pit.

Consternation. Horror. Emissaries were sent to both dressing rooms. In Enrico's, our hero talked darkly of canceling his contract and returning the advance money, of leaving Milan. The emissaries remonstrated in vain. Caruso was unyielding. However, La Scala's diplomatic corps had dealt with trickier situations than this before, and won. Now they played their trump card.

Into the scowling tenor's dressing room came Duke Visconti di Modrone, scion of the ancient Visconti family of Milan, President of the Board of Directors of La Scala, and a diplomat of extreme suavity and adroitness—distinguished, understanding, beloved. This honey-tongued ambassador—a gentleman to the tips of his aristocratic fingers —brought all his charm to bear on the petulant little Neapolitan.

"Don't let your fellow performers down," said he. "Resume your place on the stage. You are not Caruso, you are Rodolfo. The opera comes first. Sing any way you please," he urged, "but return—please return—to your singing."

Finally, begrudgingly, Caruso went back to the stage. Toscanini, somehow pacified by another group of La Scala representatives, was cooler now. The rehearsal continued, without further mishap, until one o'clock in the morning. All seemed well, at last.

In the morning, however, Enrico awoke with a fever.

The previous day's burst of temperament had been too much for him. To make matters worse, Borgatti, scheduled to sing *Tristan* on the opening night, also came down with a fever and took to his bed. *Bohème*, decided Gatti-Casazza, must be substituted for *Tristan*. But *Bohème* had no tenor either!

More emissaries brought back the information that Caruso's fever seemed to be more temperament than malady. Into his bedroom now filed a solemn ambassadorial procession, headed by Gatti-Casazza. He simply *must* sing Rodolfo that night. Always, at La Scala, the opening night came on a certain fixed date. Tradition forbade postponement. Would he, Caruso, be the first to break that venerable tradition? All this in the suavest Gatti-Casazza manner. Little by little, Enrico reluctantly let his temperament slip. It was a case of *"mon coeur s'ouvre à ta voix."* He agreed to sing Rodolfo in *Bohème* on the opening night, December 31, 1900.

It was not a success. As the curtain fell on Act II there was what Emma Carelli called "a mortal silence." The Milanese papers, the next morning, were nasty. One critic sneered at "the little tenor of the Lirico, who had tried to take the step to La Scala and found it too wide for him." Most of the commentators, however, surmised that Caruso might not have been in the best of health.

It is to the credit of Gatti-Casazza and Toscanini that they did not wash their hands then and there of the naughty Neapolitan brat. But both the manager and the conductor knew talent when they saw it, and Caruso was kept on as a member of the La Scala company.

Next he sang in Mascagni's *Maschere*. It was a failure— like almost everything else produced by its composer after his sensationally successful *Cavalleria Rusticana*. But, in it, Caruso did not fail. Whatever applause there was came mostly to him.

But Gatti-Casazza and Toscanini were once more in front of a stone wall. They had hoped that *Maschere* would be one of the big drawing cards of La Scala's season. Instead, they found that they had expended immense toil and trouble on what one sarcastic critic called "the most tremendous non-success in Italian lyrical history." Carried off his feet by the fact that *Maschere* was to have six simultaneous *premières* in six different Italian opera houses, Mascagni, its composer, had proudly announced: "With this work I shall resuscitate classic Italian *opera buffa*." This indiscreet prophecy prompted a sardonic Milan critic to write, after the fiasco of *Maschere* at La Scala:

> *Tra il dire è il fare*
> *C'e di mezzo il mare*

which, freely translated, means:

> To dream, alas, is not to do.
> An ocean lies between the two.

What were Toscanini and Gatti-Casazza to produce now? What could they substitute for the Mascagni opera? Gloomily, the two sat in the manager's office; gloomily they paced the Galleria.

"Let's dig up *L'Elisir d'Amore!*" suggested Gatti-Casazza. He had always liked that comic opera by Donizetti, almost forgotten at the beginning of this century. Toscanini nodded. *Something* had to be tried. *L'Elisir* might do as well as anything else.

Then came the problem of the singers. Caruso, the two agreed, was all right for Nemorino. But what about Dulcamara, the quack doctor, brewer of the elixir of love for which the little opera is named? Where could they unearth a *buffo* singer for that amusing role?

They decided on one Carbonetti—if they could locate him, for he had faded from the operatic scene. He was discovered after a considerable search, forgotten and poverty-stricken, but with all an old actor's resilience and fire and courage. He arrived in Milan in the dead of winter, without an overcoat—he could not afford one. "Shame on you, you young fellows!" he exclaimed, as he strode into La Scala. "Not one of you has the stuff in him to go out coatless in this cold weather. But this old fellow has it! Shame on you!"

The choices of *L'Elisir d'Amore* and of Carbonetti, when they became known, were severely criticized. Particularly that of Carbonetti. Toscanini was plunged into apprehensive gloom by a letter from a traveling salesman.

"Why do you go to the provinces for that old relic?" asked the writer of the letter. "Just the other night I saw him hissed off the stage at a provincial opera house."

"You mustn't let one traveling salesman discourage you," said Gatti.

"He is more intelligent than we are," wailed Toscanini.

Work began on rehearsals. Carbonetti tried hard to have the conductor allow him to sing some notes which Donizetti had failed to include in his score. "No!" thundered Toscanini, always furiously opposed to such liberties with composers. "They are very nice notes," persisted Carbonetti. "Let me sing them to you." "NO!"

On the night of the performance the melancholy enveloping the conductor was something prodigious. In Gatti-Casazza's book * the manager tells of that night:

"Toscanini . . . takes his place. . . . The opera com-

* Giulio Gatti-Casazza, *Memories of the Opera*, Charles Scribner's Sons, 1941.

mences. . . . The public is not interested and remains cold. . . . An ugly state of affairs. . . .

"Now it's Caruso's turn. . . . Calm, conscious that at this point will be decided the fate of the performance, he modulated his reply (to the soprano's first-act aria) with a voice, a sentiment and an art which no words could ever adequately describe. He melted the cuirass of ice with which the public had invested itself, little by little capturing his audience, subjugating it, conquering it, leading it captive.

"An explosion, a tempest of cheers, of applause and enthusiasm on the part of the entire public, saluted the youthful conqueror. So uproariously and imperatively did the house demand repetition that Toscanini, notwithstanding his aversion to encores, was compelled to grant it. . . . During the intermission only Caruso was talked about. . . .

"The romanza *'una furtiva lagrima,'* interrupted at every phrase by exclamations of admiration, is repeated by Caruso and the public almost insists upon its being sung a third time.

"Toscanini, radiant, as he was going before the curtain with the artists, to thank the public, embraced Caruso, and said to me:

" *'Per Dio! Si questo Napoletano continua a cantare così, farà parlar di se il mondo intero!'* ('My God! If this Neapolitan continues to sing like that he will set the whole world talking about him!')."

Which is exactly what *"questo Napoletano"* proceeded to do.

To make things perfect, Carbonetti, the basso (concerning whom Gatti-Casazza was so pessimistic at the start of the performance that he hid in a remote corner of the theater when the *buffo* singer went on) also made a hit that night. *L'Elisir d'Amore* was given a dozen times that season at La Scala. Toscanini forgave Caruso for his *Bohème* tantrum. He forgot all about the carping traveling salesman. All was sweetness and light. Box-office receipts leaped upward. And Gatti-Casazza, always an ardent admirer of Verdi, agreed more than ever with the Grand Old Man's dictum:

"Watch the box office! A theatre should be filled; it never should be empty. If the public comes to a theatre, that means success. If it stays away, that means failure. Watch the box office!"

And Carbonetti, I feel sure, bought an overcoat.

CHAPTER 8

NAUGHTY NAPLES

In early 1901, Giuseppe Verdi—for more than half a century the idol of opera-loving Italy, composer, patriot, and philanthropist—died, beloved and revered by Italians of every class, every walk of life, every type of intellect. Giulio Gatti-Casazza, vanguard fighter in Italy for Richard Wagner, Verdi's antithesis, had for Verdi, notwithstanding, genuine admiration. Arturo Toscanini, equally at home on the most rarefied peaks of classical music and on the podium conducting *Trovatore*, divided his highest musical allegiance, it was said, between Beethoven and Verdi. And Enrico Caruso—how often had the Voice of Gold poured out Verdian melody in *Rigoletto*, *Aïda*, *Traviata*, *Ballo in Maschera*, *Forza del Destino* and other works of the great master!

Verdi died at eighty-seven. All Italy mourned him—and when Italians mourn they do it with their hearts and feel no shame at showing their grief. They had come to believe that their Grand Old Man would live forever. A foreign visitor, driving in a horse-carriage over Milan cobblestones just after he had heard the news, called out to the driver on the box: "Verdi is dead." "No!" exclaimed the driver, dropping reins and whip—and the next moment tears were streaming down his rough cheeks.

At Milan there was a grandiose tribute to the dead

genius. Before sobbing crowds of many thousands Toscanini led an immense chorus and orchestra in the "Lament of the Captives" from Verdi's *Nabucco*. And Enrico Caruso sang in the famous quartet of *Rigoletto*, putting his whole heart into it.

When preparations were being made for this great concert, somebody had the audacity to contradict Toscanini—and get away with it! When Toscanini was telling his plans to the artists who were to participate in the Verdi concert he remarked, "The tenor part in the *Rigoletto* quartet will be sung by Borgatti." He was about to proceed to other matters, when, to the stupefaction of all those present, who were only too well acquainted with the Vesuvian characteristics of Toscanini's temper, Emma Carelli, Enrico Caruso's fellow singer, piped up: "Caruso ought to sing that part."

Dead silence. All looked apprehensively at Toscanini, the Man of Wrath. To the amazement of all present, Toscanini, after looking at Emma Carelli for a moment, as if trying to decide exactly what course he would take in order to make her sink through the floor, suddenly said: "You are right. It is Caruso who must sing in the *Rigoletto* quartet. I'll have Borgatti sing in the duet from *Ballo in Maschera*." And Caruso it was who took the role of the Duke of Mantua in the famous quartet, in which, according to Gatti-Casazza, "he sang like an angel, moving his hearers to indescribable emotion."

That same year, Caruso met the celebrated Russian basso, Feodor Chaliapin. Chaliapin had been brought to Milan by Gatti-Casazza to sing the title role in Boïto's *Mefistofele*. At the Scala production of that opera Caruso appeared in the part of Faust. Caruso and Chaliapin discovered that they were exactly the same age. They hit it

Chaliapin in Boïto's Mefistofele

off famously together. From the big Russian basso, Caruso received one of the most eloquent compliments of his career: "Your voice is the ideal which until now I have sought in vain."

Compliments were now coming to Enrico in batches. The renowned tenor Masini, feeling that he was growing old, spoke of Enrico, with that touch of pomposity so characteristic of tenors, as "my successor."

Caruso was now engaged to sing at the famous (and dreaded) San Carlo Opera House in Naples, ranking infinitely above that city's Bellini and Mercadante theaters where he already had been heard. This was in 1901, the year of his great success at La Scala. The San Carlo management agreed to pay him $600 per night (rather better than the original two-dollar rate of pay of his early days of singing in Naples). On arrival, he was received on the streets with uninhibited and uproarious welcome.

But—the San Carlo! It was a sort of Neapolitan La Scala. Its public was "uncertain, coy, and hard to please." On first nights, two factions in its regular audience, captained by two musical noblemen of Naples, monopolized all the best seats, and what was one faction's meat was all too likely to be the other's poison.

It had been pointed out to Enrico Caruso by wellmeaning friends who knew their way around in the Naples of that day, that it behooved him to pay a round of polite calls on the noble chieftains of the two San Carlo factions and their leading followers—they were known in Naples as the Sycophants—and say nice things to them, in the hope that, on the night of his first San Carlo appearance, one or both of the chieftains, together with their cohorts, would refrain from asserting their keen sense of local importance by articulate disapproval of his singing. But that sort of bowing and scraping never appealed to Enrico Caruso at any point in his career. His forthright nature rebelled instinctively against it. He demanded sincerity and directness in those with whom he dealt. If applause at the San Carlo Opera House was to be won only by such subterfuges, why, to hell with it!

On the night of Caruso's first San Carlo appearance the famous house was packed, for the news of his successes in Milan and Russia had traveled southward. Rows and rows of the best seats in the theater were occupied by the two factions of the Sycophants. Their noble chiefs were there, all dressed up, casting patronizing glances over the house, simply oozing self-esteem. "Hm—how about this new tenor? So they think very highly of him in Milan? Hm—we must be careful. We mustn't allow him to put anything over on us." That was the prevailing attitude as the curtain went up.

Caruso sang. The Sycophants took his singing calmly. He sang some more. This time, one of the factions, led by its noble commander, signified approval. That was enough for the other faction. It immediately registered violent disapproval. The first faction leaped to its feet. Awful Neapolitan epithets were exchanged. It was just another of those theater rows which were a regular occurrence in the Naples of fifty years ago.

After a while things calmed down. Ruffled tempers subsided. Nobody was injured. The performance was resumed.

But Enrico Caruso had been wounded to the heart. He had not expected anything like this. Summoned before the curtain, he bowed with a manner as icy as a Russian winter. His fellow Neapolitans had refused to give him the ovation of which he had dreamed! His implacable attitude showed how eagerly he had looked forward to that ovation.

He remained unforgiving to the end of his life. The grudge created in him by his reception at the San Carlo proved indestructible. Never did he consent to appear before a Neapolitan audience again as a professional singer.

Those who did not know this story accused him in later years of ingratitude and arrogance. "Caruso," they said, "has become so great and rich that he will not sing for us poor Neapolitans. He will sing anywhere in the world, but not for us."

His love for the city where he had been born remained unshaken—and unshakable. It was to Naples that he was to return to die. But the little boy in him refused to be placated. Naples—as typified by that audience at the San Carlo—had spanked him in public.

Years later, he said to a friend: "Of course, I'll return to Naples. Always. But never to sing. Only to eat spaghetti."

After this deplorable experience, London began fishing for Enrico—via his friend the baritone Antonio Scotti, also a Neapolitan, destined to become a prime New York favorite and one of Caruso's best friends.

"How much shall I get?" inquired the tenor of the baritone, after the latter had broached the subject of a possible trip by Caruso to sing at London's renowned Covent Garden Opera House.

"Two thousand lire," replied Scotti, who was acting as an unofficial spokesman for Covent Garden interests.

"But I got 2,500 at La Scala and 3,000 at the San Carlo in Naples," objected Caruso.

"Ah, my friend, you must think of the prestige of singing at Covent Garden! It's a golden gate to the rest of the world."

Caruso saw the point. He agreed to sing in London at the rate mentioned by Scotti.

But not quite yet. First he sang a short season of opera at Monte Carlo, "before half the Almanach de Gotha." He also became good friends with the famous diva Nellie Melba, to whose Mimi in *Bohème* he sang Rodolfo. In the book of reminiscences which she wrote after her retirement from the stage,* she speaks of Caruso as "the most wonderful tenor I have ever heard"; and she says of his voice: "It rolled out like an organ." "What a simple, lovable creature he was," she added. "There was always something of the sun of Italy in Caruso's dark, laughing eyes. . . . It may be a surprise to those who thought of Caruso merely as a fiercely temperamental artist to learn that he was full of practical jokes and his bubbling sense of humor was so irrepressible that he would make fun even in the midst of the most poignant scenes—such as the last act of *Bohème*, where Mimi is dying on the bed. Never shall I forget one night at Monte Carlo, before an immense audience, thick with grand dukes, princesses and marchesas, how I was suddenly startled in the middle of the death scene, by a strange, squeaking noise, which seemed to come from Caruso as he bent over me. I went on singing, but could not help wondering at the time if Caruso was ill, for his face was drawn and solemn, and, every time he bent down, there was this extraordinary noise of squeaking. And then, with a gulp which almost made me forget my part, I realized that he had a little rubber toy in his hand, which, at the most pathetic phrases, he was pressing in my ear!"

* Nellie Melba, *Melodies and Memories*, T. Butterworth, London, 1925.

Incidentally, some of those in the audience that evening who heard that squeaky noise thought it was part of poor Mimi's cough—that *"terribile tosse"* so poignantly pictured in Puccini's score.

Back in Milan for a short spell, Enrico sang again at La Scala in the opera *Germania*, by the Italian nobleman Baron Franchetti. But not even Enrico's excellent singing and that of his teammates, including the baritone Sammarco, later one of Oscar Hammerstein's mainstays in his operatic war against the Met in New York, could keep the noble baron's creation alive. It must have been a relief to the tenor to switch to good old *Rigoletto*.

CHAPTER 9

LONDON
AND THE UNITED STATES

London, 1902. Another big step up for Caruso. He sang at Covent Garden. He "did the town" with his old friend Tosti, the celebrated composer of popular songs, a great favorite with Londoners. For the first time in his life he gazed on Anglo-Saxons in large masses and compared them with Neapolitans—undoubtedly to their disadvantage. He ate spaghetti at Pagani's with baritone Scotti, to whom he could not resist saying: "You low-down Neapolitan! What a nerve you have!—bringing me here at a baritone's salary instead of a tenor's!"

In reality, he had no reason for complaint. Money in considerable quantities had been coming to him for so long that he had bought a villa near Florence, transferred thither Ada Giachetti and Fofò, their little son, and surrounded them with a regular squad of retainers. All quite appropriate, remarks Biographer Eugenio Gara, since "a tenor without a villa is not a real tenor."

He sang at a command performance in Buckingham Palace before King George V, Queen Mary, and King Alfonso XIII of Spain. After singing that evening Caruso went away with a diamond-ruby pin, a present from King George and Queen Mary, to add to his Imperial Russian gold cuff links.

One day when Scotti and Tosti, busy showing Caruso

the sights of London and vicinity, were preparing to have lunch at a roadside inn near Windsor, a motorcar stopped before the inn and from it stepped Adelina Patti, the Caruso of sopranos, with her husband, Baron Cederström. The trio of Italians, jumping to their feet, stuck out their left arms behind them, raised their right arms in a ridiculous theatrical gesture of adoration, and bowed from their waists, sweeping the ground with their hats. When she stopped laughing, the great diva said to them: "You're all lunching with us. But first I must photograph you. Hold that pose. Don't move, any of you." And not until she had snapped them in their absurd posture of welcome did she ask them to join the baron and herself and tell her what they wanted for lunch.

Caruso was now approaching his thirtieth birthday. His voice, with every day that passed, was becoming more beautiful, more melodious, more powerful—and its golden quality was permeating it more and more, to the delight of the thousands packed into the theaters where he sang, many of whom, realizing the phenomenal nature of his vocal gifts, were proclaiming it from the housetops, spreading his fame far and wide.

One of the most eloquent and uninhibited tributes to Caruso's singing—and it is not by a wild-eyed Latin either!—was written by Thomas Burke, author of *Limehouse Nights,* in his *Nights in London,** after attending a performance of *Bohème* at Covent Garden in which Caruso sang. Here is a condensation of Burke's enraptured outburst:

"But Caruso? What is he? He is not a singer. He is not a voice. He is a miracle. There will not be another Caruso for two or three hundred years; perhaps not then.

* Thomas Burke, *Nights in London,* Henry Holt, 1918.

Jean de Reszke would strain and strain until his audience suffered with him, in order to produce an effect which this new singer of the South achieved with his hands in his pockets, as he strolled around the stage.

"The opera in London is really more of a pageant than a musical function. On Caruso nights it blazes. There is a subdued rustle. . . .

"Campanini [the conductor] taps—his baton rises. And suddenly the band mumbles those few swift bars that send the curtain rushing up in the garret scene. Only a few bars . . . yet so marvelous is Puccini's feeling for atmosphere that with them he has given us all the bleak squalor of his story. . . .

"Two people are on. One stands at the window. . . . Downstage, almost on the footlights, is an easel, at which an artist sits. The artist is Scotti, the baritone, as Marcello. . . .

"The man at the window turns. He is a dumpy little man in black, wearing a golden wig. . . . A few more brusque bars are tossed from Campanini's baton and the funny little man throws off, cursorily, over his shoulder, a short passage explaining how cold it is. This short passage, throbbing with tears and laughter, has rushed like a stream of molten gold to the utmost reaches of the auditorium and there is not an ear that has not jumped for the joy of it. For he is Rodolfo the poet, in private life Enrico Caruso. . . .

"As the opera proceeds, so does the marvel grow. Gold swathed in velvet is his voice. He is prodigal of his powers. He flings his lyrical fury over the house. . . . There never were such warmth and profusion and display. Not only is it a voice of incomparable magnificence; it has that intangible quality that smites you with its own mood. . . . There are those who sniff at him. . . . They would like him better if he were not popular. Some people can never accept beauty unless it is remote.

"Caruso speaks to us of little things we know, but he speaks with a lyric ecstasy. Ecstasy is a horrible word; it sounds like something to do with algebra; but it is the only word for his voice. I remember hearing him at the first performance of *Madame Butterfly* and he hurt us. He worked up the love duet with Butterfly at the close of the first act in such fashion that our hands were wrung, we were perspiring, and I at least was near fainting.

"Such fury, such volume of liquid sound, could not go on, we felt. But it did. He carried a terrific crescendo passage as lightly as a schoolgirl singing a lullaby, and ended on a tremendous note. . . . As the curtain fell we dropped back in our seats, limp, disheveled, pale. . . .

"When Puccini and Caruso join forces they can shake the soul out of the most rabid of musical purists. What they do to commonplace people like myself is untellable. I have tried to hint at it in these few remarks, but I have told nothing—nothing."

And now Caruso realized that still another center of grand opera wanted him. As early as 1899 the management of New York's Metropolitan Opera House had instructed its European scouts to send in reports about the rising Neapolitan star. Later, Maurice Grau, grand opera czar of the Metropolitan, talked personally with Caruso in Milan. Galleria gossip buzzed furiously. Everything seemed settled—Caruso was to go to New York. But when the tenor looked up Grau in order to obtain a definite letter of confirmation, he found, to his surprise, that the great New York impresario had left Milan.

After a while, an agent called on Caruso and informed him that he was empowered to conclude arrangements with him. "If you don't act through the agency which I represent," he added, "you will never sing in New York."

"Go to hell," said Caruso. They parted. But soon there was a cable from Maurice Grau requesting Caruso to sign up through the agent to whom the tenor had suggested such a disagreeable travel route. The tenor swallowed his pride and acted according to Grau's suggestions.

It looked like plain sailing from there. But it wasn't. Another cable, this time from New York, arrived, stating that Grau had just died. In the several years that followed, the contract fell into neglect.

But this was not permanent. In March 1903, just as Caruso was preparing to depart from Europe for another South American tour, he learned that Heinrich Conried, Grau's successor at the Met, had accepted with slight modifications the Grau-Caruso contract and that the tenor was engaged (at nearly $1,000 per performance) to make his debut in New York in the late autumn.

In Buenos Aires, where he was by now a prime favorite, Caruso won more laurels than ever. In Rio de Janeiro, his "*La donna è mobile*" in *Rigoletto* got four encores (when Toscanini's away, the mice will play).

But one night the Rio public, hostile to one of the members of the visiting opera troupe, stayed away from the theater in large numbers. Caruso sang to long rows of empty seats. After the curtain went down he started teasing the manager, a taciturn North Italian.

"I'm not accustomed to sing to empty houses," he complained.

The manager merely grunted. He did not believe that breath was made for words.

"I think I'll get the terms of my contract changed."

That made the manager sit up. He grunted twice.

"Suppose we see about changing the clause about my salary."

"I knew it!" thought the manager to himself. "He wants a raise."

"Suppose we change that clause to read as follows: The fee per performance for Enrico Caruso is to be—*nothing at all.*"

And he meant it. Luckily, there were no more half-empty houses. But the singer's offer was no joke. It was typical of his impulsive generosity, characteristic of him all his life.

From Brazil, he returned to Italy for a short stay at his villa, with Ada Giachetti and Fofò and the squad of servants and other satellites. And then—on November 11, 1903—he looked for the first time on the harbor and water front and massed marvels of New York.

When Enrico Caruso, having conquered Europe and South America, was girding himself to conquer New York, what was the world like? What sort of backdrop was it providing for him?

On the throne of the land of his birth sat King Victor Emmanuel III, who had succeeded his father, King Humbert I, after the latter's assassination in 1900 by an Italian anarchist. In England the long reign of Queen Victoria ended, ushering in the short reign of her son, Edward VII. (Incidentally, while Edward was Prince of Wales, it is said that, having heard the boy Enrico Caruso sing in his native Naples, the prince advised him to study singing in London.)

In the years 1901 to 1903, Guglielmo Marconi transmitted the first wireless signals across the ocean. The death of Pope Leo XIII brought Pius X to the Vatican. In what was called Serbia, in 1903, King Alexander and Draga, his Queen, were murdered in their royal palace. Henry Ford

put his first cheap car on the market. The relations between Russia and Japan were growing steadily more strained
(they went to war early in 1904). In the French West
Indies, the eruption of Mount Pelée killed thousands. Cuba
assumed the status of an independent nation. Panama became a republic (just short of three weeks before Caruso's
first operatic performance in New York). In Kitty Hawk,
North Carolina, Orville and Wilbur Wright made the
world's first airplane flight.

The world as mankind knew it was about to be stood on
its head. Complacent sages prognosticated: "The price of
the horseless carriage will probably fall, but it will never
come into as common use as the bicycle." "The example of
the bird does not prove that man can fly." "I do not think
it at all probable that aeronautics will ever come into play
as a serious modification of transport and communication"
(that one came from a prominent man of science of fifty
years ago). Thus wagged the tongues of the ultra-conserva-
tives when Enrico Caruso made his first appearance in New
York's Metropolitan Opera House.

When the bewildered Italian tenor was eyeing the spectacle of New York and trying to assimilate it into a life
which up to then had known only Europe and South America, Theodore Roosevelt was in the White House in Washington. But it seemed to his fellow citizens that he was
never in it for more than a few hours at a time, such was
his whirlwind activity in rushing from platform to platform, pouring out fiery speeches, shaking his fist, baring his
assertive teeth, calling multimillionaires "malefactors of
great wealth" and other endearing names, electing them to
membership in his "Ananias Club," giving his fellow
Americans the distinct impression that he was perpetual
motion on two legs. Incidentally, he managed to find time,

Theodore Roosevelt

before the end of his feverish tenure of the presidency, to present Enrico Caruso with an autographed photograph of himself, which was to be useful later.

The New York that presented itself to Caruso's gaze on that November day was a very different city from the one we know. There was, with the exception of the Williamsburg Bridge, then still under construction, only one bridge to Brooklyn: the East River bridge of the lofty stone towers and network of steel cables. It is antiquated now, but still as beautiful as when local Italians first displayed it to Caruso with a proud air of proprietorship. Over the North River there was no bridge at all. There were no tunnels under East or North Rivers. Ferryboats, chugging to Brooklyn and New Jersey and Staten Island, were still the principal means of transportation to and from Manhattan Island. As they floated and tooted and gingerly felt their way in and out of their slips, they were as typical of the New York confronting Heinrich Conried's new Italian tenor as were the trains running above the streets of New York City and the hansom cabs moving by the hundreds along its pavements. The Elevated was the last word in urban transportation, to be pointed out by New Yorkers to visiting foreigners with the pride of a child showing a country cousin the hippopotamus at the zoo. As yet there was no subway, although great gashes in metropolitan streets presaged its arrival.

Everywhere in the city hansom cabs and a dozen other versions of horse-drawn vehicles lorded it over the few motor-driven freaks that wheezed and snorted and looked apologetic along the Fifth Avenue of the beginning of the twentieth century and smelled very bad indeed. This Fifth Avenue of fifty years ago had long rows of be-stooped brownstone residences. Horse omnibuses jogged up and down the avenue, and, from the great hotels—the Holland

House, the Victoria, the Buckingham—spectacular four-in-hand coaches, driven by New Yorkers from the higher brackets of the Four Hundred, sped up and down the avenue amid fanfares of bugles *pour épater les bourgeois*. At the Buckingham, the head waiter knew the exact state of the stomach ailments of all the old ladies who lived there. The Plaza which Caruso saw was not the gleaming white edifice of today, but a big, squat, red brick building. At Forty-second Street there was no grand Public Library, but a reservoir enclosed within drab gray walls. And dotted up and down the great street stood the Vanderbilt palaces, the sumptuous Daly château, the impressive Huntingdon mansion, Mrs. Astor's haughty citadel of the Four Hundred, the vast Gerry palace, and the architectural hodge-podge of Senator Clark of Montana, the copper multimillionaire, which looked like something out of a hangover.

As Caruso walked along Broadway on his way to the Metropolitan Opera House to pay his respects to Heinrich Conried, he saw the great Broadway hotels—the Metropolitan, the Sturtevant, the Marlborough, the Normandie, the Continental. Not for some years yet were they to include the imposing Knickerbocker at Forty-second Street, where Caruso was to be a resident during season after season of grand opera. In front of the Opera House itself, at Thirty-ninth Street and Broadway, ran electric cars instead of buses, with their wires laid underground—never would Manhattan allow overhead trolley wires. Opposite the main Broadway entrance of the Metropolitan was Browne's Chop House, oasis of male operagoers bent on a "quick one" between acts. Indeed, many among them rode out entire operas at Browne's, leaving to their wives and daughters across the way the task of absorbing enough musical stimulation for the whole family.

CHAPTER 10

"THERE IS A TIDE . . ."

At Caruso's first encounter at the Metropolitan Opera House offices with Manager Conried, the translating services of the Italian banker Pasquale Simonelli were necessary, since Conried could speak neither Italian nor French and Caruso neither English nor German. Conried took the newcomer on a tour of the opera house and "briefed" him in preparation for his appearances there. At a subsequent meeting of the two, Conried, notoriously ignorant about grand opera, suggested to Caruso that, when he sang the part of Alfredo in *Traviata,* it would be well, perhaps, for him to interpolate some agreeable *romanzas,* because "Alfredo has not enough music to sing in the opera."

"If there is not enough music in Alfredo's role to suit you, it's not my fault but Verdi's," was Caruso's comment on this bizarre proposal. But this suggestion of Conried's gives a hint, perhaps, of the workings of the Metropolitan Opera House in those days. Although it was in the days of its greatest glory, the motives underlying its success were not entirely musical.

When Caruso first strode out from the wings onto its stage, the Met was twenty years old. It had come into being in 1883 because of the jealousies between the old New York aristocracy and a new rising group of millionaires.

The old aristocracy had, for thirty years before the advent of the Met, attended operas at the old Academy of Music, at Fourteenth Street and Irving Place. Here there had been enough boxes so that the elect of society could see one another and be seen by the multitude of ordinary opera-goers who, poor souls, attended the opera merely to hear the music. The aristocrats hung onto their boxes, year after year, like barnacles. There they could come, these proud families, to sneer down at the members of the new aristocracy of mere wealth, sitting in their seats in the orchestra. Of course the latter could sneer back. But a sneer going down is far more effective than a sneer going up. The newcomers offered many thousands of dollars for the privilege of sitting in the boxes, but they were haughtily rejected.

Eventually, the rich occupants of the orchestra stalls at the Academy of Music got tired of the sneers of the nabobs seated above them and, unable to endure their sufferings any longer, purchased a plot of ground at Broadway and Thirty-ninth Street, where they proceeded to build an opera house which would be bigger and better in every way than the old Academy of Music. On its completion, their hopes were realized. Here was an opera house with more boxes and bigger boxes than had ever been seen before. These, in fact, overshadowed every other feature of the building, including the stage.

On October 22, 1883, twenty years before Caruso's New York debut, the beginning of New York's 1883-1884 opera season was marked by *two* opening performances. At the Academy of Music, Colonel Mapleson, its veteran manager, put on Bellini's *Sonnambula*, with Etelka Gerster, an extremely popular diva, in the star role. At Broadway and Thirty-ninth Street, Manager Henry E. Abbey produced Gounod's *Faust* with Christine Nilsson, also a tremen-

dously admired prima donna, as the principal star. "My
audience is the Faubourg Saint-Germain," boasted the
Colonel. "My rival is supported, I understand, by a number of rich persons who want a new way of spending
money. And he sneeringly called the new Metropolitan
Opera House "the new yellow brewery on Broadway."

At the end of that season the Mapleson-Abbey fight
looked like a draw. Abbey was somewhat in the position
of General Meade after the Battle of Gettysburg. He was
badly shaken (the season had cost his backers around
$600,000), but he still held his lines. Mapleson, though his
losses were less, was proportionately as badly shaken. But,
unlike Lee after Gettysburg, he did not retreat. Instead,
he prepared defiantly for the season of 1884-1885 with the
renowned Adelina Patti as his most formidable asset.

The new opera house opened its second season under
the aegis of Dr. Leopold Damrosch, who was not only its
executive director but one of the leaders of its orchestra.
One of the most ardent disciples of Richard Wagner, Damrosch wanted to introduce the Wagnerian operas into New
York in proper fashion (up to that time they had been
performed there only occasionally and in an unsatisfactory
manner). The directors of the Met voted in favor of the
Damrosch proposal. The musical dictatorship of Wagner
in New York had begun. It received what might have been
a serious setback when Damrosch died early in 1885, with
his first season in full swing. But the Wagnerites put in his
place as musical director the famous Anton Seidl, one of
the greatest of German Wagnerian conductors.

At the close of this season, the Academy of Music struck
its flag. "I cannot fight Wall Street," sneered Colonel
Mapleson. For its 1886-1887 season New York had only
one opening night instead of two—and that one was at
the "yellow brewery on Broadway."

For several seasons thereafter Anton Seidl labored mightily to add the conquest of America to the triumphs already achieved by Wagner in Europe. Filled with a fanatical zeal, Seidl met for a while with sweeping success.

But during this Wagner period there was rising discontent among the grand tier box-holders. How could they assert their importance adequately against the crashing orchestral opposition supplied by the Master of Bayreuth? How much easier it had been to do so in competition with the music of the average Italian or French opera! Thus they grumbled, while Wagner rumbled. In their disgruntlement they began to undermine Richard Wagner and Anton Seidl, his prophet. Their efforts were successful. Soon Henry Abbey was put at the helm of the Met again.

In August 1892 there was a fire that almost ended the opera house's career. Much of the orchestra floor and many of the boxes were devastated. But the restorers of the building reasserted the tremendous importance of the boxes in relation to everything else. At the brilliant reopening of the opera house on November 27, 1893, the year after the fire, the Diamond Horseshoe burst on the metropolis in all its gorgeousness and for many years it was to glow and shine and sparkle in matchless glory. Prominent and prodigiously rich families and individuals figured all through that Golden Age of Opera among the Met's box-holders. They drove up to the portals of the opera house in costly carriages; and after they had seated themselves, the rest of the audience gazed in awe at the splendor of their apparel or the magnificence of their jewels. From 1893 onward the members of the audience found printed on their programs, to add to their enjoyment of each performance, a plan of the boxes with their numbers and the names of those holding them. From then onward the grand tier parterre boxes came to be known as the Diamond Horseshoe and the tier above as the Golden Horseshoe.

The renowned Box Number Seven in the Diamond Horseshoe, sacred to the Astors, was occupied on that opening night in 1893 by "the current Mrs. Astor." She appeared at 9 P.M., well after the opera (*Faust*) had got under way. Thenceforward, as the opera progressed, the boxes gradually filled, and the interior of the opera house likewise filled with the uninhibited chatter of the expensively bedecked box-holders and their guests. In those boxes, averred a suitably awed commentator of the period, "a total of half a billion dollars was represented."

But, despite the fact that the Metropolitan seemed to have been rebuilt to serve as a mere showing-off place for the rich of New York, it should not be forgotten that these were also the years of the Metropolitan's highest musical glories. Henry Abbey, back in his post as director, assembled an extraordinary number of excellent singers: Nellie Melba, Jean and Edouard de Reszke, Lillian Nordica, Antonio Scotti, Emma Calvé, Pol Plançon, Tamagno, Scalchi, Maurel. Under Abbey, singers in German were obliged to yield precedence to these artists, although Seidl and his Teutonic contingent held sway on some nights. The all-star casts of this period at the Metropolitan were remarkable. One performance of *Don Giovanni* in 1898-1899 presented Nordica, Sembrich, the two De Reszkes, and Victor Maurel. A performance of *Les Huguenots* that same season enlisted Nordica, Sembrich, Jean and Edouard de Reszke, Maurel, and Plançon. This situation continued through the reigns of Maurice Grau and Heinrich Conried, who took over the Metropolitan in 1903. With casts like this, what could one expect the audience's reaction to be on November 23, 1903? "It was understandable," remarks

Irving Kolodin,* "that the evening performance was all but ignored, for it offered only Sembrich and Scotti in *Rigoletto*. . . . An unfamiliar Italian tenor attracted little notice from the smart set, though he had the mellifluous name of Enrico Caruso."

Caruso and Ada Giachetti first stayed at the Hotel Majestic on Central Park West. There, soon after his arrival, the Italian banker Pasquale Simonelli shepherded into the tenor's presence an eager gathering of reporters and photographers. Simonelli did the interpreting, for Caruso's English in 1903 was almost nonexistent. Whenever there was a lull in the questioning and answering, the tenor made caricatures of those around him. Later, in New York and elsewhere, Caruso was to do excellent work as a caricaturist, and many people averred that had it not been for his golden voice he could easily have made a living with his pencil. At the Hotel Majestic, his caricaturing made an instant hit with the reporters. They crowded around him, looking over his shoulder as he dashed off amusing sketches of them and himself. These sketches broke the ice: they served to humanize the singer.

But it was not difficult, once his reputation grew, to make of Caruso a popular figure. "He was, for all his travel and varied experience," wrote Pierre Key, "essentially of the people. Much newspaper *réclame* having been made for him as a singer upon whom the mantle of the renowned Jean de Reszke was likely to fall, much naturally was expected of him. . . . Where De Reszke was aristocratic, Caruso decidedly was not; there was the widest possible physical difference in the two men; and, finally, the one

* Irving Kolodin, *The Metropolitan Opera 1883-1939*, Oxford University Press, 1940.

was undertaking in the middle period of his career to succeed a consummately finished artist—perhaps the greatest exponent of the highly polished intellectual school of tenors the world has ever known. . . . His appearance [Caruso's] was decidedly plebeian; and he was undeniably fat."

Jean de Reszke had abdicated his throne just before Caruso's arrival in New York. He proved that he knew how to read the future. De Reszke remarked of Caruso, as he departed from Manhattan, "This boy will be my successor." (Only an operatic tenor would be capable of so patronizing a statement.) All through his first weeks in New York the shadow of Jean de Reszke hovered over the new tenor, making him very uncomfortable indeed. "Almost every time I sang," said Caruso afterward, "some of the critics would write: 'Yes, a beautiful voice of wonderful quality. But—Jean!' "

All Enrico could do was to try to win the critics and audiences by his own kind of singing and his own kind of personality. Little by little his singing at the Metropolitan won him wide respect; but still there were few signs of the Caruso craze soon to swamp New York. Critics and public remained calm. When H. E. Krehbiel of the New York *Tribune* wrote, "The name Caruso is beginning to have professional value," he was, as it were, letting himself go. At the tenor's first New York appearance the only auditors who made a noise worthy of comparison with what was to come later on were fellow Italians who, aware of the triumphs which Caruso had already won in Europe and South America, had formed themselves into a volunteer "claque." In fact, more than a year after the tenor's first appearance at the Metropolitan Opera House there were many Americans conversant with grand opera who still failed to realize the transcendent talents of Enrico Caruso. When the casts selected for the Metropolitan company's nation-wide 1905 tour were announced, the representative in Los Angeles wired to Heinrich Conried in New York: "Can't you substitute Dippel for Caruso? I am sure he will attract larger audiences."

Caruso soon, however, settled down to the highly individual life which he was to continue to lead in New York, though he did not then know it, for many years. True to his Neapolitan background, Enrico could not stomach New York's regular cuisine. Having moved from the Majestic to an apartment in the Murray Hill section of the city, he proceeded to make it a shrine of Italian cooking. There he cooked spaghetti in a way all his own. And he served miles of it to visitors, mostly Italians, who filled the apartment at all hours.

Caruso was settling himself in in America, despite the lukewarm reception he was getting. It is surprising that, accustomed to the encomiums of critics and audiences in Europe and South America, he did not give up New York after that first season and return to those places that had most applauded him. "There is a tide in the affairs of men which, taken at the flood, leads on to fortune." Caruso by returning to New York for a second season was unwittingly traveling with the tide.

CHAPTER 11

CRESCENDO OF SUCCESS

After finishing his first New York season without as yet setting either the East River or the North River on fire Enrico Caruso returned to the European continent, where by this time the Caruso craze had taken on in some places noteworthy proportions—as it had also in southern South America. One of those places was Monte Carlo, his first European singing stop after landing from the steamship which had brought him across the Atlantic from New York. Monte Carlo acclaimed him rapturously.

But Barcelona, his second stop, did not. Barcelona prided itself—still does—on its excellent musical taste. It considers itself the musical capital of Spain. Caruso made his Barcelona debut—which was also his first appearance anywhere in Spain—in *Rigoletto*, as he had done the previous year at the Metropolitan in New York.

After his singing of *"Questa o quella"* there was cheering. But, as he finished his next important piece in the first act, there were—*hisses!* Substantial, unmistakable Spanish hisses. Caruso was stunned—and deeply offended. So much so that, in the last act, after *"La donna è mobile"* had brought him an ovation and unanimous demands from the audience for an encore, he refused to sing the aria again.

"An insult!" stormed the audience. Still Caruso refused

the encore. He sulked in the wings. As the last curtain fell there was a silence which may be described as stentorian.

Taking advantage of this unfortunate situation, the Barcelona impresario, who, ever since he had signed up Caruso, had been viewing with alarm the fee which he had agreed to pay, informed the tenor the next day that, on account of what had happened the night before, any further singing by him before Barcelona operagoers must be done at half price.

"Not one penny less than the fee agreed upon!" snarled the tenor. He added: "You have announced me for a second *Rigoletto*. I sing. I sing at the full price. Then I go." At his second appearance the same peculiar rigmarole occurred. At first they cheered. Then they hissed. Again Caruso sulked. Again he refused to repeat *"La donna è mobile."*

Barcelona opera lovers formed themselves into two schools of thought: those who maintained that Caruso at the two *Rigoletto* performances had slipped off the key and subsequently climbed back onto it again, and those who maintained that he had stuck to it all along. The dispute grew hot. The Mayor of Barcelona begged the sulky tenor not to leave town in a huff. But there was no shaking Caruso's decision.

Off he marched to Paris. It was the San Carlo incident in Naples all over again. And his huff was so solid and durable that he not only refused to sing again in Barcelona, but turned down offers to appear in Madrid. Madrid is 350 miles distant from Barcelona, the city of his misadventure. Far too near, thought Caruso.

In Paris he cheered up. He sang at the Sarah Bernhardt Theater there with tremendous success. So far as Paris was concerned the Caruso craze was on. Peasants in rough smocks and hobnailed boots and soiled berets appeared at the box office of the theater and tendered 100-franc notes, representing to them a small fortune, in the hope of getting seats to hear the Neapolitan nightingale. Many of them were turned away disappointed.

Next came Prague. *Rigoletto* again. In the cast was the tenor's old comrade of Russian days, the gigantic Vittorio Arimondi; also Pignataro, the baritone who had sung with Caruso in Caserta of dreadful memory, had recommended him to the management of the Teatro Bellini in Naples, and had helped to get him so drunk in Trapani that he had warbled about the foxes of Scotland.

After that came a richly deserved rest at his villa in Italy (originally called the Villa Pucci, it became known later as the Villa alle Panche, and, finally, as Villa Bellosguardo). There, Ada Giachetti, little Rodolfo, and the squad of retainers welcomed him. That same year (1904) in September, a second son was born at the Villa Bellosguardo to Enrico and Ada—Enrico, Jr., nicknamed Mimmi.

After a short rest at his villa, Caruso returned to London, opening there in *Rigoletto* (that opera was getting to be a regular choice with him for *premières*) on May 17, 1904. With him sang Melba, Mme. Kirkby-Lunn, Maurice Renaud, and Marcel Journet. In the audience were the King and Queen of England, Princess Victoria, and the Duke and Duchess of Connaught.

Caruso won another great victory, and the Covent Garden management signified its appreciation of his prowess as a drawing card by billing him twenty-six times during London's opera season of that year. Besides the eminent artists already mentioned, his fellow singers at Covent Garden included Emmy Destinn, Pol Plançon, and Antonio Scotti. And this time he had no occasion to remark to

Scotti, with whom he was becoming constantly friendlier, that he was being paid merely a baritone's salary in lieu of a tenor's.

Now, looking for more worlds to conquer, he arranged to visit Germany for the first time.

Already he had come, seen, and conquered in Latin lands (not including Spain) and Anglo-Saxon countries; he had showered his golden notes on Egypt. Now for the Teutons.

On October 5, 1904, he made his first appearance in Germany at the Theater des Westens in Berlin, in—*Rigoletto*. He was received with storms of deep Prussian approval. One Berlin critic wrote: "Caruso has the typical Italian art of singing, now so rare." He made another Berlin appearance in *Traviata*—he was playing safe with well-tested Verdi vehicles.

One day, in Berlin, a German woman asked Caruso to add his signature to the collection in her autograph album.

"Let me see it," he requested.

She handed him a large album, containing the autographs of many persons, labeled "first among the world's harpists," "first among the mandolinists of Italy," et cetera, about whom the singer had never heard in his life. After looking over a batch of the signatures of these "firsts," he took up a pen and wrote in the album:

"Enrico Caruso, second tenor."

Also, in Germany, Caruso became a great admirer of Herr Blech, the pint-size assistant manager of his tour, autocrat of rehearsals, a veritable Prussian disciplinarian. One day, after going through an entire act of an opera in rehearsal, Blech remarked: "Now we must do the whole thing over again." Emil Ledner, the manager, looked apprehensively at Caruso. After all, the tenor was working very hard and showing signs of great fatigue. Perhaps, thought Ledner, he will explode like Vesuvius. But all Caruso did was to smile affably at the little Prussian drill sergeant and remark: "The king has spoken." And he rehearsed the entire act again without the slightest objection.

Back in London, he sang with the visiting opera company from the San Carlo Opera House of his native Naples. What an enormous satisfaction to be engaged by the management of the theater where he had suffered so sorely shortly before at the hands of the Sycophants! What a pleasant revenge for San Carlo slights! Revenge on his fellow Neapolitans now took the form of a glorious burst of Carusian warbling for Londoners, beginning on an October night in 1904, when he appeared in Puccini's *Manon Lescaut* with Sammarco and his boon companion, Arimondi.

London closed its 1904 season on November third. And, as New York was to open its season that same month with the Caruso First Night that was soon to become a New York tradition, it behooved Enrico Caruso to hustle across the Atlantic again. This time he put up, after arriving in New York, at the Hotel York, on Seventh Avenue (it is still doing business there), only a few blocks from the Metropolitan Opera House.

In this, his second New York season, his extraordinary merit as a singer was becoming more apparent every day to New Yorkers. The city which was to acclaim his singing more loudly and take him as an individual to its heart more enthusiastically than any other city, now began to gauge him at his true worth—and Enrico Caruso reciprocated with genuine Neapolitan gusto.

One of those who by this time realized Caruso's value was Manager Heinrich Conried of the Met. Conried played the new vocal phenomenon to the limit. The tenor of the hour, during that second American season, made fifty-four appearances, apportioned as follows: thirty to New York; five to Philadelphia; three to Boston; two to Pittsburgh; one to Cincinnati; three to Chicago; one each to Minneapolis, Omaha, Kansas City, and Los Angeles; and six to San Francisco. His voice was rapidly approaching the fullness of its glory. "From 1905," wrote an American operatic commentator, "Caruso was established on his singer's throne."

His second Metropolitan season concluded with a gala performance. The house was packed. Crowds were turned away. Act IV, *Gioconda*, Caruso as Enzo. Act I, *Pagliacci*, Caruso as Canio. One critic declared that he had never sung so well before. After establishing itself in Europe and South America, the Caruso craze was gripping New York.

Caruso's next Covent Garden season brought him twenty-four times before London audiences, with Melba, Destinn, and the American singer, Clarence Whitehill. On July 10, 1905, Covent Garden saw Puccini's new opera *Madame Butterfly* for the first time, with Caruso as Pinkerton. It was an immense success. Yet it had been a failure at its Milan world *première* shortly before, to the astonishment and consternation of Giulio Gatti-Casazza and Arturo Toscanini, who had produced it with their usual conscientiousness.

After London, Paris. There, his old friend of early Neapolitan struggles, Nicola Daspuro, had arranged a season of opera for his employer, the great publisher-impresario Eduardo Sonzogno. His prime offering was Giordano's *Fedora*, which had swept Enrico Caruso to fame in Milan. Six performances of *Fedora* with Caruso were advertised.

"As soon as they were announced," wrote Daspuro in his memoirs long afterward, "all tickets disappeared as if by a miracle." Speculators offered them at an outrageous profit. They had guessed correctly the tenor's box-office appeal. Paris raged. But it paid. It dug into its pockets and acquired seats for Caruso *Fedora* nights at a cost which, by Paris standards—or any others—were fantastic.

Those who have been to the theater in the French capital will remember that, in the theaters there, on crowded nights, narrow extra seats, straddling the aisles, are let down, enabling persons perched insecurely on them to get whatever enjoyment from the show they can under such uncomfortable conditions. These revolting perches, known as *strapontins*, sold, on Sonzogno's Caruso nights in Paris, for 100 francs—*twenty dollars!*

On the tenor's opening night in *Fedora* everybody who was anybody in Parisian political, artistic, aristocratic, and wealthy circles was on hand—and the spectacle of beautiful women in extremely expensive jewels was breathtaking. Lina Cavalieri, that dazzling apparition of loveliness, was in the cast, likewise Titta Ruffo, the celebrated baritone.

Cavalieri sang excellently. Titta Ruffo gave of his best. But—Caruso! It was his night. He sang at the top of his form, inspiring his fellow Neapolitan, Daspuro, to this molten Mediterranean outburst:

"The really culminating moment was Caruso in the second part of Act II. In a voice filled with vehemence, with the furious aspect of a wounded lion, he sang—

> *La fante mi svela*
> *L'immondo ritrovo—*

"To describe that crushing finale is beyond any pen. Through the entire theatre ran an uncontrollable thrill. His voice, pouring out in gusts of indignation, yet filled at the same time with heart-rending anguish, rings out in a full-throated torrent of such brilliancy and power that it seemed to surpass the lightnings of the heavens. All those in the house held their breath; it was as if the life of everyone who heard him vibrated through the theatre; all felt within themselves a rising ardor, a growing intoxication, violent and irresistible. Caruso was giving vent to the passion that all of us feel in ourselves, deep down in our most hidden depths. Only Caruso could unchain it in our souls with his aggressive exuberance; only he could arouse it in us with the sonorous accents of his flaming emotion.

"When he reached the '*t'amo*' at the end of the second act . . . a tremendous roar burst out all over the theatre. The entire audience, in the stalls, in the boxes, in the gallery, in the corridors, surging to their feet as if in obedience to unseen steel springs, seemed to have lost their minds, as they applauded in an uncontrolled frenzy, as they shrieked 'Encore! Encore!' "

Besides his appearance in regular operatic performances during that sensational Paris visit, Caruso sang at a monster outdoor performance. He was paid $4,000—a record for him up to then. The audience attracted by him numbered 122,000! Then and all through his fabulous years Caruso more than justified Gatti-Casazza's remark about him: "No matter how much you paid him, he always turned out to be the least expensive of singers."

The next Caruso Opening Night in New York was on November 20, 1905. Enrico was now starting his third consecutive New York engagement. His fee per performance had risen to $1,344. From now on he was to pocket earnings which, in view of his Neapolitan beginnings, must have seemed unbelievable to those who had known him in those days—including himself.

After the close of New York's 1905-1906 season the Met singers, including Caruso, went on a tour that took them all the way to the Pacific Coast—and smack into the San Francisco earthquake and fire.

Caruso and Scotti and a number of other important members of the troupe, who were staying at the St. Francis Hotel, were awakened a bit before 5 A.M. on April 17, 1906, to find the earth apparently planning to get rid of all the buildings and human beings cluttering up its surface. While several of the singers—Scotti, Marcella Sembrich, Pol Plançon—who had left their rooms in attire far from formal, were clustered in the hotel lobby, Caruso suddenly appeared, very much excited, with a towel around his head and a silver-framed photograph under his arm.

They began to discuss what to do next; but, when they looked around for Caruso, to get his opinion, he had vanished. He reappeared as suddenly as he had disappeared, still with his towel and photograph, babbling incoherently of adventures which, he said, he had had during his short absence from the group; they included, according to him, a tremendous fight with a Chinaman. Then he vanished again.

Scotti, remembering that he had a friend who lived in suburban San Francisco—and hoping that the earthquake would draw the line at joggling suburbs—found an automobile after a long search. He asked the driver how much he would charge to take him to that suburbanite's home.

"Three hundred dollars," replied the driver.

Scotti paid without a murmur. Caruso reappeared. He and the baritone climbed into the automobile. They found the suburban home of Scotti's friend in a fair state of preservation. Scotti prepared to go to bed in one of its rooms. But Caruso refused to cross its threshold. He had been born in the shadow of Vesuvius. What? Trust a roof over his head or a floor under his feet that night? Never! He slept in the back yard under a tree, with the towel still around his head, and the photograph in the silver frame still under his arm.

Next day, after returning to the central part of San Francisco, Scotti successfully concluded negotiations for the hire of a launch to take him and other agitated songbirds, including Enrico Caruso, to Oakland, whence they could get back to New York, where, they hoped, the ground knew its place. Caruso disappeared.

As the launch was about to start, he reappeared. Once more he had got into a fight—not with a Chinaman this time, but with policemen on the dock who questioned his right to join those in the launch. Pulling the silver-framed photograph from under his arm, the wild-eyed Neapolitan brandished it in the faces of the policemen. They drew back. They bowed politely. Respectfully they asked him to get aboard the launch.

As it puffed away, Scotti and its other occupants surrounded Caruso, demanding an explanation of the miracle of his embarkation. Caruso held up before them the silver-framed photograph, which he had salvaged from his swaying room at the St. Francis Hotel, kept by his side under his suburban tree, and revealed with such immense success to the obstructing policemen. It was the photograph of a man with a bellicose expression and assertive teeth, inscribed: "To Enrico Caruso. From Theodore Roosevelt."

After arriving in New York, where, to his relief, no earthquake was waiting to welcome him, Caruso again crossed the Atlantic for a rest at his Villa Bellosguardo.

He needed it! Around the villa—to his unbounded gratification—he found the earth on its best behavior. He invited Marcellino Caruso, his father, and Maria Castaldi, his stepmother, to visit him. They declined. Signa was too far for those home-bodies, Marcellino and Maria. Enrico had to console himself with the heterogeneous company flocking to Bellosguardo—composers, singers, conductors, theatrical agents, reporters, favor-seekers.

His system was feeling the strain of his Arabian Nights career. Undoubtedly it would have done him good at this point not to yield completely to the sedentary life. A little physical exercise was indicated. As usual, he listened politely to those who suggested it, and failed to give their admonitions a second thought. As Pierre Key remarks, "The physical exercise he needed to keep in condition was as repugnant to him as water to a kitten."

His next singing engagement was at Ostende, Belgium, which he visited now for the first time. At his debut (*Rigoletto*), Albert, King of the Belgians, was present with his Queen. Another listener was the Duke of the Abruzzi, of the royal family of Caruso's Italy. All the singers in the cast sang in French except Caruso, who had not yet tackled that language as a vehicle for song. A Belgian critic was so enchanted with the tenor's performance at Ostende that he wrote: "He sounds like a clarinet played by an archangel."

In the early autumn of 1906 Caruso departed from Europe for New York to get ready for another season at the Metropolitan Opera House, which was to begin with something which by now was already a social and musical fixture in the American metropolis—the Caruso First Night.

In November 1906, one week before the opening, Caruso got mixed up in an incident which, had it taken another turn, might conceivably have wrecked his career—at least in the United States.

From his earliest days in New York he liked to walk in Central Park and spend some time looking at the animals in the cages there. One afternoon, while he was strolling in the Central Park Monkey House, a woman beside him, turning toward him angrily, accused him of annoying her. A policeman came up, she repeated her accusations against the tenor, and Caruso was taken to a nearby police station, where, at the angry woman's behest, he was held. Immediately he got in touch with the Metropolitan Opera House management, and somebody connected with it, rushing to the police station, gave surety for the necessary amount of bail, whereupon Caruso hurried in great agitation to his hotel (at that time the Savoy, at Fifth Avenue and Fifty-ninth Street).

Soon the newspapers came out with big headlines; the consensus of the versions of what had happened was that the tenor had pinched his accuser. And on that theme they embroidered day after day.

Before going on as Rodolfo in the opera chosen for the Metropolitan's opening night, the tenor told the Mimi of the evening that there was not a word of truth in the accusation against him. When the curtain went up on the first act he was terribly agitated, wondering how the public, having read the papers, would receive him. At the start of the first-act duet, he was deadly pale, and his hand, when he took Mimi's, was cold and trembling. Yet he sang marvelously—perhaps his agitation helped his voice. Anyhow, as he paused after his part of the aria, there was a tremendous spontaneous ovation.

When Mimi began her part, Caruso's eyes were streaming with tears—tears of relief. "New York is still my friend," he sobbed behind the scenes.

A few days later, Caruso appeared at the Yorkville Police Court. There was a big, excited crowd on hand. They expected—hoped for, perhaps—something sensational. But the woman who had accused the tenor did not appear.

At a second hearing, on November 22, 1906, another woman, wearing a white veil, swept it aside and asked the tenor: "Do you remember me? Do you recall what happened on February 4, 1904?" Then she accused him of having annoyed her at a performance at the Metropolitan on that date. Her complaint was dismissed. The upshot of the first accusation against Caruso was a fine of $10.00.

The Monkey House incident has never been forgotten in New York—indeed, there are many persons there and elsewhere who know practically nothing about Caruso's career except that bizarre detail in it. Yet New York as a whole—and the United States as a whole—and the rest of the world as a whole—refused to get perturbed by it. They went on admiring and acclaiming and liking Enrico Caruso.

If he *did* pinch the lady (and, knowing something about male Latins, I sometimes suspect that he did), part of the blame for his conduct, I think, should be placed on the metropolis of Argentina, Buenos Aires, a city well known to Caruso at the time of the Monkey House contretemps. In Buenos Aires the art of lady-pinching has been brought to a perfection unattained elsewhere, so far as I know. In fact, I wrote once in an article: "The colors of the Argentine flag are blue and white; the colors of the Argentine woman must be black and blue." Is it not possible that the thoughts of Enrico Caruso went wool-gathering and he imagined himself for an unfortunate moment not in New York but in Buenos Aires, the pincher's paradise?

Forever after, Caruso was very sensitive about the Monkey House. Once a man who for years had collected Carusiana and had a big scrapbook filled with them asked the famous singer to look over the collection, write down some comment on it, and add his signature. As Caruso turned the pages he seemed at first to be pleased with what he saw. But suddenly he slammed the book shut and leaped to his feet white with rage.

"Get out!" he thundered. "Take it away. Get out!"

He had happened on a lot of headlines pasted into the book which dealt with the Monkey House incident.

Another time, when he was at a party entirely composed of men (so he thought), he entered a room to mix with a group of them, when he noticed a lady—just one. At sight of her he fled—literally fled—turned his back, forgetting manners and etiquette, and ran right out of the room. It was learned afterward that, ever since his adventure at New York's Monkey House, he had developed a horror of lone females.

CHAPTER 12

GRAND OPERA WAR

New York's second Grand Opera War broke out in 1906. Until then, the "new yellow brewery on Broadway" had reigned supreme in the operatic doings of the American metropolis. From 1885, when Mapleson threw up the sponge, to 1906, there had been none to question its lone eminence.

But, in the latter year, Oscar Hammerstein, veteran builder and operator of theaters, opened his Manhattan Opera House on West Thirty-fourth Street, with the avowed intention of competing with the long-established monarchs of the Met and, if possible, driving them ignominiously out of business. During four years, punctuated with a fair amount of success and an enormous accretion of personal advertisement, Hammerstein fought his powerful foe at Thirty-ninth and Broadway.

As a fledgling, just-out-of-college journalist, I wrote a number of stories for the New York *Times Sunday Magazine* on the activities of the warring armies of song. As a result of this—and of the fact that I was well acquainted with Bill Guard, Hammerstein's famous press representative—I was "put on the door" at the Manhattan Opera House. That is, Guard instructed the ticket collectors at the Manhattan's front portals to let me in free of charge, whenever the spirit moved me to imbibe operatic melody.

As I already enjoyed that priceless privilege at the Metropolitan I was plunged into an orgy of operagoing such as I had never known before. There was one week during that dual season in New York when I was present, within a space of four days, at five operatic performances—four of them in the evening, one in the afternoon.

Against Hammerstein, the Met arrayed its glittering star casts of which, by now, the undisputed chieftain was Enrico Caruso. Against his rival, Oscar Hammerstein pitted, as his foremost shock troopers in his audacious attack on intrenched privilege, Mary Garden (soprano) and Alessandro Bonci (tenor), the latter already mentioned in these pages, especially in connection with Bologna's War of the Tenors. Later on, stars of the first magnitude, including the great Nellie Melba, joined Hammerstein. He engineered a campaign in the newspapers (masterfully stoked by Bill Guard) telling all about the great fight, round by round. So lively did the warlike doings become that the Sunday *Times*, I recall, published a fanciful hodgepodge by me, describing how the Hammerstein troupe, in full force, sallied forth one day from the Manhattan Opera House, bent on kidnaping Caruso, and got into a pitched battle at Thirty-fourth Street and Seventh Avenue with the Met warblers, in tremendous strength, bent on kidnaping Bonci.

As for Mary Garden, she won sensational success in roles like *Thaïs* and *Salomé*, long on art and short on clothes, and raised high the hopes of Hammerstein that he would eventually overcome the Metropolitan organization.

Managing Mary Garden was not easy. She was of temperament all compact. Once, when I was buzzing around Oscar Hammerstein's offices at the Manhattan Opera House, trying to get a Sunday story for the New York *Times* involving Mary, Grenville Vernon of the New York *Tribune* informed me dramatically that he had the prima donna's private telephone number and generously allowed me to copy it into my pocket notebook.

Feeling that we were important cogs in the making of local operatic history, we went to a nearby telephone booth, where I asked for that private number. Mary Garden in person came to the phone. I told her that I wanted first-hand information from her regarding doings at the Hammerstein citadel of song for inclusion in the story I intended to write.

"Sorry," said she icily, "I am no longer connected with the Manhattan Opera House." Whereupon she hung up with a bang.

I looked at Vernon. Vernon looked at me. What a sizzling hot platter of front-page opera war news! We rushed back to the Hammerstein offices and told Arthur, son of Oscar, what Mary had said. He turned white with rage. He used language of exceptional strength.

Next day, the story of Mary's defection blazed on newspaper front pages. And the picturesque progress of the Hammerstein-Garden hostilities caused me to use the temperamental lady's private telephone number again and arrange for a chat with her at her residence on Madison Avenue, to which she had been confined by doctor's orders.

She was in bed. I sat on a chair, wrapped in my best bedside manner. "Only five minutes," a severe nurse had decreed, as I entered the royal bedchamber.

Mary was wearing a beribboned, belaced nightgown, which would have pleased Thaïs. She was affably communicative. Her remarks about Oscar Hammerstein and all his works waxed steadily more unfriendly. But, just as they showed signs of becoming sulphurous and hence

Grade A journalism, that nurse loomed majestically in the doorway.

"Time's up," she snapped. And it was Madison Avenue for me.

Later, under Gatti-Casazza's Metropolitan regime, that Mary Garden scene had a Caruso counterpart. One night, Caruso sang divinely—or, at least, he thought he did. Next morning, at breakfast, he settled back comfortably in his chair, to hear his secretary translate the reviews of his performance by New York's music critics. He expected a wild outburst of enthusiasm. Instead, to his amazement, the critics declared, in croaking unison, that his singing the night before had been bad, very bad.

The effect on the tenor was cataclysmic.

"Finish!" he ejaculated. "They no like me! I go away! I resign! I never come back! Finish!"

At once the news was rushed to Gatti-Casazza at the offices of the Met, and he came galloping diagonally across Broadway to the Caruso apartment at the Knickerbocker Hotel. There was a tremendous scene. Gatti stormed, implored, threatened, wheedled, wept. Otto H. Kahn, Chairman of the Met Board of Directors, hastily summoned, plunged into the battle. No use.

"I go! I resign! Finish!"

Finally, as in the analogous case of Mary Garden during the Grand Opera War, the storm cleared. The clouds vanished. The sun shone. Caruso promised not to resign. And Gatti-Casazza trudged back to his offices with several new gray hairs in his beard.

Oscar Hammerstein finally abandoned his anti-Met campaign. He was bought off. The Metropolitan-Hammerstein negotiations preceding his elimination were so protracted that eventually New York ceased to believe in them at all. But, suddenly, words gave way to deeds. Arthur Hammerstein, son of Oscar, appeared one day among his fellow negotiators of the Manhattan Opera House team with a check for $100,000, tendered him as advance payment by the Metropolitan magnates as a proof that they meant business. He immediately set off, followed by his retinue, and he bought champagne for everyone in sight.

The news was transmitted to Oscar Hammerstein, who was in Europe, in a 750-word cablegram. "Yes, we cabled 750 words," mused Arthur Hammerstein years afterward. "And yet, the day before, we hadn't $7.50 among us!"

Thus ended New York's Second Grand Opera War. After the elimination of Hammerstein competition, several star members of the disbanded Manhattan Opera House troupe joined the Met forces—Nellie Melba, John McCormack, Maurice Renaud, the Spanish tenor Florencio Constantino.

Now, many, many years later, I look back nostalgically to my early days around Times Square. Memories of Bill Guard, that colorful character, and his constant ballyhoo about the Opera War, will not leave me. I brazenly wrote thousands of words about this pitched battle, and Bill, wearing a sort of conspirator's cloak over his shoulders as he strode along Broadway, remains foremost in my memories.

Ah, those days! How I reveled in their rich operatic fare! How I loved to tell my friends, constrained to pay for their operagoing, all about my delicious and incredibly inexpensive evenings listening to Caruso and his colleagues. And my friends liked to hear my reports—provided that they did not include whistling. I have an idea that the

William J. Guard

difference between Caruso's singing of "*Celeste Aïda*" and my whistling of it was one of the most terrific perpendicular plunges in the realm of music.

Although Caruso was now established as a permanent attraction of the Metropolitan Opera House, he was still free, outside the Met's season, to travel and sing where he liked. Accordingly, in the summers he went to Europe for singing and to visit his beloved Villa Bellosguardo. After more success in London and Paris in the summer of 1907, Caruso triumphed in Germany—and failed in Hungary.

Never in his previous career, never in the subsequent part of it, was there such a violent contrast as that between an *Aïda* appearance by him in Berlin and his first (and last) performance in Budapest, for which *Aïda* was again the opera selected.

The tenor's manager for Central Europe was Emil Ledner, prominent in German grand opera circles, who became his good friend and adviser. In Berlin, Caruso scored one of his most brilliant triumphs as Rhadamès. After the third act, in which he sang superbly and was magnificently seconded by Emmy Destinn, there ensued, wrote Ledner later, the most extraordinary scene he had ever witnessed in his life.

The Berliners, he pointed out, can hardly be classified as "temperamental southerners." Yet they went insane with joy after the duet in that act, stayed insane for five, ten, fifteen minutes, and seemed resolved to stay insane all night.

"They did not applaud—they went into paroxysms," wrote Herr Ledner. "I saw the whole audience, which filled the house to the roof, rise up as one individual, yelling and stamping. They did not call for Caruso. They stood there and howled like maniacs. They rioted. They screamed. It

was the same after the tomb scene. I have seen many Caruso
riots, but never anything like that one."

But—Budapest!

A dreadful memory, moans Ledner, in his book of Caruso
reminiscences.* The tenor's singing showed none of its
usual fire and splendor. When he finished *"Celeste Aïda"*
in the first act the audience remained "ice cold." Caruso
was fully aware that he was doing badly. Catching sight
of his manager in the wings he called out to him "an
unprintable French word."

In the Nile scene (which had brought him such an in-
credible ovation in Berlin) he was even worse. "And that,"
said Ledner, "sealed the fate of the whole performance."
After the final scene, the one in the tomb of the two
lovers, Rhadamès and Aïda, Caruso confessed that all he
thought about while singing it was to end the ordeal and
get out of the theater and back to his hotel as fast as he
possibly could.

Ledner was confronted with a dreadful situation. His
Caruso campaign was just beginning. There were several
cities in Austria and Germany to be visited. In a few days
the tenor was to face the veteran operagoers of Vienna,
who know all about music including opera and are corre-
spondingly hard to please. The manager realized that something drastic must be done. And he did it.

Then and there, with the echo of Caruso's Hungarian
fiasco still ringing in his ears, he constructed the Legend
of Budapest. Through interviews and articles in the newspapers, by word of mouth, he built up a cock-and-bull story
to the effect that it was not Caruso who had failed in the
Hungarian capital but the audience which had listened to
him. The leitmotiv of this brazen blast was that the Buda-

* Emil Ledner, *Erinnerungen an Caruso*, P. Steegemann, 1922.

pesters had expected too much, that their coldness to Caruso merely betrayed their glaring deficiencies as music critics, that they hadn't had any idea of what was going on that night and didn't know fine singing when they heard it. Et cetera, et cetera—in a crescendo of heroic, outrageous mendacity.

It worked.

And it probably saved the Caruso-Ledner tour from ruin. When the tenor and his manager arrived in Vienna, the Viennese had no inkling of Enrico's flop in Budapest, for the tales about it which had seeped through to their city had gone unnoticed in the flood of Ledner's press barrage.

At his Vienna debut, Caruso had got over his indisposition, his nerves were unjangled. He achieved a huge success.

Through the years, the Legend of Budapest, says Ledner, flourished unchecked. It was told again and again in many places by many narrators. It was adorned with frills and embroidery as fictitious as its foundation. Not until after Caruso's death did its creator divulge the true story.

One evening in Munich, Germany, while he was playing in *Bohème*, Caruso was struck on the back of the head by a falling piece of heavy scenery, which knocked him out completely. For twenty minutes he lay unconscious, while management, co-singers, and doctors worked over him in vain. Emerging at last into consciousness, he grinned amiably, and pointing to his occiput, remarked: *"Testa dura"* (a thick skull). There was talk of ringing down the curtain, or sending on a substitute for the last scene of the opera, but the iron-willed tenor would not hear of it. "I will sing," he announced.

Arrangements were hurriedly made to have him remain seated during the death scene by the bedside of Mimi, instead of striding all over the place, as tenors normally do when acting the part of the distracted Rodolfo. While everybody was on pins and needles wondering how Caruso could possibly sing to the end of the opera, he stuck to his job, though obviously in excruciating pain, with the perspiration pouring down his face, until at last the curtain descended.

The only ill effect on him of this alarming adventure was that it left him firmly convinced that the Black Hand was responsible—that a trusted agent of that unsavory organization, lurking somewhere above the stage, had dropped that heavy piece of scenery on his skull. So sure was he of this that for some time afterward, whenever he played in *Tosca,* he insisted that the rifles of the firing squad which is supposed to shoot the tenor offstage must be carefully examined, in case some Black Hander masquerading as a soldier had smuggled a real bullet into his rifle.

Caruso in Germany figures in a book * by the renowned and beloved Lotte Lehmann. She first heard him as Don José in *Carmen.* "His complete abandonment to his part," she wrote, "communicated itself to his audience, breathless under the spell."

When she was appearing in Hamburg in Gluck's *Orpheus,* which was to be followed on a double bill by *Pagliacci* with Caruso, the tenor, who always dressed early for his parts, was listening in the wings to Lehmann's singing. As she came off, he rushed up to her, exclaiming: "Bravo! Bravo! What a beautiful, magnificent voice. It is an Italian voice." (Doubtless his high-water mark of praise.) Lehmann was overwhelmed with joy—for, at that time, she was still in her early epoch as a singer.

Next day, she was invited to a small dinner in honor

* Lotte Lehmann, *Midway in My Song,* Bobbs-Merrill Co., 1938.

of Caruso. "Why am I asked?" she inquired modestly. "Caruso himself wanted you to come," she was informed. At the dinner, she sat next to him, but "my school French and English dried up from sheer nervousness, my Italian was limited to the text of a few songs, and Caruso did not speak a word of German."

Next day she got a letter inviting her to Caruso's Hamburg hotel for supper after her performance that evening in *Carmen*.

"I was just a great baby and imagined that temptation had come to me in the guise of the loveliest voice in the world. . . . So I fetched my French dictionary and wrote a polite refusal. Quickly, before I could regret it, I took it around myself to the hotel.

"On the way there I heard Hindermann [a fellow singer] saying to Fleischer-Edel [another]: 'Will you be at Caruso's after the performance tonight?' "

Lotte Lehmann stopped in her tracks. She asked whether Caruso was giving a party that evening. Yes—an enormous dinner at his hotel.

"Oh, what luck that I had found out in time! So it was not for me alone—my dark yet dangerously alluring presentiments of a *chambre séparée* were quite unjustified. My letter of refusal fluttered to the ground in little pieces."

At the dinner she sat opposite the host. Unfortunately, Caruso, quite exhausted by his strenuous Hamburg singing feats, spoke at the supper in a weary voice and only in words of one syllable. But, when Lotte Lehmann shyly pushed a post card of him across the table and requested an autograph, he flashed her a friendly smile, asked her address, put it on the card, pocketed it, and, taking up a menu, did a caricature of himself for her, which he autographed and handed to her across the table. Next day, she received "a huge, lovely photograph" with an autograph dedication.

According to Emil Ledner the Caruso craze gripped Germany early and held its grip right through the famous tenor's German tours. The nights when he sang in Berlin and other big German cities were considered of such high social importance that it became a habit there among female society leaders, as soon as they learned the dates of his appearances, to start planning their "Caruso dresses" well in advance.

Apropos of Caruso in Hamburg, somebody revealed that on nights after he had appeared at the local opera house, the average number of persons arrested by the police for singing operatic selections in bars, thus disturbing silent drinkers at their devotions, totaled 263—as against an average on nights when the tenor was not in town of only 83.

CHAPTER 13

CARUSO THE LOVER

New York's 1907-1908 season brought Enrico Caruso another series of spectacular triumphs. His life was at its brightest. When he departed for Europe in April 1908, no cloud was visible in his skies.

On the steamer carrying him across the ocean was Father Tonello, a priest, a close friend of his. They sat together at table. Enrico laughed and joked continually. He was in high good humor. He had arrived. He was on the pinnacle of operatic glory. Renown such as had come to no other singer was encompassing and delighting him.

One day a wireless message was handed to Father Tonello. Caruso saw him open and read it. "How important you are!" he chaffed. "Getting a message in mid-ocean!"

The priest was in a quandary. The message was as follows: "Inform Enrico Caruso that his father is dead."

Pulling himself together, Father Tonello broke the news to Caruso. The tenor burst into tears. Marcellino Caruso had not been a good father to him. He had scoffed at the thought that his son might become a professional singer. The showers of fame and gold which afterward poured down on Enrico, whom he wished to make into a mechanic, failed to change him basically.

But—he was Enrico's father. All the child of nature in

Marcellino's son came to the surface as he gave way to his sorrow.

When he landed in England, a letter was handed to Caruso. He tore it open eagerly—he had recognized the handwriting on the envelope. As he read it, tears again came to his eyes; and when he reached the end of it he was crying openly, unashamed.

The letter was from Ada Giachetti. The woman whom he loved, with whom he had lived for eleven years, the mother of his sons, his companion and counselor in good and bad fortune, had left him. She had left him for another man—her chauffeur.

"I do not love you any more," she wrote to Enrico. "I shall never return to you."

He was distracted, he was beside himself, his life seemed to be crumbling away.

"I can't sing any more," he sobbed. "Everything is ended. Finish!"

Two faithful friends stood beside him in his grief, two friends who knew him well and sympathized with him from their hearts as he wept—Father Tonello, who had crossed the ocean with him, and Paolo Tosti, the composer of popular songs, who had come from London to meet him when he landed in England.

They reminded him that he had agreed to sing at the Albert Hall in London. Melba was to sing with him, and Sammarco, and other renowned stars. It was to be one of the most brilliant events of the London season.

"Impossible! I can't do it!"

They spoke to him gently, understandingly, they reasoned with him, those two good friends of his. They reminded him of his uncompromising rectitude in matters of business, of his high sense of honor. "Enrico, you *must* sing. Never have you failed to keep your word."

"Good. I sing."

He came on the stage at the Albert Hall amid tumultuous applause. He started—by a savage stroke of irony the song was "*Vesti la giubba*" from *Pagliacci*—the song of the lover betrayed by his sweetheart, the song of the brokenhearted clown compelled to laugh and joke in his agony.

The audience sat tense, rapt. Tosti and Father Tonello trembled as they wondered how Enrico could possibly reach the end of his aria without breaking down. They, and they only, knew that up there on the stage was their friend Enrico, crushed and broken, singing his own desolating tragedy.

"He began the recitative of the *Pagliacci* aria," wrote Father Tonello, "in a voice touched by an emotion deeper than any he had known before. Yet only Paolo Tosti and one other friend who were of the thousands who thronged the auditorium realized what Caruso was experiencing during those moments. He sang the Lament with a pathos and passion I had never heard him put into an aria before. It was not to be wondered at that the people went mad. If they had only known! All they saw, as they applauded frantically, was a man, with a face unnaturally pale, who came again and again before them."

Many years after that, when his American wife asked him the secret of his power as a singer, Enrico Caruso said:

"I suffer so much in this life. . . . That is why they cry. People who have felt nothing in this life cannot sing. Once I had a great suffering and from it came a new voice. It was in London this thing happen to me. . . . That night I must sing *Pagliacci*. Already I had been singing for many years, but that night was different. I became something more than a good singer that night."

✦

Eleven years had passed since Enrico Caruso, singing Rodolfo to Ada Giachetti's Mimi at Livorno, found out that he loved her and she him. Ada was already married. She and her husband were separated. But absolute divorce was difficult in the Italy of Ada and Enrico.

Snapping their fingers at convention, they had set up a home together. That home, for each, had been wherever the other was. Ada Giachetti accompanied Enrico to Russia, to Argentina, to the United States. She lived the gypsy life of the opera singer. After the birth of her children Ada was compelled to stay in Italy, while Enrico toured the world in triumph. So he bought Villa Bellosguardo, filled it with treasures he had picked up all over the world, made possible for her a life of luxury and glamour.

But one day, on his return from a foreign tour, he heard that Ada was unfaithful to him; that she was living with her chauffeur. Frances Alda, of the Metropolitan Opera House forces (who became the wife of Giulio Gatti-Casazza, the Met's manager), told about the shattering of the Ada Giachetti-Enrico Caruso romance.[*]

"The emotional shock of the discovery almost unbalanced his mind," she said. "He told me the story himself, as simply as a child. He went and stood before the gates of the villa and called Giachetti's name over and over, till she came out. He prostrated himself in the dust and begged her to send the man away and not to see him again.

"She promised to do so. They were reconciled. That autumn, Caruso returned to New York, while Giachetti remained in Italy with the children. Presently it was reported to the tenor that the same handsome young chauffeur was being seen with Madame Giachetti. Instantly all the intensity of his love was turned to hate and to a fanatic

---

[*] Frances Alda, *Men, Women and Tenors*, Houghton Mifflin, 1937.

desire for revenge. The memory of his recent bitter experiences overwhelmed him at times and cast a darkness over his naturally gay, fun-loving disposition."

According to others, Enrico's love did not turn to hate—never—neither just after she abandoned him nor at any time during the rest of his life.

At first, in his despair, he flitted from one light-o'-love to another, trying to forget Ada and the days of their happiness. He had an affair with Rina, Ada Giachetti's sister, also a singer, but they did not get along. When, in Rome, Rina met Nicola Daspuro, Caruso's old-time friend of Naples days, she sputtered to him: "Enrico is as jealous as Othello. If he sees me chatting for a moment with any man, he becomes terribly irritated. Now, isn't that just wonderful for me! What business is it of his what I do?" In less than a year Rina Giachetti and Enrico Caruso went their separate ways.

Shortly after Ada Giachetti left him Enrico decided that it would be only right for him to inform her estranged husband, a prosperous Italian businessman, of what had happened. Probably the thought that this other man knew Ada well was an impelling motive in this decision—doubtless, in Enrico's eyes, it set the husband apart from other men, invested him with a very special halo. So Enrico wrote to him.

But the prosperous businessman apparently had outlived any grief or resentment at the break between himself and Ada. His letter in reply to Enrico's exuded calm detachment; he advised the distracted lover to apply the balm of philosophy to his lacerated feelings. For Enrico, however, there was as yet no balm in philosophy or anywhere else.

He shut himself up. He suffered in solitude. He kept away from his friends. He refused to commit himself to further agreements for singing. All the flavor seemed to have gone out of his life. He shunned all company except that of his valet, Martino, who knew him and understood him and adored him and now stuck to him in his grief with selfless fidelity. Martino and Caruso ate together. They took walks together. When Enrico shook off his moodiness for a bit and showed that he felt like talking, Martino led him on, tried to keep him from reverting again to black silence. And, when Enrico slept, Martino lay down for the night just outside the door of his master's bedroom.

Slowly the time for fulfilling a contract in Berlin approached. The tenor, in his desperation, had been thinking of canceling it. But now he received a letter from Emil Ledner, his German manager, informing him that Kaiser Wilhelm II, knowing that the famous singer was engaged for the German capital, wished to have him as a guest for dinner at his imperial palace. It was to be a very intimate little dinner. Only the Kaiser and Enrico Caruso.

At first the despondent tenor was all for refusing. What was a dinner with an emperor to him in his affliction?

"I won't go," he told Martino.

Silently, the valet laid before him pen and ink. "You must go. There is no way out," he said.

Finally, Caruso compromised. He would go, he wrote to Emil Ledner, if the Kaiser would allow Martino to be present at the contemplated dinner *à deux*. Martino had become absolutely indispensable to him. Through diplomatic channels Ledner made the necessary inquiry. "Certainly," replied Kaiser Wilhelm II—shedding the pomp which usually encompassed him.

Enrico Caruso went to Berlin. In the tremendous success which he achieved in his singing at the opera house there he found a little solace for his sorrow.

He dined with the Kaiser. Behind his chair, Martino

served him—and the knowledge that the faithful valet was there, close to him, meant to him all the difference between a small portion of enjoyment and blank, hideous despair.

And the Kaiser was human. He understood. All through the meal he tried to make Caruso forget. He showed no obsession of superiority, of eminence, of the divine right supposedly separating monarchs from other mortals—of which, in his usual moods, he was always so arrogantly aware.

And, when his guest arose to go, he said: "Signor Caruso, if I were not the German Emperor I would like to be Martino."

Caruso returned to New York early in November 1908. The news of the defection of Ada Giachetti had shaken him badly. His face had lost much of its cheerful expression; seldom was there the old twinkle of fun in his eyes.

On the credit side, however, instead of the pudginess previously characteristic of his features, there was a new firmness of the flesh, as if suffering had hardened him.

When he arrived in New York he found his old associate of Milan's La Scala, Giulio Gatti-Casazza, who had been made co-manager of the Metropolitan with Andreas Dippel. Heinrich Conried was no longer in the managerial picture. And there was another old comrade of exciting and glorious La Scala days to greet him when he strode into the Metropolitan Opera House offices—Arturo Toscanini, who had been appointed the Metropolitan's principal conductor.

At the very beginning of that season Caruso ran into a bit of trouble. When it became known that Dippel's contract as co-manager was not to be renewed and that, consequently, Gatti-Casazza was soon to be in sole charge, there were murmurs among some of the Met singers. Dippel was well known to most of them and he was popular, whereas Gatti-Casazza, to the majority, was unknown and untested. Moreover, Dippel had expressed a certain hostility to his Italian colleague in the management.

So some of the prominent members of the opera house's troupe sent to the Board of Directors a round robin protesting against the coming elimination of Andreas Dippel. They included Eames, Farrar, Scotti, Sembrich, and—Caruso. This was strange, in view of the fact that Caruso knew Gatti well and Dippel not at all. Probably, with him, it was a case of the line of least resistance—colleagues had asked him to sign the round robin and that was enough for good-natured Enrico.

The Board of Directors showed Gatti-Casazza the round robin. Gatti must have put up a convincing argument against continued employment of Dippel, since the Directors not only refused to sign up the latter beyond the single year for which he had been engaged but also backed his Italian colleague when the latter sent to the protesting singers a snappy little missive, the gist of which was:

"Dear Artists. Continue to sing, which is your job. Do not trouble yourselves with things that do not concern you."

Quite a rap across the knuckles for Caruso and the other signers of the round robin!

The tenor now installed himself at the Hotel Knickerbocker, at Forty-second Street and Broadway, which was to be his New York home for a dozen years more.

The opening night that autumn of 1908 was a grand gala occasion. The opera selected (*Aïda*) was the first production at the Metropolitan under Gatti-Casazza's management—he was not to make his last production there until a full quarter of a century later. Also, at that performance, Arturo Toscanini made his first appearance as a conductor of opera in the United States.

But of much greater importance—in the eyes of the Met's society-conscious box-holders—was the fact that, on that night, for the first time in recorded history, in Box Number Seven in the Diamond Horseshoe, the sacrosanct Astor box, *there was not a single Astor present.* For the first time the box had been sublet for part of that season. That sad proof of the impermanence of tradition undoubtedly spoiled the performance for many. With an Astorless Number Seven on an opening night at the Metropolitan, what was to become of the great opera house's prestige and glory? What hope was there for the traditions, hallowed by decades, of New York's Four Hundred? "Terrible!" "What are we coming to, my dear fellow?" "Why bother about going to the opera any more?" "Soon there will be nothing left of it." Such, in a considerable section of the audience, was the general trend of comment. Caruso sang.

After that performance, and the performances that followed it, faithful Italian friends crowded into the great tenor's apartment, surrounded him at Italian restaurants and on strolls through New York's streets, seeking to cheer him up. They played cards with him. They smiled. They joked. But only now and then did he give them a smile or a joke.

During that 1908-1909 Met opera season Enrico Caruso received a visit from Ada Giachetti. Her New York visit was not a success. It did not contribute to a reconciliation. There were violent quarrels with him at the Hotel Knickerbocker. Eventually he made a large cash payment to her and she returned to Europe. Still he could not stifle his love for her—but it was also impossible for him to think of living with her again.

He, who had hardly ever missed a performance, who had been able always to tax his strength with impunity and pour out his golden notes no matter how carelessly he drew on his health and his endurance, now discovered again and again that he had to give up appearing on some of his scheduled singing nights; something new in him was warning him to spare himself, to conserve a power which, before, he had come to believe was inexhaustible. During that season the announcement that he was unable to sing was made on twenty-one nights. What had happened to Caruso, the Man of Steel with the Voice of Gold? He wrote to his brother Giovanni in Italy, when the season was half over: "You can understand how nervous I am. Pray for me."

When he sailed for Italy in the spring of 1909 he was frankly worried. Something was wrong with his throat. On arrival in Milan he went to Professor della Vedova, a specialist who, some time before, had removed an obstruction on one of his vocal cords. Now the specialist told him that he had the same trouble again.

In great secrecy he was taken from his Milan hotel to a private house, where Della Vedova again operated; and soon the patient was back at his hotel with nobody (so he thought) the wiser.

To his astonishment, the *Corriere della Sera*, Milan's leading newspaper, came out with a story about the operation. Caruso was enraged. He strongly suspected that the specialist was responsible for letting the cat out of the bag. Caruso declared that Della Vedova had merely *said* that he had removed the throat obstruction the first time— that there was no *proof* that he had. After the first operation, the tenor claimed, he had gone to an unknown young doctor in Florence, who, having scraped some matter from his vocal cords, afforded him prompt relief. Indignantly he called attention to the fact that when Della Vedova first operated on him, he had charged fifty lire ($10.00), whereas now his charge was 60,000 lire ($12,000).

Della Vedova denied furiously that he had violated his promise of secrecy about the operation; and he pointed out that, since he was making it possible for Caruso, the world's most renowned tenor, to resume his lucrative singing career, his charge was by no means exorbitant.

Eventually, through the efforts of diplomatic friends, the specialist's fee was reduced by one-half—to 30,000 lire— which the tenor paid amid angry grumblings. He was tasting not only the rewards but the penalties of renown.

After some anxious waiting, when the question as to whether his voice had been hurt or not hung in the balance, it came out as strong and beautiful as ever. All was well along the vocal cords. So the clouds vanished from his horizon for the time being, at least so far as singing was concerned. But not as regards Ada Giachetti.

Following a short stay at his Bellosguardo villa, he took the waters at Salsomaggiore and Montecatini, where his health improved visibly. After a concert tour through England, Scotland, and Ireland, which wound up with a highly successful appearance at the Albert Hall in London, he sang brilliantly in a number of German cities. Then he embarked for New York. He arrived there in a more cheerful frame of mind than the year before. Laughing was easier to him; and again he was able to joke. But not often.

On November 15, 1909, with the Diamond and Golden Horseshoes transformed into gorgeous semicircles of light and beauty, another Caruso First Night opened the New York opera season. *Gioconda* was the opera. The great tenor sang gloriously. The rumors that his voice was not what it used to be—some of them from worried friends, others from malicious ill-wishers—disappeared like mists in morning sunlight. New York thrilled and wept and thundered its joy as the Voice of Gold rang out in all its magnificence.

During that season Enrico Caruso got into trouble strongly suggestive of detective fiction. In February 1910, he received a Black Hand letter instructing him, under pain of death, to take with him on his way from the Knickerbocker to the Metropolitan Opera House a package of greenbacks and hand it to a man who would meet him en route. Surrounded by a hollow square of detectives Caruso made the trip from hotel to theater. Nobody molested him.

Then a second letter arrived, ordering him to send a large sum of money over to Brooklyn, where it was to be placed on the steps of a certain house.

Martino, Caruso's valet, took across the East River a package with greenbacks at top and bottom, but, stuffed between these, were strips of ordinary green paper. Having located the house specified by the Black Handers, Martino placed the package on its front steps. The entire block had been surrounded by detectives—they were in doorways, hallways, around corners—peeking, concealed, from windows.

For half an hour nothing happened. Then three men appeared.

They walked past the house, retraced their steps, passed it again. As they did so, one of them scooped up the package on the steps. Immediately, from all directions, armed detectives closed in on the three men. One escaped, but two were seized.

Months later, after the tenor was back in Europe, the two men were tried. One, named as the ringleader, was sentenced to seven years' imprisonment; the other got the same sentence plus deportation from the United States.

Some time after, a petition was circulated asking for the pardon of the criminals. A large number of persons signed it. One of them was Enrico Caruso.

CHAPTER **14**

CARUSO THE NEAPOLITAN

The late Commendatore Salvatore Cortesi, for uncounted years Associated Press correspondent in Rome, dean of American correspondents in Europe and a very charming Roman gentleman, once wrote a book * about his journalistic adventures which included a chapter on Enrico Caruso. He gave me a copy of it, with an autographed dedication, describing me as one *"chi ama Roma e a Roma sempre ritorna,"* which made me feel pleased and proud.

The next time I saw him I told him that his Caruso chapter was the best thing in his book. A peculiar expression came over his face—part pleasure, part not; for, after all, did not his book contain chapters describing meetings with Pope Leo XIII, whom he knew well; with that grimly growling Teuton, Bismarck, from whom he had wheedled an interview famous in newspaper circles; and with other extremely august celebrities? Was Cortesi on Caruso better than Cortesi on the Vatican?—or than Cortesi on the Iron Chancellor's growlings? But I stood my ground.

"Your description of Caruso in Naples," I insisted, "is the best thing of its kind about him that I ever read."

Cortesi met Caruso in the sunshine of Naples, in the

* Salvatore Cortesi, *My Thirty Years of Friendships,* Harper & Bros., 1927.

full tide of the great tenor's glory; and he has put that sunshine and glory into his report of their meeting.

In an open horse-carriage Caruso and Cortesi drove along the Toledo, the main street of Naples.

"Everybody knew him, and he knew everybody, and everybody saluted him, from princes and plebeians, with that southern familiarity which is not separated from respect. 'Don Enri,' 'u Signore ve bendica' was heard on all sides, and wherever I looked I saw men and women pointing and gesticulating at the great singer. . . . He answered all in Neapolitan accent, calling everyone by his Christian name, grinning and laughing and generally behaving like a schoolboy.

"Suddenly he stopped the carriage and said to me: 'How can I enjoy my Naples if I go about in a cab?' As soon as he had set foot on the ground he was surrounded by a crowd of admirers, and for all he had a smile, a joke, a handshake. The more people gathered around him the heartier was Caruso's laugh, the more obvious was his enjoyment.

"But Caruso afoot was soon too much for the traffic on the Toledo. . . . Those who wanted to get near him took up the whole street, and all were excited and talking at the top of their voices and gesticulating in typical Southern Italian style, so that anyone unaccustomed to Neapolitan demonstrations of affection and respect would have thought that a riot had broken out. . . . Caruso found himself obliged to hire another cab. . . . Some of his ardent admirers hired other carriages and drove after the singer, while others still, who were either too poor or had found no free cabs, ran after him on foot.

"Caruso drove to a little restaurant in Posilipo, where, overlooking the bluest bay in the world, he awaited those enthusiasts who had followed him all the way from Naples.

Several cabfuls of them arrived, besides the athletes who had run the mile and a half from the Toledo."

Caruso gathered everybody around him and then said more or less these words:

" 'Friends, your demonstrations of affection have touched me. The long journey from the Toledo here, especially in the case of those who footed it, must have waked up a mighty hunger in you. This hunger must be satisfied. What more suitable spot could be found than this, with the blue sky above us and the bluer sea before us, and old Father Vesuvius in the distance? And what in the world soothes hunger better than macaroni with vongole? [Typically Neapolitan shellfish.] Therefore, I invite you all to lunch with me.'

"To Caruso's great surprise this invitation did not evoke the enthusiasm which the thought of macaroni usually engenders in all true Neapolitans. . . .

" 'We want song, not food. . . .'

" 'You shall have that as well. To the tables, my friends!'

"He kept his promise. Between one course and the other, between pulls at his everlasting cigarette, he would sing. It did not matter what he sang; the effect on his audience was always the same. Whether he tried operatic melodies or whether he would burst forth with a Neapolitan song, the macaroni would equally be forgotten on everybody's plate, and everybody's mouth would open, not to receive food, but in ever-growing astonishment at the singer's powers and art. The singing would not only enchant the bystanders, but one could see all the womenfolk of the establishment come forth from their various occupations; the proprietor would leave his office, the cook would abandon his pots and pans. At the end of one song, in the midst of delirious applause, he turned to me and said: 'The cook's praise is the one I love and respect most of all. Women will even weep when I sing, but they do so largely because it is Caruso who sings. But if I can draw the man who cooks my macaroni from his fire and if I can make him forget that there is such a thing as food in the world, then I know that I am touching the heights of my art. . . .

"'On days like these, with such a scene, with such macaroni, and such an audience, I wonder why I ever leave Naples!'"

Naples! How Caruso loved her! The adored city of his birth was seldom out of his thoughts. Her hot sunshine warmed him in cold St. Petersburg, in damp, foggy London. Her smiling bay got mixed up in his mind with the East River and the North River whenever a ship brought him into New York.

"I was happiest," he used to say in years of fame, "when I was earning ten lire as a boy in Naples. I spent seven and saved three. And my reputation did not run any risk if I sang a false note. When I was unknown I used to sing— modesty be hanged!—like a nightingale. And I sang for the sheer joy of singing, with untortured nerves, without a worry in the world.

"Now, on the other hand, weighed down by a reputation which cannot be increased, but which the slightest deterioration in my voice can threaten, I sing, so to speak, with my nerves. When I finish an evening's singing I am always exhausted. And I think of those who come to hear me at exorbitant prices—who consider me a phenomenon, a creature of an exceptional kind, to be looked at with the wide open mouth of astonishment—who is to be envied— and I don't like it!"

During his career, innumerable photographs were made of Enrico Caruso—in full operatic splendor, in flamboyant street attire, in formal evening dress—once, even, on Long Island, in yachtsman's garb. But none of them are as typical of the happy Neapolitan lad who always stayed alive in him than his first photograph as a professional singer at the very outset of his career.

It was taken in Naples. The photographer, working for a local newspaper, walked one morning right into the tenor's bedroom where he lay asleep, shook him, and demanded that he pose for his picture then and there.

It was a tough moment. Enrico Caruso owned only one shirt. It was being washed. So, draping himself in the bedspread, as if it were a magnificent stage costume, he struck a regal dramatic attitude. The photographer finished his work, then dashed away to the office of his employer. And next day the photograph was printed.

Always there was a spirit of boyish mischief in Enrico Caruso. It persisted long after he had left boyhood and early youth and Naples behind him. It kept breaking out with a suddenness and irreverence calculated to keep the men who tried to manage him on pins and needles—especially Giulio Gatti-Casazza, who tried longest.

Will anybody who saw the renowned tenor in *Pagliacci* ever forget his antics with the bass drum, when the strolling players make their first appearance? Once, in that scene, the donkey accompanying the players refused to cross the stage decorously, as required by the libretto. Instead, giving way to an intransigent, *j'y suis-j'y reste* mood, it stood stock still, obliging the dignified Scotti to tug frantically at its bridle, to the delight of Caruso, who gave an impromptu variation of his usual clowning by throwing himself with special energy into heaving, pushing, and shoving at the other end of the animal.

On another night, at a critical point in an opera in which he was performing, Caruso sidled surreptitiously close to the baritone and put an egg in his hand. Imagine! The baritone couldn't throw the egg on the floor. He couldn't toss it among the members of the orchestra. He couldn't stuff it into his pocket. So, when he whirled his arms about, with the dramatic abandon characteristic of grand opera principals, the egg whirled with them. Whether he eventually deposited it on some inconspicuous piece of scenery, or presented it to the soprano, or hurled it at Caruso, doubled up with laughter in the wings, I do not know.

Then there was the time while *Bohème* was being given, when the singer playing the role of Colline, having informed the audience, in the famous *"Vecchia zimarra"* song, that he was going out into the freezing Paris night in order to pawn his overcoat and buy medicine for the ailing Mimi, found himself utterly unable to get into the garment. Caruso had sewed up the sleeves.

Another time, when Caruso's good friend, the big basso Arimondi, was playing Colline, he fell a victim to the irrepressible tenor's pranks. Having sung the overcoat song, Arimondi put on the garment—on this occasion Caruso had not tampered with it—and started to don the high hat that goes with it. To his consternation, water trickled from the hat all over his face and overcoat and the back of his neck. Caruso had been at work.

Once, however, Enrico's mischief boomeranged. As Nemorino, in *L'Elisir d'Amore*, he used to play all sorts of amusing tricks with the bottle of love potion, which is so important in that gay little Donizetti opera. One night Caruso decided that the liquid looked altogether too tranquil in its bottle. If Donizetti sparkled, why shouldn't the love potion? He felt that it ought to act up in the scene when he drinks it down. Turning his back for a moment on the audience, he put something into the bottle to make the liquid fizz—and fizz it did, to such alarming effect that it deluged Caruso's face and the adjacent parts of his clothing.

Also, the laugh was on Caruso in this case:

He was up to his ears in that melodramatic scene in *La Forza del Destino,* in which Don Alvaro (tenor), busy trying to put through an elopement with a highborn Spanish lady (soprano), is suddenly confronted by her father (basso) and a heavily armed retinue, bent on thwarting the elopement at all costs. The retinue are supposed to start shooting, whereupon Don Alvaro, in self-defense, returns their fire, killing the lady's father.

Caruso, as Don Alvaro, stood ready to shoot as soon as the retinue went into action. But—not a sound came from the pistols of those confronting him. Something had gone wrong somewhere. Resourceful as usual, Caruso leaped into the breach.

"Bang!" he exclaimed, pretending to be a burst of small-arm fire. "Bang! BANG!" Unfortunately, his resourcefulness fooled nobody. The audience rocked with laughter.

At one time, Caruso decided to learn to play the flute. In the course of his apprenticeship, a man with a phonograph came to him. "Play your flute into the horn of my phonograph," he told the singer. Caruso did so. When he had finished his flute selection, the man played back the reproduction to him.

"Is that how I sound?" asked the tenor.

"Yes. Can I sell you the record?"

"No," answered Caruso. "But I'll sell you the flute."

Always a child himself, Enrico Caruso adored children. In Hamburg, he lost his heart to the little son and daughters of the proprietor of the hotel where he was staying. He told them stories; he laughed and joked with them;

he did magicians' tricks; he ransacked the city's toy shops for new toys to present to them; he got down on the floor and squatted with them there, to make new gadgets work or play new games. And they reciprocated, as if he were someone their own age, instead of a famous, grown-up singer.

One day, in New York, the little son of a friend asked Caruso point-blank: "Is it true that you have the finest voice in the world?"

"Come to the opera house to hear me tomorrow evening," said Caruso, "and judge for yourself. I will send you tickets."

"But I am only eight years old," wailed the child, "and I'll be in bed when the opera starts."

"Well, come to my hotel at three o'clock tomorrow afternoon and I will sing for you."

Next day the little boy and his father appeared at Caruso's hotel apartment. The tenor turned to the father. "Oh, no! Not you! I am singing for your son alone. If you insist on listening, it will cost you $1,500." Exit father, to read newspapers and kick his heels in an anteroom.

Meanwhile, inside the apartment, Caruso sang *Tosca* in full-throated splendor. When he finished, the little fellow, tears trickling from his eyes, jumped up, ran over to the singer, climbed on his lap, and covered his face with kisses. "Papa didn't tell me *anything* about your voice!" he sobbed. "It's wonderful!" Caruso returned his kisses with the greatest enthusiasm. And he gave the little boy an autographed photograph of himself, in a silver frame, on which he wrote: "To my little friend ——, to whom I owe the greatest satisfaction of my life."

The tenor's Neapolitan mischievousness showed itself sometimes when reporters crowded around him.

"How do you live?" asked one, pencil poised.

"By breathing."

"Do you snore?"

"No, I don't have to. It isn't required in my contract."

On a gala night at London's Covent Garden Opera House, the right-hand stage box was occupied by ex-King Manuel of Portugal, the left one by the Prince of Wales; and other celebrities were sprinkled generously all through the audience. The opera was *Rigoletto*, with Caruso playing the Duke.

That night he was not in good voice. He did not sing well at all. When the third act started, the ex-King of Portugal, leaning over the rail of his stage box, asked audibly of the tenor: "Signor Caruso, are you going to start to do some real singing now?"

Everything came to a dead halt. Sir Thomas Beecham, the conductor, signaled to the musicians to stop playing.

Imperiously, Caruso signed to the conductor to go on with the music. Then he walked over to the ex-monarch's box, leaned his elbow impudently on the railing around it, and, without so much as a glance at the royal interrupter, began to sing—divinely. After a short while, still without looking at the ex-King, he calmly walked away, still singing.

That is in a book by an author who, obviously fearing skepticism on the part of his readers, adds, "I know that this really happened at Covent Garden. I was there."

Naples was always cropping up in Caruso's conversation.

"When I was a boy," he told his wife in New York, "I wanted to take singing lessons. But I had no money. So I used to sit on the sidewalk under a street lamp after working hours [he was employed at that time by Signor Meuricoffre, the Swiss manufacturer] and copy songs for students, who used to pay me a few lire. Much of what I earned went to buy shoes. I had to walk far in those days for my lessons."

At times Enrico was the victim, not the perpetrator, of Neapolitan street-urchin tricks. On one occasion, after his engagement for a series of operatic appearances—an honor which had been ardently coveted by a considerable number of rival local singers—he came out on the stage to find, to his consternation, that the whole front row was occupied by—*tenors*. There they sat, a long line of them, arms folded, scowling. They had hit upon this outrageous device in the hope of making Enrico come down with stage fright. But he managed, somehow, to get through the evening without serious mishap.

A friend of mine likes to tell about the time when she was a little girl and paid a visit with her two little sisters to their great-aunt, who was staying at the Hotel Knickerbocker, Caruso's New York home. That great-aunt was a severe lady, a great-aunt of the old school, who did not believe in spoiling little girls and making them feel important. So, after admonishing them on what they should and should not do in order to be successful in life, she gave them each a large red apple and signified that the audience was over.

The three little girls emerged from the elevator into the grand lobby of the Knickerbocker, blushing with embarrassment, after the manner of children, at being in such a gorgeous place with big plebeian apples in their hands.

They held a whispered conference in a corner of the lobby. Enrico Caruso, lounging in another corner, watched them with a twinkle of understanding in his Neapolitan eye. Then, in single file, they walked over to an ornate receptacle, out of which grew a plant, unobtrusively deposited the three apples at the foot of the plant, and unobtrusively stole away, thinking that nobody had noticed them.

They were mistaken. Enrico Caruso had noticed them. To their horror, he threw back his head and roared with laughter. The whole lobby was full of sophisticated people. Caruso's laugh was so musical, so unrestrained, that the children heard it all the way down the street as they left the Knickerbocker.

"I hate Caruso!" said one child. "I never want to hear of him again!"

"I loathe him!" said one of her little sisters.

The next week they went to a Caruso matinee at the Met. Caruso was forgiven—but their aunt was not.

Enrico Caruso was born a Neapolitan, he lived a Neapolitan, he died a Neapolitan. No matter in what city he was, Naples was what he saw. She peeped out in irresistible beauty as he sang her songs, gay or melancholy; and she brought to his Voice of Gold when he sang them a caressing quality, a torrent of genuine feeling, which no rendering by him of the most famous arias in the most famous operas ever surpassed.

One day he went with friends to an Italian restaurant in New York's Little Italy. In a short time the group around him numbered twenty-odd joking, wine-quaffing comrades; and to them, even to those whom he had never seen before, Enrico Caruso spoke as if there had never been a time when he had not known them.

As he sat there, a hand organ on the street outside struck up an old Neapolitan song. "Don't you love to sing Neapolitan songs sometimes, instead of airs from the operas?" someone asked him. "I certainly do," replied the tenor, "but not that one. Never again will I sing the song which that organ-grinder is playing. If I did, I would tarnish one of my sweetest and saddest memories."

And he told the group around him how, one day during World War I, five rough Italian workmen came to his New York hotel and asked his secretary to be allowed to see him.

"They want money, I suppose," thought Caruso, who was experienced in such matters; and, placing his checkbook in readiness to be called into action, he had the five visitors ushered into his living room.

They were miners working in New Mexico, the spokesman of the five said. Many years before, they had come from Naples to America; always they had hoped to return; every day they had saved a little money for the homeward trip. Now they were in New York to sail to Naples, having been called to serve in the Italian army fighting by the side of Britain and France. In a few days they would be on submarine-infested seas. Perhaps they would die without seeing Naples again. They had raised among them two hundred dollars. Would Caruso take their money and sing for them? It would be, to them, like a day spent in Naples.

The tenor was so overcome that for a moment he could not speak. He knew it would be impossible for him to sing for them that day—his emotion was too great. "Come back tomorrow," he told them. "Bring as many friends as you wish. I will sing to you—free."

Next day not five but one hundred Italians showed up. And Caruso, back in Naples, swept them all back to Naples, as he sang typical Neapolitan songs of joy and grief. Everybody laughed and cried; and, when he had finished, they crowded around him, with tears and smiles, and they clasped his hand and some of them wanted to kiss it.

The last song he sang to them was a melancholy little

ditty about a Neapolitan emigrant, who, as his ship is carrying him away from the Naples water front, sings his heart out to her beauty, puts his whole soul into the expression of his love for her as she fades away in the distance and he realizes that he may never see her again. When he finished, Caruso buried his head in his arms and wept like a child.

"That song," he told his tablemates in the restaurant in New York's Little Italy, "was the one which that organ-grinder outside there was playing a few minutes ago. It is a sacred thing to me. Never will I sing it again as long as I live."

When Caruso was making phonograph records of his voice in the United States, he told Frances Alda that he wanted to make some additional records of duets with her —that her voice and his blended to perfection in recordings. Alda was willing. The records were to be made in Camden, New Jersey. The two arranged to meet on a ferryboat plying between Manhattan and the opposite Jersey shore. It was a cold, rainy day. Caruso pointed to the prima donna's shoes.

"You have no rubbers on," he remarked.

"I don't like to wear rubbers," said Alda. "I have pretty feet and I'm proud of them. I'm a woman."

"You ought to be wearing rubbers."

"I tell you I don't like them."

No more was said on the subject until they reached Camden. There Caruso, bowing Alda into a taxi, said to the driver: "To the best shoe store in town."

Inside the store, he told one of the clerks—all of whom knew who he was; there was no mistaking that face and figure any more—to bring an assortment of the best ladies' rubbers. Then he knelt at Alda's feet, and tried on one rubber after another, looking up at her while he did so, waving ladies' rubbers over his head in Neapolitan gesticulation, and humming some of the most impassioned love music in grand opera, while she shook with laughter.

When he had finally decided on the right pair, he escorted her to the waiting taxi and they continued their drive to the place where the recordings of their voices were to be made.

At a performance at the Metropolitan in New York, in which Alda was singing with Caruso, the tenor led her onto the stage after the curtain had fallen on the second act, and she bowed to the audience and received from the ushers a number of baskets of flowers and bouquets, sent by her admirers. Instantly Caruso the Neapolitan saw a grand opportunity for clowning.

Walking up to one of the baskets, he eagerly scrutinized the card attached to it. Then he shook his head, as if grievously disappointed, whispered to Alda, "For you," and handed it over to her, simulating extreme reluctance.

Another big basket was brought onto the stage. Again Caruso, all eagerness and anticipation, walked up to it. He read the card on it. Sadly, he shook his head. His face registered acute disillusionment. Again he whispered to Alda, "For you." Again, he handed over the basket to her, with a melancholy gesture of renunciation.

A big bouquet of roses was now placed on the stage. But this time the prima donna was too quick for Enrico. Striding forward, she got between him and the roses, plucked one from the bouquet, and presented it to him with a formal curtsy. He bowed from the waist, registering mock gratitude. And the audience, who had by this time guessed what was going on, smiled and chuckled delightedly.

✦

Many and variegated were the honors lavished on Caruso in the years of his phenomenal triumphs in New York, but it is safe to say that none of them pleased him more than Police Commissioner Enright's calling on him one day at his grand apartment in the Knickerbocker Hotel and formally handing him a gold badge, which, the Commissioner informed him, made him an honorary member of the New York police force.

That delighted Enrico Caruso, the perennial little boy of the streets of Naples. Proudly fingering the badge, he inquired: "Am I now a policeman?"

"You are," replied Enright.

"Can I arrest people?"

"You can."

"Ah! Very good!" The tenor started toward his hat and coat. "I go now to find Gatti-Casazza."

CHAPTER 15

HECTIC YEARS

After the close of the New York 1909-1910 opera season, the steersmen of the Metropolitan Opera House, headed by Otto H. Kahn, Chairman of its Board of Directors, resolved to send the Metropolitan opera troupe to Paris for a season of opera at the Châtelet Theater there. Mr. Kahn offered to foot 50 per cent of the expenses of this daring and unprecedented venture. Gabriel Astruc, the manager at the Paris end, wired: "If Caruso comes, success is sure." The tenor agreed to contribute his services. He was to sing in *Aïda, Pagliacci,* and *Manon Lescaut.*

Paris got much excited about the projected invasion. And it became apparent from the start that the excitement was almost entirely caused by the prospect of hearing Caruso.

Monsieur Astruc resorted to a neat ruse. He informed the Paris public that, in addition to every ticket purchased by anybody for an *Aïda* night with Caruso singing, another ticket must also be purchased for a performance of *Otello* without Caruso. Similarly, all who wanted a ticket to hear Caruso in *Pagliacci* must buy likewise a seat for a Caruso-less *Falstaff.* Finally, to get to hear the renowned tenor in *Manon Lescaut* the Parisians were told that they must buy, in addition, a ticket for one of several other operas in which Caruso was not to sing. This trick brought an advance sale totaling 600,000 francs (about $120,000, at the current rate of exchange) before Enrico Caruso had so much as opened his mouth. And it undoubtedly contributed mightily toward swelling the audiences in the Châtelet when Enrico was not in the cast.

For the first performance—*Aïda*, with Caruso as Rhadamès—the Châtelet was jammed to suffocation. Destinn was the Aïda, Homer the Amneris, Amato the Amonasro. The attitude of Paris, despite its overpowering desire to hear Caruso, was not entirely friendly. There was a feeling in some quarters that Otto Kahn and his colleagues wanted to teach Paris how to give opera.

But Caruso carried all before him. He swept away disapproval in a torrent of superb singing. He alone received undiluted praise. The audience cheered itself hoarse. Next day's newspapers raved in unison. "The other artists did well," declared one critic, "but it was a Caruso night. He carried the whole opera. Thank God, he has strong shoulders."

Every time he sang receipts averaged over 60,000 francs, whereas, on non-Caruso nights, they ran to only 45,000 francs. And that latter figure was largely due, it must be remembered, to Gabriel Astruc's little box-office trick.

As the Paris season drew to a close the demand for Caruso became so terrific that he had to appear six times in eight days. He was under a tremendous strain, but his fatigue was counterbalanced by the sweet music of the cheers of those delirious Châtelet audiences. Praise was poured on him. The great French actress Réjane wrote him: "I would like to grasp your hand and thank you for an unforgettable evening."

After Paris, the Villa Bellosguardo. But without Ada Giachetti. A desolate existence! Enrico Caruso might have capped the assertion, by his biographer Eugenio Gara, that "a tenor without a villa is not a tenor" with "a villa without Ada is not a villa."

His spirits, however, were improving—a little. He was more talkative, funnier. Once he gravely informed a visitor that he kept in a chest of drawers, a whole set of different voices—a dark *Aïda* voice in one drawer; a light, gay *Elisir d'Amore* voice in another; his *Bohème* voice in a third; and so on.

After a few appearances in Brussels Caruso again toured Germany. In Berlin, Kaiser Wilhelm II, having summoned the singer to the imperial box at the opera house, remarked to him: "Caruso, why don't you give up going to America and stay all the time in Europe?"

"Your Majesty," replied the tenor, "my gratitude to America will end only with my death."

There is a story to the effect that Caruso's chain-cigarette-smoking behind the scenes of the Berlin Opera House so alarmed the management that they had a fireman follow him around with a bucket of water. But Emil Ledner, who was manager of the Berlin Opera House, gives the following story:

Before going on the stage to sing Caruso suffered from the most acute stage fright; and the extent of his suffering could be gauged by the number of cigarettes he smoked while waiting for his cue. When about to sing exacting roles, such as Rhadamès, Canio, or Cavaradossi, his cigarette seemed to be a regular feature of his face. His hotel rooms and dressing room were dark and rank with smoke clouds. Before going on in *Aïda* he smoked fifteen or twenty cigarettes, which littered his dressing table and his whole dressing room.

"But I never saw a fireman follow him with a bucket," declared Ledner. "However, I did station two theater employees outside the door of his dressing room, with orders to watch him closely as he smoked, and I myself, whenever I could, kept an eye on him. It was useless to remonstrate with him. 'If I can't smoke, I can't sing,' he used to say." Perhaps the manager would not have minded so much if the tenor had smoked decent cigarettes; but what Caruso considered a cigarette, says Ledner, was as a matter of fact *"ein fürchterliches Kraut"* (a fearful weed), the fumes of which were bearable only in the open air—if at all.

The stage fright which, said Emil Ledner, plagued Caruso just before he went on the stage at the beginning of an opera, is typical of opera singers in general—according to Caruso himself. He used to tell tales about how it, combined with superstition, affected some of his fellow singers. One prima donna, he declared, always crossed herself devoutly just before making her first entrance. Another invariably bade her mother, whom she insisted on bringing with her to her dressing room every night on which she sang, an affectionate, elaborate, and lachrymose farewell— as if she were about to be led to execution. Still another, before leaving her dressing room for the stage, never failed to fasten around her wrist a gold bracelet, explaining: "It will bring me good luck. Gounod gave it to me."

"Unfortunately," Caruso used to add in telling his story, "that prima donna eventually got so fat, and so many extensions had to be grafted onto that bracelet that, finally, there was practically nothing left in it of the gold contained in the original gift from Gounod. But she never lost her faith in its efficacy as an amulet."

In his book of reminiscences about Enrico Caruso, Herr Ledner makes an important disclosure—and he makes it with the solemnity of a statesman whispering a state secret. Caruso, it seems, when he went on to sing, always carried, in pockets occupying strategic points in his apparel, a number of little flasks containing a special mixture, which he would sip if he did not feel well, availing himself of some friendly piece of stage architecture or conveniently placed clump of stage shrubbery, behind which he could sip unbeknownst to the audience.

"I know what that mixture was!" announces Emil Ledner dramatically. "Its ingredients have never been revealed before. Here it is: a little warm water, heated just before he went on the stage; five drops of anise; a small quantity of orange juice, passed through a very fine-meshed sieve; and as much salt as would cover the tip of a knife."

In Frankfort-on-the-Main, Caruso turned suddenly to Emil Ledner and remarked: "I'm engaged to be married."

"Oh, I know all about those engagements of yours," scoffed Ledner, who, in the course of several years of dealings with the tenor, was not entirely unacquainted with the latter's way with a maid. "You have at least one of them every year."

"But this is a real engagement."

Ledner said "Tut, tut" in German.

Caruso was offended. He requested his manager to make no more slighting comments. He told him that the lady's name was Signorina Gianelli, that she had been his guest for a while during the preceding summer at his Villa Bellosguardo.

"I love her," added Enrico. "She is a virtuous, beautiful, good girl. She will join me with her father in Berlin in a few days. There—I ask you urgently—please announce my engagement—not at my hotel, but in your own home."

Ledner shrugged his shoulders. There was no more to be said. In Berlin he reserved an apartment at the Hotel Bristol, consisting of two bedrooms and a salon, for Miss Gianelli and her father. It was entirely separate from the tenor's apartment, reserved at the same hotel.

Miss Gianelli and her father arrived in Berlin in due course. The girl, according to Emil Ledner, was really beautiful. She and her father were all dressed up for the Berlin visit. The girl was fairly at ease. But not the father. It was perfectly apparent that formal attire was something wholly new to him, also something extremely uncomfortable. He had all sorts of difficulty managing his stiff collar. And as for his high hat! He and it simply could not get along together. Obviously, they were Italians in very modest circumstances, unable to cope adequately with the strange situation in which they suddenly found themselves. Caruso told Ledner that he had met Miss Gianelli in a Milan department store, where she was employed as a saleslady. He had hoped, he added, that her visit to Bellosguardo would help him to forget Ada Giachetti.

Father and daughter kept very much to themselves. Both seemed embarrassed and worried. They used to see Caruso at the theater, in the hotel, on walks together, at meals. Caruso, according to his German manager, behaved impeccably. He treated the young girl like a great lady. He seemed to be very much in love. He spoke a lot about getting married the following spring after his return to Italy from New York; about how hard it was for him to wait for the wedding.

A few days after the arrival of the Gianellis in Berlin Emil Ledner gave a party at his house, at which he announced Enrico Caruso's engagement to Signorina Gianelli. Shortly after, father and daughter left for Milan, Caruso and Ledner for Bremen, from which port the tenor was to depart for the United States, to star in the 1910-1911 Met season in New York.

"One hour before the departure of the steamer," writes Ledner, "he handed me a telegram and asked me urgently to dispatch it by a reliable messenger. But first, he insisted, I must read it.

"It was for Miss Gianelli. It read: 'There must be no marriage between us. After careful deliberation, I must break off our private engagement, which has never been made public. Let us forget what has happened.'"

Emil Ledner was struck speechless.

"Do you want me to send this?" he asked.

Caruso answered nervously in the affirmative.

"Please don't ask many questions," he added. "I am fed up with the whole thing."

The telegram was sent.

1910-1911. Another Metropolitan Opera season. Enrico Caruso's eighth in a row. He had returned to America with a fresh crop of European laurels.

And he returned to find his American reputation higher than ever. "His place in the Metropolitan was seemingly as fixed as the very foundation upon which the opera house was reared," wrote Pierre Key. Again the great singer installed himself at the Knickerbocker, just up the street from the scene of his operatic triumphs; again his faithful valets, Martino and Mario, efficiently served him.

That season was opened with Gluck's *Armide*. Caruso did not feel at home in it. Classical Gluck was not for him.

In the season's second month came the world *première* of Puccini's *La Fanciulla del West* (like *Madame Butterfly*, fashioned from a play by David Belasco and John Luther Long, which, with Blanche Bates starring, had been a success on Broadway). Caruso played the part of Dick Johnson. Obviously, Puccini had intended to tickle Americans, from whom he drew a fat slice of his income as the most popular opera composer of the day, by successfully setting to typical Italian music a typically American story.

Caruso as Renaud in Gluck's Armide

But *La Fanciulla del West* was no *Madame Butterfly*. Even Caruso's excellent singing (which particularly delighted Puccini, who had crossed the ocean to be present at the *première*) could not keep it alive. Soon it disappeared from the playbills; and never since then has there been serious talk of putting it back.

On February 6, 1911, Caruso made his last appearance of the season in Franchetti's *Germania*—the stillborn opera which he had tried to sing to life in Milan a few years before. It was not scheduled as his last appearance. The New York public had looked forward to much more of him. But, suddenly the Gatti-Casazza offices announced that the tenor had a cold. Something fishy about the announcement caused the New York papers, always hot on the scent of Caruso news, to get busy. Once more they speculated, guessed, suspected; all through the city which he had made his second home the old rumors ran and multiplied.

Was something wrong again with Caruso's vocal cords? In vain, Bill Guard, now chieftain of the Gatti-Casazza press department, scoffed; in vain, physicians pooh-poohed. The rumors persisted. And when the report came that the tenor was going to Europe for a rest, their number and volume took on unprecedented proportions. "Now," groaned Caruso, as he read the New York dailies at breakfast, "my enemies will say that I have lost my voice."

In February 1911, he left New York for Europe—much earlier than usual. Rumors reached high-water mark. "Aha! He has been singing too strenuously." "He sang too much, I tell you." "Poor Caruso! Finished!" While his enemies gloated and his friends grieved and worried, he went, immediately on his arrival in Europe, to Professor Della Vedova in Milan—apparently Caruso had allowed his respect for that specialist's skill to overshadow grudges against him.

Another operation was performed on the tenor's vocal cords, similar to the two that had gone before it. And Caruso kept busy denying a flourishing crop of new rumors. Again an Italian doctor—not Della Vedova—had circulated a story about the end of Caruso's career as a singer. "Pure invention!" exclaimed the angry tenor. "The doctor who started that yarn did it merely to advertise himself! The yarn he gave a reporter about my having a 'corn' in my throat is absolutely false! My vocal cords are in excellent condition."

Gradually the rumors subsided. Credence began to be given to denials by doctors, friends, business associates, Caruso himself. In an editorial about the Golden Voice, *Le Figaro* of Paris said: "He has not, thank Heaven, lost it!"

For some time Caruso had been maintaining a home in the Maida Vale section of London, where his younger son, Enrico, Jr. (Mimmi), now seven years old, lived with an English governess. The sharp-eyed collectors of Britain's income taxes, arguing that this residence, though he was seldom in it, made him a resident of London, assessed against him what he considered an outrageous tax. Flying into one of his Neapolitan tantrums, he stripped the house of all its furnishings and got rid of his lease on it. Mimmi and the governess went first to live elsewhere in England, and, later, to make their home with Rina Giachetti, Ada's sister, who had a villa near Livorno, the town where Enrico and Ada had first met and loved. Later still, the tenor installed the two at his Villa Bellosguardo.

Caruso was fond of his two little sons, the children of Ada Giachetti, and tried to be with them as much as his nomadic life would allow. Once, when Enrico, Jr., was living in London with his governess, Caruso, interrupting an afternoon of storytelling and playing with the little boy, prepared to depart for his hotel to get ready for the evening's opera at Covent Garden.

"Where are you going, Papa?" asked the little boy.

"I am going to work so you can get food to eat."

Some time later, when Mimmi was asked where his father was, he replied: "He's gone out to get the dinner."

Caruso hired governesses for his sons and, when they were old enough, sent them to good schools in Europe, and—in the case of one of them—to a school in the United States. He impressed upon them constantly the necessity of work, hard work, as a road to success and happiness.

Rodolfo, the eldest son, was a rather moody little individual, inclined to sulking and sudden outbursts of weeping. But Enrico, Jr., was full of laughter and gaiety, continually engaged in singing and playing with the toys with which his generous father kept him bountifully supplied.

Caruso arranged with the successive governesses employed to care for his little boys to have photographs of them sent to him as frequently as possible during his extended travels. Once, Miss Saer, Mimmi's governess in London, took a snapshot of him when his face was wearing a serious expression—which was most unusual. When Caruso, away in distant parts, saw that picture he instantly got alarmed. "I do not like his expression," he cabled. "I am coming immediately to London to cheer him up."

He liked to have the little boy hear him sing. And, whenever at Covent Garden he took a curtain call, he always made a point, while tremendous applause was thundering all around him, to look toward the box where Mimmi was sitting and smile at him and throw him kisses.

As an employer of governesses and others, Caruso was

a kind but firm master. He wanted them to do their work faithfully and well. When, on leaving him for employment elsewhere, they asked for references he gave these willingly. And he often used to say: "And I want a reference from *you* also."

In July 1911, Signorina Gianelli, she who had gone from Italy to Berlin to visit Caruso, accompanied by her father in the incompatible hat, brought suit in Naples against the tenor for breach of promise of marriage. Caruso was compelled to be present and give testimony. From Naples he wrote to Emil Ledner: "Yes, Miss Gianelli haled me into court for material and moral damages. She wanted to have me compelled to pay her 250,000 lire. As a matter of fact, it is not she but her father, that attractive gentleman. It is simply an attack on my fortune."

The suit gave rise to acrimonious action on both sides. Many letters from Caruso were produced in court. The case dragged along for some time. Finally, one day, an elated Enrico Caruso wired to Ledner: "Gianelli case ended with complete victory for me. Miss Gianelli sentenced to pay expenses incurred by me, costs, etc.—10,000 lire."

True to his Neapolitan nature and his Southern Italian blood, Enrico Caruso was always deeply interested in the female sex. And he was an impetuous lover. He showed that by his conquest of Giuseppina Grassi in the old Salerno days; by his whirlwind wooing of the little ballerina who supplanted Giuseppina in his heart; by his wooing of Ada Giachetti (via Puccini's melting *Bohème* love music); by his ardent though ephemeral affair with Miss Gianelli. And he showed it later by his tempestuous storming of the New York social fortifications surrounding the second of his great loves—which I shall describe before long.

Unwittingly, he summed up his amorous philosophy one day at his Hotel Knickerbocker apartment, when he was rehearsing with his accompanist (at that time Richard Barthélemy) the role which he was to sing that night at the Met. Barthélemy told him that the word *"amore,"* occurring in one of the arias which he was to sing, must be sung pianissimo.

Caruso was splashing about in his bath when the accompanist made this pronouncement. Leaping out of the water, wearing nothing but a large towel, he strode to the piano at which Barthélemy was seated, shouting: "What's that? Sing *'amore'* pianissimo? Who says so?"

"It's so marked in the music."

"Well, it's a mistake! Do they take me for an old soprano? When I sing of *'amore'* I think of something that burns me up, overwhelms me! That word makes me picture something that is a madness, that is destroying me, that makes me weep, that assassinates me! And you tell me to sing it pianissimo! Never!"

It was significant that at this time Caruso temporarily gave up all singing at concerts. He had emerged without mishap from a third throat operation, but even he, with all his lighthearted recklessness and contempt for the morrow, knew at last that he must mend his ways if he was to continue being the undisputed monarch of the world of song. He turned down all offers from concert managers in England for appearances on the platform. Indeed, he sang not a single note anywhere in Europe, because he wished to be sure that he would do himself justice at the next Caruso First Night at the Met.

That night came on November 13, 1911. Caruso, singing in *Aïda* with Destinn in the title role and Matzenauer as Amneris, was magnificent. Besides his marvelous singing, he was now giving the public something else—better acting.

For years he had been overcoming the crudity, the lack of polish and elegance of his histrionic beginnings. All too often he had been portraying dukes without making them ducal. Now—without sacrifice of any of his inborn, unrivaled qualities—he was endowing his acting with more and more polish and elegance, yet not losing one iota of the tremendous vocal power of his portrayals.

It must be remembered that, as an actor, Enrico Caruso had to fight a serious handicap. Physically he was unimpressive; in some parts, in fact, his undistinguished physique invested his roles, lyrical as well as heroic, with a touch of the ludicrous. He was too squat for Rhadamès, too fat for Faust. It is enormously to his credit that he both knew this and fought it. That he was fighting it he now proved in his ninth successive Met season. That he was aware of it he proved constantly by his jokes about himself, entirely free from false vanity; and, above all, by his caricatures, in which the caricaturist repeatedly made himself the butt.

After the New York opera season of 1911-1912, during which Caruso did not miss a single scheduled performance, he sang at a big memorial concert to commemorate the sinking of the *Titanic*. With him on the program were Lillian Nordica, Mary Garden, Bella Alten, and Andrés de Segurola. The German Hertz and the Italian Sturani conducted.

Caruso astonished his hearers by *singing in English* for the first time. He chose for his debut in this province of song Sir Arthur Sullivan's "Lost Chord."

After Caruso's return to Europe in the spring of 1912 he was asked by his old admirer Arrigo Boïto, the renowned composer-librettist, to sing the tenor role in his opera *Nero* (usually called by its Italian name, *Nerone*), scheduled for production at Milan's La Scala during 1913, as a feature of the celebration of the Verdi centenary that year. Caruso accepted. But there was no *Nerone* production until many years later; and, when it was finally given at La Scala in 1926, there was no Enrico Caruso to sing in it.

At the height of his New York renown Caruso gave an interview to a representative of the American musical magazine, *Etude*,* in which he said:

"Anyone who has traveled in Italy must have noticed the interest that is manifested at the opening of the opera season. This does not apply only to the people with means and advanced culture, but to what might be called the general public. In addition to the upper classes the same class of people who in America would show the wildest enthusiasm over your popular sport, baseball, would be similarly eager to attend the leading operatic performances in Italy.

"[In Italy] the opening of the opera is accompanied by an indescribable fervor. It is 'in the air.' The whole community seems to breathe opera. The children know the leading melodies and often discuss the features of the performance as they hear their parents tell about them, just as the average small American boy retails his father's opinion on the political struggles of the day or on the last baseball game. . . .

"I find that, as far as manifesting enthusiasm goes, the world is getting pretty much the same. If the public is pleased, it applauds, no matter whether it is in Vienna, Paris, Berlin, Rome or New York. An artist feels his bond with an audience very quickly. He knows whether they are interested, or whether they are delighted, or whether

* "Italy, the Home of Grand Opera," *Etude*, Jan. 1912, p. 112.

they are indifferent. I can judge my own work at once by the attitude of the audience.

"No artist sings exactly alike on two successive nights. That would be impossible. Although every sincere artist tries to do his best there are, nevertheless, occasions when he sings better than at other times. If I sing particularly well the audience is particularly enthusiastic. If I am not feeling well my singing indicates it and the audience will let me know at once. . . .

"There is something about an audience that makes it seem like a great human individual, whether in Naples or San Francisco. If you touch the heart or please the sense of beauty, the appetite for music common to all mankind, the audience is yours, be it Italian, French, German or American. . . .

"I am told that many people in America have the impression that my vocal ability is a kind of 'God-given gift'— that it is something which has come to me without effort. This is so very absurd that I can hardly believe that sensible people would give it a moment's credence. Every voice is in a sense a development and this is particularly so in my case.

"The marble that comes from the quarries of Carrara may be very beautiful and white and flawless, but it does not shape itself into a work of art without the hand and the heart and the intellect of the sculptor.

"Just to show how utterly ridiculous this popular opinion really is let me cite the fact that at the age of 15 everybody who heard me sing pronounced me a bass. When I went to Vergine [his singing teacher in Naples] I studied hard for four years . . . then I studied repertoire for three years and made my debut. Even with the experience I had had at that time it was unreasonable to expect great success at once. I kept working hard and working for at least seven years more before any really mentionable success came to me. All the time I had only one thing in my mind and that was never to let a day pass without seeing some improvement in my voice. The discouragements were frequent and bitter, but I kept on working and waiting until my long-awaited opportunity came in London and New York.

"The great thing is not to stop. Do not think that because these great cities gave me a flattering reception that my work ceased. Quite on the contrary. I kept on working and I am working still. Every time I go upon the stage I am endeavoring to discover something which will make my art more worthy of public acceptance. Every act of each opera is a new lesson. . . .

"I have no favorite roles. I have avoided this because the moment one adopts a favorite role he becomes a specialist and ceases to be an artist. . . ."

CHAPTER **16**

ALARUMS AND EXCURSIONS

Following her return to Europe after her trip to New York to see Enrico Caruso, which resulted in that stormy and anything but satisfactory meeting between them, Ada Giachetti sang in Italy with an opera troupe performing there and also went on a singing tour to South America. Caruso continued to send her checks regularly for herself and their two little sons, supplementing the cash which he turned over to her in New York.

Now—in 1912—she decided to take a drastic step. Over three years after her meeting with Enrico in America, she brought about the publication, in the *Corriere della Sera,* Milan's famous newspaper, which circulates all over Italy, of an article accusing Enrico Caruso of having prevented her from getting singing engagements in America by interception of letters and bribing of third parties. She also declared that he had stolen articles of jewelry belonging to her and tried to wreck her life.

After this article appeared in the *Corriere della Sera,* Caruso brought suit against Ada Giachetti for slander. Thus, Caruso, the very next year after Miss Gianelli had sued him for breach of promise, found himself involved again in legal proceedings.

The case came before a Milan court. It was the sensation of the hour. Enrico Caruso was present. Ada Giachetti was

not; she had gone to Buenos Aires—Hamlet without
Ophelia. The proceedings lasted from October 25 to October 30, 1912. In order to obey the court's summons to
appear before it Caruso was compelled to cancel arrangements for a tour in Central Europe under the management
of his old friend and admonisher, Emil Ledner.

The defendants were:

Ada Giachetti, accused of slander.

Vincenzo Turco, accused of false testimony.

Cesare Romati, Ada Giachetti's chauffeur (the cause of
the break between Ada and Enrico).

Gaetano Loria, accused of bribery of witnesses.

An action for slander brought by Maria Carignani, accused by Ada Giachetti of helping Caruso to intercept
business letters, also figured in the proceedings.

Reports in the case took up thirty-one large folio sheets.
They seemed to Emil Ledner (who took a deep interest
in the case and wrote copiously about it after the trial was
over) like chapters from a lurid crime novel.

At the opening session, attended by an excited Milanese
crowd which packed the courtroom and included a liberal
percentage of artists and musicians, Enrico Caruso was
seated close to the judge, between his lawyers. A statement
from the absent Ada Giachetti was read, in which she called
Enrico names which (according to Ledner) were mostly
unrepeatable. The mildest among them was "shameless
tenor." In this statement she maintained her charges of
interception of letters by Caruso and Maria Carignani,
basing them on a letter to her from Gaetano Loria (one of
the defendants), an operatic agent, expressing surprise that
he had received no answer to a letter about a contract form
sent to her in America by him. She also repeated her
accusation against Caruso of the theft of jewelry.

The article in the *Corriere della Sera* was then read aloud.

Caruso's lawyer submitted to the court a document signed by Ada Giachetti on June 26, 1909, stating that she would make no demands on Caruso for the return of jewelry, or of letters or anything else; and she also agreed not to go to America. Another statement by her was read making serious accusations against Caruso and Maria Carignani, alleging that the latter had played a double game, by helping Romati (the chauffeur) in his dealings with herself while at the same time reporting constantly to Caruso on her alleged relations with Romati.

Ada Giachetti having denied, in the *Corriere della Sera* article, all misconduct with Romati, three documents from her to Caruso were shown next. In the first, she asked the tenor's forgiveness, stating that she could no longer return his love, since the sons born to her in their relationship had given her the strength to forget her love for him; and adding that she hoped, however, that Caruso, who had always been kind to her, would continue his kindness. Furthermore, she asked him how she was to live in future, whether he would aid her, or whether she must look about for some means of making a livelihood. She added that she had already forgotten Romati; and she asked Caruso, as a good and magnanimous man, to forgive her.

In the second document, written in New York, where both she and Caruso were at the time, she complained of a scene made by Caruso when she tried to see him, the upshot of which was her getting thrown out of his hotel. In the third document she sent him kisses and praised him.

The testimony of Loria, the operatic agent, was then read. He said that Romati had threatened him to make him testify favorably to Giachetti. He said that Romati actually followed him in Milan; and, one day, in a bar, they met the journalist Turco, who tried to borrow from

Loria five lire ($1.00). Loria introduced Romati and Turco, after which the two became very close.

Loria stated that he had never asserted that Caruso had confiscated the letter from him to Ada about a contract or tried to have another person confiscate it. He added that he had addressed the letter to Giachetti at the Pension Excelsior in Milan, owned by Maria Carignani, and had never received an answer. He stated that Romati, in order to prejudice him (Loria) against Caruso, had declared that the famous tenor had stated to all and sundry that Loria had been discharged by the Cook firm in London because of theft. Loria closed by appealing to the magnanimity of Caruso to show that he was never anything but a tool in the hands of his enemies.

Next the journalist Turco took the stand. "I think," he said, "that the darkest day in my life was when I met Loria and Romati." He added that he was at the time in the most wretched circumstances; that he had met Loria, who had said to him: "You are in a bad way. How about making a statement that you had heard that Caruso had in his possession a bulky letter addressed to Ada Giachetti. To make such a statement is a mere trifle; if you make it, it will clear up everything."

The court asked Turco whether he had received money. He replied: "Yes. One Napoleon" ($4.00 at that time).

"From whom?"

"From Romati."

The court asked further: "Did you receive any more from Romati?" Answer: "Yes, from time to time—five, ten, twenty, and thirty lire." Question from the court: "Did Caruso's lawyers ever approach you?" Answer: "No." Question: "Who asked you to write to your brother-in-law and get him to state that he also had heard from you about the 'bulky letter'?" Answer: "Cesare Romati."

Here Romati and Turco were confronted with each other. There ensued a scene which Ledner calls "disgusting." They denounced each other in violent terms. Turco said that Romati belonged in the electric chair. Romati hurled himself at Turco, shook his fist in his face. "Say that I urged you to give false testimony!" he exclaimed. Turco replied: "Once more I maintain what I have testified."

The former chauffeur (who had become a flyer) was then called. The accusation against him was read to him. "I am very sorry," he said, "that I have caused unpleasantness to Caruso and Carignani. I entered the service of Giachetti, not of Caruso."

Then Romati proceeded ("in a manner somewhat reminiscent of Boccaccio," says Ledner) to describe his intimate relations with Ada Giachetti; and he told how Caruso suddently left Giachetti alone in the villa with a dog and took away with him everything else. Ada Giachetti, he said, was left with nothing to wear but one slip. He told how Caruso had got into a scene with Giachetti, beaten her, and grabbed her by the throat, after which came a "financial reconciliation," Caruso agreeing to give his former sweetheart 500 lire monthly.

Romati added that Ada Giachetti had told him that Caruso was in possession of the intercepted letter.

After Romati, Caruso took the stand.

Amid the absorbed attention of the crowd, which filled the court to overflowing and was passionately excited, he said:

"I became acquainted with Ada Giachetti in 1897 and lived with her until 1907. It was a life replete with happiness, and, for me, of inspiration. We had four sons. Two are still alive. To them I have given my name.

"One day my happiness ended. I came to Milan, alighting at the Hotel Milano, where Giachetti awaited me. She said that she had done something which might displease me. 'Whatever you do, is well done,' I said, because, as a matter of fact, that is the way I had thought about her up to then."

Here Caruso stopped, overcome with emotion. The court encouraged him to go on. In a short while, he resumed:

"Giachetti then told me that she had bought a 40 HP car, which I actually saw when I stepped out of the hotel, with this gentleman [Romati] at the wheel."

He then spoke of his break with Giachetti, caused by her fatal acquaintance with Romati. He declared that, during his absence in New York, she had taken a trip with her lover to Nice, whence she had asked him for 10,000 lire and later for another 10,000. She denied all relations with Romati. Later, pressed by Caruso, she had admitted her relations with the chauffeur, but added that she had yielded to him only for the good of Caruso, because Romati had been sent by a secret society to murder Caruso and she wanted "to save herself and their love."

Caruso then stated approximately the sums sent by him to Giachetti at Nice, London, and Milan, after Romati's advent in his home ("an impressive succession of 1,000-lire notes," says Ledner). The only way to account for his generosity, the tenor added, was his strong love for Giachetti, which had robbed him of all reasoning power.

The court then asked Caruso about his alleged theft of Ada's valuables. He answered: "When I saw that all was over between me and Ada Giachetti and had assured myself that she had definitely left me in order to stay with the chauffeur, I took my belongings, also hers, among which were articles of jewelry, which I had given her over a period of years. But I had not given them to her as presents, because presents are given only outside one's home and not to one who lives in one's house and is the mother of one's children. Am I to be accused of theft, because I was unwilling to place those valuables at the disposal of Mr. Romati?"

When Caruso had finished, Romati stood up and asked: "Does Mr. Caruso know that Ada Giachetti, in the villa, had a lot of servants and gave them at least 1,000 pounds sterling in three months?" Caruso replied: "I do not know about that. What I do know is that I laid down in my cellar wine costing 800 pounds sterling, and, when I returned, there was not enough of it left to fill a glass."

Enrico Caruso won a victory in the case. Ada Giachetti, found guilty of slander, received a sentence of one year and a 1,000-lire fine. Vincenzo Turco, found guilty of giving false testimony with extenuating circumstances, was sentenced to serve three months and twenty-six days in prison. Cesare Romati, Giachetti's chauffeur, was sentenced to one year and fifteen days for bribery of witnesses. The agent, Gaetano Loria, was also found guilty on the same count as Romati; he received a sentence of eleven months and twenty-three days in prison.

Emil Ledner was not satisfied with the verdict. Though he admitted that Ada Giachetti's guilt was brought out in the proceedings, he was not at all pleased with the fact that she did not speak at the trial in her own defense. He also felt that the matter of the letter containing a contract form for her in the United States, which, it was alleged, had been intercepted, was not investigated with sufficient thoroughness. It *was* sent, Ledner points out, from New York and *was* delivered at the Pension Excelsior in Milan, of which Maria Carignani was the proprietress. "Who received it?" asks Ledner. "Who undertook to hand it or forward it to Ada Giachetti?"

On October 26, 1912, the day after the close of the

proceedings instituted by Enrico Caruso against Ada Gia-chetti and the other persons accused, a statement by Maria Carignani was read in court to the effect that Ada Giachetti had lived at her pension, that they had become friendly, and that Giachetti had told her that she was financially embarrassed because Romati had spent all of an inheritance received by him; and she asked Maria Carignani to write to Caruso and request him to send her (Giachetti) some money.

Ledner is not sure that Caruso was not concerned with the going astray of the letter containing the American con-tract for Ada Giachetti—after all, the German manager remarks, Caruso did not want her in the United States. "When I questioned him later," Ledner added, in his com-ments on the case, "he either left my questions unanswered or managed cleverly to evade them. I have always felt that there was no doubt that Caruso had some connection with this matter—but I had no right to interfere in the tragedy of this love affair."

After his court victory in Milan Caruso resumed his interrupted singing engagements (under Emil Ledner's managership) in Germany. Ada Giachetti was now out of sight—but not out of mind.

Her absence from his life, after eleven years of intimacy, was a cruel blow to him. He simply could not forget her. Whenever he was forced by his commitments to appear in either *Pagliacci* or *Bohème*, says Ledner, all those around him went through an ordeal that was "fearful." During and after a performance of either one of these operas he would burst into violent fits of weeping, which brought on a fever that sometimes lasted several hours.

According to his German manager, he saw in Nedda (*Pagliacci*) the living Giachetti and in Mimi (*Bohème*) the

Giachetti who, for him, was dead. His attacks of fever, instead of becoming lighter with the passage of time, grew ever more violent—sometimes they were almost unbearable to him. "Finally," says Ledner, "we had to omit *Pagliacci* from our Caruso repertoire for an entire year."

In Munich and in Hamburg the tenor complained for the first time of headaches, which later became combined with something like brain fever, a shocking development in a man who, all his life, had enjoyed vigorous, apparently impregnable good health. At times, in Germany, three doctors were in attendance on the tenor. But his sense of duty was such that he refused to cancel any of his appearances at German opera houses. Again and again he suffered acute tortures, which made him, in his agony, beat his head against the bedposts in his hotel room or strike his forehead with his clenched fists.

Yet he used to get up from his bed of agony at the Hotel Bristol in Berlin and be taken from a rear door, in his pajamas, straight to the stage door of the opera house. There, his dresser would hastily put on the tenor's costume, make-up would be hurriedly applied, and, still in torture, he would go on the stage in *Aïda* or *Carmen* or *L'Elisir d'Amore*. He did well—a miracle, under the circumstances —but "he was not Caruso."

"I kept telling him to cancel his appearances," adds Ledner, "but here he showed his iron will power.

" 'If I cancel, I'll make a hundred enemies,' he would say. 'Many of the tickets for my performances have been obtained by operagoers from speculators. Everyone receiving at the box office a refund of only one-half the price paid by them for tickets will automatically become my enemy.' "

Even when his headaches were at their worst he would blurt out: "I want no talk of my illness!" His consumption of sedatives was unbelievable. "Never," declared his manager, "would I have believed that a human being could absorb into his system such quantities of aspirin, pyramidol, etc. When he left Berlin Caruso took with him twenty tubes of aspirin."

Having found out that only the aspirin made in Germany really helped him, he wrote to Ledner from America begging him to send him more. And, after the outbreak of World War I in 1914, he wrote his German friend again, imploring him to find some way of sending him German aspirin, despite the Allied blockade of Germany, because he was still beset by torturing headaches.

All this, Ledner was convinced, was due to the suffering caused him by Ada Giachetti's defection—and by what he had gone through at the Milan trial.

"Though, in later years, he seldom spoke of her," Ledner wrote, "and though, I have heard, he eventually was happily married, I think that it took him a long, long time to get over Giachetti's betrayal. In fact, I think it likely that he never got over it."

Apparently, Enrico Caruso and Ada Giachetti never saw each other again after those stormy New York scenes in 1908, following her leaving him for the chauffeur Romati. Some years later, her voice deteriorated so much that she had to give up singing in opera; and she also lost her good looks. Eventually she died in South America.

According to Ledner, Caruso was much run after by women and young girls. He adds:

"I never understood why. His personality was certainly not such as to arouse interest. Possibly he might greatly influence a certain type of woman by the sensual charm of his voice and his artistic temperament. But there were many women whose social standing demanded the greatest caution on their part in their actions, yet who sought, through acts and words which sometimes were positively importunate, to become acquainted with him—and more than that.

"Caruso was no friend of 'adventures,' particularly with really elegant, charming, personally attractive women. On the contrary. Often, when we were with beautiful and genuinely desirable women he would whisper in my ear: 'My Ada! None can compare with her!'

"As he knew not a word of German, and all his letters were handled by me, I nipped in the bud some obviously foolish love affairs in process of development; and I put an end to amorous aberrations which had in them an element of danger. I owed it to myself to avoid possible 'incidents.' And I succeeded in avoiding them."

With the great tenor in the cast on the Metropolitan's next Caruso Opening Night in November 1912 were the soprano Lucrezia Bori and Enrico's faithful friend, the baritone Antonio Scotti. The opera chosen was that Puccini work which was getting to rival that same composer's *Bohème* in Caruso's affections—*Manon Lescaut*. For the rest of that season he stuck to it and to other well-tested items in his regular repertoire—except for an excursion into Meyerbeer's *Les Huguenots*.

As for concerts, he continued to cold-shoulder them in his new role of Caruso the Prudent. So his income for the year ran to only $100,000 or so.

At the end of June 1913, he was at Covent Garden in London again, warbling wonderfully, with the effective support of Nellie Melba, Emmy Destinn, and Scotti, in *Aïda*, *Tosca*, and *Bohème*. In fact, so admirable was his warbling that the rumor-mongers were comparatively out of the picture. "My boy, do you know the latest?—Caruso has lost his voice." That croak that had been heard around the world popped up only occasionally at this stage in his career. And his next burst of golden song usually silenced it.

Two performances in Vienna—his last, as it turned out, in that city. A few more in Germany in the autumn of 1913—and they too were to be his last in that country. Unheeded for the most part, the clouds of World War I were massing, with their stored lightning and thunder.

That farewell tour of Caruso in Germany had electrifying moments. One night, after he had sung magnificently in a big German city, an immense crowd filled the street outside his hotel suite, begging Martino, his valet, every time he showed himself at a window: "Please! Let us see Caruso!" After they had kept this up a long time and were giving signs of meaning to keep it up all night if they were refused what they wanted, Caruso showed himself. He got a delirious reception. It touched him to the heart.

"If only I did not have to take care of my voice all the time now," he called out to them, "I would sing to you." How he must have thirsted for the old days when he could sing when and where and as long as he pleased.

The New York opera season of 1913-1914 was the last before the outbreak of World War I in Europe. So was the Covent Garden season that followed it. By this time Caruso was showing signs of serious fatigue. "The doctors call my trouble a nervous breakdown," he told Giovanni, his brother.

Complete rest was emphatically indicated.

In obedience to doctors' orders—how he must have hated to pay heed to those importunate gentry!—he went to the Italian resort of Montecatini, to take the waters and get a thorough rest. Then—the villa at Bellosguardo. He asked

Giovanni Caruso to join him there. "But promise to tell nobody where I am. I want no letters. And no visitors."

While he was still in Italy, World War I engulfed Europe. During its opening months Italy stayed neutral.

Caruso gave his willing consent, at the start of hostilities, to take part in a big concert in Rome to raise funds to get Italian workers stranded in Germany back to their native country. Also on the program were Lucrezia Bori and Battistini, with whom Enrico had sung in Russia. Toscanini was the conductor.

When Caruso had sung *"Vesti la giubba"* the audience went wild. Toscanini, opposed as always to encores, tried to go on with the show. One good look at that theater, filled with temporary lunatics, made him change his mind. He signaled to Caruso to repeat. Again the tenor sang that thrilling lament, the most famous feature in his repertory —and the house was rocked to its foundations.

To sing in Rome at that charity performance Caruso had cut things very close. Immediately after he had finished, he had just time enough to dash, costume and all, to a special train, which rushed him to Naples, to the steamer which was to take him to New York.

He did not even have time for a few minutes of praying at the church of Sant' Anna alle Paludi, near his home (a regular custom of his), where he had sung some of the first of his songs. At the pier were Assunta, his only sister, and Maria Castaldi, his stepmother. He barely had time to hug and kiss them before rushing up the gangplank of the steamer.

CHAPTER 17

CARUSO CONQUERS
NEW YORK

There can be no doubt that, deep down, Enrico Caruso asked little from life but the sun, sociability, and spaghetti of Naples; that, provided he could eat, drink and be merry, he really craved little beyond her bright sky, shimmering bay, and pet, private volcano; that he would have been content always to hear, speak, and sing nothing but the liquid Neapolitan dialect of his childhood and youth.

But the second half of his life was such a vortex of change and motion, such a maelstrom of internationalism, such a phantasmagoria of foreign sights and sounds and food and beverages and people that there must have been mornings when he woke up wondering in what country he was, what language the strange persons hemming him in on all sides were talking, and how the devil he was to push them out of his path and get back, in headlong flight, to Naples, with his Neapolitan soul undamaged and his Neapolitan speech uncontaminated.

Beyond the frontiers of Italy he sang in twenty-three foreign lands: Argentina, Austria, Belgium, Brazil, Canada, Cuba, Czechoslovakia (known as Bohemia in Caruso's epoch), Egypt, England, France, Germany, Holland, Hungary, Ireland, Mexico, Monaco, Poland, Portugal, Russia, Scotland, Spain, the United States, and Uruguay.

The Italian cities in which he sang before or during his years of renown included Bologna, Caserta, Florence, Genoa, Livorno, Mantua, Milan, Naples, Palermo, Padua, Pisa, Rome, Salerno, Trapani, Turin, Venice, and Verona.

In Europe and Africa outside Italy, he appeared in operas or concerts in: Alexandria, Amsterdam, Baden-Baden, Barcelona, Belfast, Berlin, Brussels, Budapest, Cairo, Dublin, Edinburgh, Frankfort-on-the-Main, Glasgow, Hamburg, Leipzig, Lisbon, Liverpool, London, Manchester, Monte Carlo, Moscow, Munich, Nuremberg, Paris, Prague, St. Petersburg, Stuttgart, Vienna, and Wiesbaden.

In the Americas, he sang in dozens of cities, including Atlanta, Boston, Brooklyn, Buenos Aires, Chicago, Cincinnati, Cleveland, Denver, Detroit, Havana, Houston, Kansas City, Los Angeles, Mexico City, Montevideo, Montreal, New York, Omaha, Philadelphia, Rio de Janeiro, San Francisco, St. Louis, St. Paul, Toledo, Toronto, and Washington. There you have a list which even those Britons most addicted to understatement would probably consent to call "not unprovided with a certain variety."

What a whirl it must have been! What relief he must have felt, in his era of near-perpetual-motion, at the thought of relaxing in Naples again, or, in default of Naples, at his Villa Bellosguardo, not so very far north of his beloved birthplace, where he could sleep around the clock, hear only Italian, see only Italians, and devour as many miles of Italian macaroni as he wished!

Of all the cities here and abroad visited and revisited by Caruso in his whirlwind years of glory only one held him for more than a few days or weeks at a time—New York.

During his golden era New York hung onto him four months or more out of every twelve. He sang at the Met in New York 607 times—to say nothing of his frequent appearances at concerts. At New York's opera house he sang his most popular role, Canio in *Pagliacci*, seventy-six times, and that of Rhadamès in *Aïda*, which ran second to it in popular appeal, sixty-seven times.

No wonder New Yorkers considered Enrico Caruso their own special property. No wonder they got all puffed up at the realization that he could not sing anywhere else until they had had their fill every year of his matchless voice.

After his comparatively slow start in New York, Caruso's fame had accelerated with a vengeance. As early as the third or fourth of his Metropolitan Opera seasons it took on that unique quality which no other singer, before, during, or since his heyday has succeeded in capturing.

It was then that he began to cash in on his unequaled ability to shine both as singer and individual; as a most marvelous tenor and a most human human being; as a god of song, inhabiting a golden world of his own, and as a man-in-the-street, thinking the everyday thoughts of everybody. *That* is what made his renown unique. He "put himself over." By that I do not mean at all that he worked at becoming celebrated, that he resorted to artful, calculated tricks to win the public. Artifice repelled Caruso's simple, uncomplicated nature. He utterly vanquished, in the race for fame, contemporaries who schemed for it, who lay awake nights planning to snare it. He got it without trying. He was born to it—to dual fame as singer and human being.

But he paid a high price for it. He had practically no privacy. Everywhere he was recognized. That broad smile, that pudgy body, that peculiar gait and extravagant attire were unmistakable. "I have my name written all over me," he used to say. Much of the time he (or at least the little Neapolitan urchin inside him) was pleased when people stopped in the street to stare at him and point him out to others, to follow him, to crane their necks at him and comment audibly about him. Sometimes, however, he was annoyed and bored. Privacy, like salt, is not really appreciated until it is unobtainable.

So dazzling was his celebrity, so acute the interest aroused by all his actions, that, as soon as inquisitive New Yorkers and out-of-town visitors in New York during the days of his operatic glory found out where he was taking his meals, they flocked there in large numbers, open-mouthed and goggle-eyed, hoping to get a glimpse of him. Whereupon, with Italian oaths of high temperature on his lips, he would ferret out some other Italian restaurant and bestow on it his patronage until that one also began to take on, among sightseers, some of the attributes of Grant's Tomb or Fraunces Tavern. Then—more Vesuvian language and still another Carusian gastronomic hegira.

For some time, his favorite eating place was Del Pezzo's, in the vicinity of today's Pennsylvania Station. There he used to leave a standing order: "Reserve for me every night until further notice a private dining room and prepare enough Italian food for me and half a dozen guests."

He might not show up. His guests might not show up. But Caruso didn't care. He paid the bill just the same. And he never looked at it twice. That was one of the many habits which endeared him to New Yorkers and gave him a unique niche in their hearts. It was such a grand gesture —yet so human. It revealed simultaneously the darling of the gods and the boy of the streets.

One night at Del Pezzo's, Caruso was wearing a pair of new shoes, rather vociferous in style, of which he was obviously very proud. Walking up to the well-known cartoonist Oscar Cesare, he inquired: "My shoes. You see them? You like?"

"I do," said Cesare, who probably did not.

"These shoes, I buy them at —" and he mentioned the name of a footwear establishment which he had discovered in the course of his Manhattan wanderings. "But—please—you promise?—you swear?—not to tell Antonio Scotti where I buy them. Because, if you tell him, he buy a pair for himself just like mine—and that I will not like—oh, no, not at all. You promise?"

Cesare bound himself by a solemn oath. And Caruso went away, radiant, to show off his shoes to somebody else.

Caruso lived at a number of places in New York during his many stays there. After the Hotel Majestic and his Murray Hill apartment and the Hotel York he settled for a while at an apartment on West Fifty-seventh Street and then moved to the Hotel Savoy, at Fifth Avenue and Fifty-ninth Street.

Then he stayed for a bit at the Plaza, where, he discovered on arrival, a suite had been reserved for him on the *thirteenth floor. Dio mio!* No place for a Neapolitan! Yet, instead of exploding and moving out, he bravely consented to occupy the suite after the management had solemnly assured him that he would be changed to other quarters as soon as possible.

Next came the Hotel Knickerbocker and there he stayed year after year until forced to leave because of its transformation from a hotel to a business building. Last of all, he lived at the Vanderbilt, at Park Avenue and Thirty-fourth Street.

Stories clustered around Caruso. As his fame grew, their number increased in proportion. This applies especially to New York, where he spent the longest time each year, where he was best known and admired and liked. In New York Caruso anecdotes multiplied like mushrooms after rain.

The great majority of Caruso stories that sprang up in his days of glory were true. But some of them were made up out of the whole cloth (and often enraged the man about whom they were told). Some, which had done duty already in connection with other celebrities, were taken down from the shelf, dusted off, and put into circulation again with the fabulous singer as their hero, in place of the personages who had figured in them before.

But, I repeat, most of them were bona fide Caruso stories. He was the sort of person who inspires such things. And many Caruso stories are invaluable as aids in shaping a picture of the man, in making one realize the radiance through which he moved, in helping one to measure the success of Caruso the Artist and the irrepressible humanness of Caruso the Individual.

When that eminent Teuton, Engelbert Humperdinck, composer of *Hänsel und Gretel* and *Königskinder*, visited America to attend the first performance of the latter opera, Caruso, with his overcoat collar turned up, a thick muffler swathing the lower part of his face, and a big black slouch hat pulled down over his eyes, went to the pier posing as a reporter for a New York paper. With notebook in hand and pencil poised over it he shot at the visiting German a volley of the most ridiculous questions. Humperdinck, having doubtless heard dreadful tales about American reporters, backed away from his interrogator in a state of wild alarm, thinking that the "American" must be crazy. Whereupon Caruso turned down his collar, pushed back his hat, pulled away the muffler, and welcomed the composer to New York with a fervent Neapolitan hug.

Late in Caruso's career, Otto H. Kahn, Chairman of the Metropolitan Opera Board of Directors, suggested to Giulio Gatti-Casazza, the Met manager, that the tenor sing in *Rigoletto* since he had not done so for some time.

"His voice is too heavy now," objected Gatti. And when it was put up to Caruso, he is quoted as saying: "Oh, no, for the love of God! *Rigoletto* is no longer for me."

But Otto Kahn was suavely insistent. Finally, Caruso consented to do as he wished.

He sang in *Rigoletto*. His singing, he thought, was awful. So did all those in his vicinity. Dense gloom shrouded the behind-the-scenes regions of the opera house. Caruso started back to the Knickerbocker in a vile humor, which was shared by his entourage (he almost always traveled around in New York with an entourage—numerous, voluble, obsequious, Italian).

Next day, all the papers declared that the performance of *Rigoletto* had been wonderful. Particularly Caruso's part in it.

The tenor was radiant. Gatti was all smiles. Kahn was beaming. The entourage was prevented with difficulty from dancing in the streets.

"We must repeat *Rigoletto*," said Gatti-Casazza. "We must," agreed Caruso, Kahn, and the entourage in unison.

Rigoletto was repeated. In the opinion of the opera house inner circle, Caruso sang infinitely better than at the first performance.

Next day the papers said that the performance had been awful. Particularly Caruso's part in it.

Years after their stormy scene at the rehearsal of *Bohème* in Milan, Caruso and that stern perfectionist, Arturo Toscanini, clashed again—this time in New York. It was on a night when Caruso was in top vocal form and knew it. In the course of an aria, he held on lovingly to a very choice high note, obviously reluctant to let the beautiful thing go out of his life forever. In a voice audible to those seated in nearby orchestra seats, Toscanini acidly inquired: "Have you quite finished, Caruso?"

Usually, if there was any poking of fun when Caruso was about, he did the poking. At times, however, he was the poked. As, for instance:

Once he met the little son of John McCormack, his famous fellow singer. Before the meeting, efforts had been made to have the lad realize the importance of the great Enrico Caruso. But they didn't "take." After looking Caruso over from head to foot in a sniffy and disdainful manner, young McCormack remarked: "You're only the greatest *Italian* singer in the world, but my father is the greatest *Irish* singer."

Edward L. Bernays, now a prominent consultant on public relations, was for some years press representative for the famous tenor. (The late music critic, Pitts Sanborn, used to call him, "the Caruso of press agents and the press agent of Caruso.") Mr. Bernays described Caruso to me as a "big, kind boy. Caruso," he continued, "was a perfect example, it seems to me, of what Freud called a 'godhead symbol.' He concentrated upon himself all the frustrations, hopes, and aspirations of everybody who heard him sing. He was ego-motivated but not egotistical. What I mean by that is that he was not one to force his personality on others. His egotism was that of a child."

He did things, Mr. Bernays recollected, in the grand style. Once, in a New York shop, he was attracted by some Russian lace. "Give me, please, twenty yards of that lace," he said to an astonished clerk. He explained the lavish order by adding that he was to sing in Buenos Aires that summer and wished to wear Russian blouses, which were the fashion there. On another occasion he was shopping with a New York lady of his acquaintance who, he knew, was extremely partial to a certain perfume. He steered her into a shop which stocked it and paralyzed a salesgirl by remarking, "Please, Miss, that perfume over there—one gallon, please."

"When I first worked for him," Edward Bernays told me, "I wished, of course, to establish pleasant personal relations. When he appeared one day with a splendid array of jewelry scattered all over his person, I said in a flattering tone of voice, 'Why, Signor Caruso, those jewels are as good as Diamond Jim Brady's.'

" 'Better!' he snapped crossly. And he refused to speak to me all the rest of that day.

"The idea of getting caught in a draft of air terrified him. Once, at a banquet, I turned to say something to him and found his chair empty. He had disappeared completely. Then I heard a rustling under my feet, and there—under the table—was Caruso. Pointing to a window at one end of the banquet hall, he complained, 'That window—it is open.' And not until somebody shut it would he leave his unconventional refuge.

"His delight in caricaturing everybody around him was so well known that, at some restaurants, as soon as he sat down, a waiter would hand him pencils and a pad of paper. At one restaurant he did a caricature of the coatroom girl and gave it to her. 'It's horrid,' she wailed. 'What a mean man you must be!' Leaping to his feet, he rushed over to the girl and apologized abjectly. 'I send you nice autographed photo of me,' he promised. Next day she received it.

"As soon as he set foot in the street he was recognized. Newsboys—they were all over the place in his day—would rush up to him brandishing newspapers and shouting,

'Buy your picture, Mr. Cruso. Right here on this page!' And Caruso would buy the paper—for one dollar.

"Once a man stepped up to him on the street and informed him, 'I have a ticket for your concert tonight. It cost me $20.00. I want you to sing these encores.' And he handed the great singer a formidable list of songs, including 'Silver Threads Among the Gold,' 'Mother Machree,' and 'Loch Lomond'—not exactly typical items in the Caruso repertoire. Bowing politely, Caruso pocketed the list.

"When I accompanied him on a tour of the western United States I sometimes found difficulty in finding premises big enough to accommodate the huge crowds eager to hear him sing. In Toledo, Ohio, I remember, I once hired a big skating rink. When touring, he was especially nervous about his voice. One night, in addition to tucking him into thick blankets, I had to build a barricade of pillows on each side of him and at his feet. 'I feel a draft,' he insisted.

"At one western hotel he complained of noise in the rooms on the floor above him. I notified the manager. 'It is a wedding party,' he told me. 'I'll move Mr. Caruso to another apartment.' When I informed Caruso of this, he shouted angrily, 'No! Move the wedding party!' And moved it was."

His quick-wittedness stood Caruso in good stead one night in New York when he was singing in *Martha*. The prima donna forgot to bring onto the stage with her a flower which, in the course of the action, she must hand to the hero. The hero (Enrico Caruso) instantly noting the omission, realized that the situation might (to borrow a phrase beloved of solemn historians and American foreign newspaper correspondents) be fraught with the gravest consequences.

So, standing close to her, he whispered: "Take a flower from your hat." She was mystified.

"Take a flower from your hat," he repeated urgently. Her mystification continued.

Unabashed, Caruso, just before the flower-handing incident was due, deftly picked a flower from the lady's hat, put it into her hand, and motioned to her to give it to him. She did. Nobody in the audience noticed anything out of the way.

Caruso used to write on the backs of canceled checks covering payments to him for Metropolitan Opera performances short and crisp bits of self-criticism. On a check for $2,500 in payment for his singing in an evening of *Carmen* he wrote "*buona*" (good); on another, for an appearance by him in *Manon*, "good in general—Act III magnificent." But he really let himself go in connection with one of his many performances in *Rigoletto*. "Meravigliosa" he scribbled across the back of the fat check which that performance brought him—"marvelous."

One evening in New York, fed up with the glitter of his daily life—though it was extremely well-paid glitter— he stole away from it all and took an aisle seat at a Broadway theater where a popular comic opera was being given. Scarcely had he done so before a man sidled up to him, tapped him on the shoulder and whispered in his ear: "Want to make a lot of money this evening?"

"I do not. I want to see this show."

"I have been instructed to take you to the home of Mr. ——"—here the man mentioned the name of a well-known multimillionaire. "You will be paid $1,500 for three-quarters of an hour of singing."

"Please don't bother me. I want to see this show."

"Mr. ——'s car is at the door. You will be back in time for the second act."

"No!"

"I double the offer."

What could poor Caruso do? He got into the waiting car with the insistent stranger and, within the hour, was back at the Broadway show with $3,000 in his wallet. What a harassing life!

As his New York fame grew, local evidences of it multiplied. A chain known as the Caruso Restaurants sprang up. Spaghetti à la Caruso became a regular item on metropolitan menus. Made with chicken livers, it was alleged by those serving it to be practically the renowned tenor's staff of life, an assertion quite sufficient to cause thousands of Americans of Caruso's Golden Age to go to great lengths (literally) in eating it.

Out of Tin Pan Alley came a popular song entitled "My Cousin Carus'." That title, moreover, was borne by a moving-picture play, in which the tenor starred at the pinnacle of his celebrity. Another song, published just after the tenor's death, with the mawkish refrain, "They wanted a songbird in Heaven, so they took our Caruso away," provided further proof of where he stood in the estimation of thousands, most of whom had never heard him sing.

Among the many traits which endeared Caruso to Americans was his generosity in singing free of charge at benefits for charitable purposes. He was a busy man, a very busy man indeed, but he refused to let that interfere with his helping toward turning such benefits into successes—and the mere mention of his name as one of the participants was enough to do that. During World War I he sang for the Red Cross and a number of other organizations.

Before that war some of the organizations which engineered benefit performances paid singers for participating in them. Once the Italian banker Simonelli asked Caruso to sing at such a performance. Sembrich and Scotti were also on the program. The treasurer of the organization getting up the benefit feared that the expense of having three such eminent singers would be too heavy. When Caruso heard of his alarm, he said, "Don't worry any more. I will sing free."

Such was the combined magnetism of Caruso's fame and personality that, in New York, crowds followed him wherever he went. Reporters for metropolitan papers snatched up every tidbit of news about him, for it was sure to be food for headlines. Special articles about Caruso filled Sunday supplements (I wrote some of them). The public was copiously informed (or misinformed) about the great tenor's diet and habits and opinions and theories and plans and pranks.

"Bill, have you heard this one? Caruso is such a chain cigarette smoker that he has offered $500 to anyone who will tell him how to smoke while he is having a shower." "Fred, here's a new Caruso yarn. It seems that once, while he . . ." New Yorkers delighted in swapping Caruso yarns. And, by so doing, they gave further proof that Enrico Caruso was an integral part of the New York of his day— like vaudeville and Vanderbilts, elevated trains and trolley cars and hansom cabs and ferryboats and derby hats, like George M. Cohan and J. P. Morgan the First, Mayor Gaynor and Fire Chief Croker and Diamond Jim Brady.

Better than the complicated legal wording put into contracts with Enrico Caruso by managers and their lawyers was the spirit of integrity put into them by Caruso himself.

All his life he was swayed by instincts grounded in honor. When, early in his career, he said to Carlo d'Ormesson, the theatrical agent, in Milan: "I would rather die than break a contract," his words were no dishonest poseur's ranting. They were the truth.

Giulio Gatti-Casazza, who knew Caruso if any man on earth did, said when he learned of the great singer's death: "Caruso was a truly noble-spirited man." That, too, was no rhetoric. And Otto H. Kahn declared that a verbal assurance from Caruso was "just as good as a written contract."

Caruso was generous. Constantly he reached into his pocket to help friends in need—to help many, in fact, who could lay no claim to possessing his friendship, who might indeed be concealing enmity while accepting his help. But Caruso did not care. Always averse to analysis, he was least analytical when he lent or gave away money.

Once, when his wife saw him signing check after check for persons whom he knew only slightly or not at all, she remarked to him: "But surely they can't *all* be deserving." "No," he agreed, "of course not. But tell me something: how can I know which deserve and which do not?"

His generosity was sometimes calculated, sometimes impulsive. After his break with Ada Giachetti, he used to hand to his secretary for mailing, to the very end of his life, checks made out to her for large amounts, remarking: "For the mother of my sons."

One evening, while changing in his dressing room at the Metropolitan Opera House in New York from his street clothes to an operatic costume, he tossed a roll of $500 bills on a table. He noticed his wigmaker, an elderly humble Italian, eyeing them.

"You like?" he asked.

"Yes."

"If you had one what would you do with it?"

"I would send my wife to Italy to see her mother, who is old and ill."

"Ah, very good." The tenor handed the wigmaker a $500 bill.

"And now you send your wife to Italy? Yes?"

He was sensitive. Under his jollity, under his mischievousness, lay sensitiveness worthy of a Spanish grandee.

On Long Island, where he was staying during the summer after his marriage, he was asked to sit in a booth and do caricatures at ten dollars each for the benefit of the local hospital. He accepted with alacrity. "This holiday I like," he said. "I will make funny drawings and have a nice time."

On arrival at the booth, with a happy smile on his face, he found that it was festooned with fringes of dry spaghetti. He stood stock still. The smile left his face.

"I am sorry, madame," he said to a member of the entertainment committee. "I cannot draw unless you remove that spaghetti. Spaghetti is for the kitchen." The committee, considerably flustered, removed it. On his way home Caruso said to his wife: "They do not imagine such thing will offend because many people think of Italians only like that. What surprise me is that such nice people make such mistake."

He was humble. In St. Petersburg, after he had sung magnificently the part of Rhadamès in *Aïda*, the rest of the company crowded around him, beside themselves with enthusiasm, shaking his hand, patting him on the shoulder, smothering him with praise. He waved them away. "Don't praise me," he said. "Praise Verdi."

He could be fickle in love. He jilted at least two women. Often, in the fields of love, he flitted from flower to flower, taking honey where he found it.

Also he could be faithful. With Ada Giachetti he stayed for eleven years; and, at the end of their love affair, it was she who left him, not he who abandoned her. To his American wife he gave unstinted devotion. And there was another woman whom he loved all his life, for whom his love even after her death, remained steadfast as a rock—his mother.

He had a temper. When, in the clutches of temperament he lost it, he could be violent and unjust. But his gusts of anger soon blew themselves out. Soon the sun shone again and his broad smile was back on his face and all was forgotten. And for his violence and injustice he was always glad to make amends.

He loved children. When he was with them—playing, joking, laughing, doing magicians' tricks—the perennial child in him came out into the open. He loved his two sons. He adored his little daughter Gloria. He understood a child's heart. He knew how to win it. He delighted in children's talk, in their naïve sallies of unpremeditated wit. Often he quoted their sayings.

He liked to tell this story: One day, when he was walking outside Naples, he came upon a ragged little boy, lying lazily against a roadside wall, who begged him for a penny. Caruso stopped beside him.

"Suppose I don't give you a penny," he said.

"Why, then, signore, I'll still have the sunshine."

✦

He was not a reader. He owned scarcely any books. One, which he kept by his bedside, was a book of facts. "When I was young," he explained, "I had little time to learn." Books for him were largely for ornament, not reading. Once he remarked: "I learn from life, not from books."

He had courage. When airplanes were in their infancy and a flight in one of them was a most hazardous adventure, he did not hesitate to accept an invitation in London from the daring flying pioneer Grahame-White, "the darling of the clouds," to fly with him in his flimsy and shockingly unsafe plane.

And, with his courage, as with the rest of his manly traits, Caruso mixed an amusing, childlike touch. Geraldine Farrar, the famous American prima donna, who knew Caruso well and was in London when he flew with Grahame-White, revealed that, before he took off, as a precaution in case the need for the disposal of his remains should arise, he had stuffed his pockets full of little scraps of paper, on which he had written instructions covering just what should be done in case of fatal accident.

He had a will of steel. Fainting from pain, drugged almost to insensibility, staggering like a blind man, he would get into an automobile at the rear entrance of his hotel in Berlin, where he had been lying deathly ill, and rush to the stage door of the opera house where he was to sing, having flatly refused to disappoint immense audiences eagerly waiting to hear him. As his dresser put him into his costume, he lay on a couch, nearly unconscious from suffering.

The door of the room opened. The stage manager made a sign from it. "Signor Caruso, are you ready?" His cue. Pulling himself together, with a superhuman effort, Caruso would grope his way toward the stage. As he stood for a moment in the wings, he braced himself, in another effort of unbelievable self-control, which strained all the iron in him.

Then—he strode onto the stage, eyes flashing, head up. Another moment—and out poured the golden notes, throbbing with beauty and power. And the audience, sitting tense and enthralled, had not the remotest idea that anything was wrong.

He was a man.

CHAPTER 18

VOICE OF GOLD

When those who knew Caruso's singing talked about it or wrote about it, the words "gold" and "golden" cropped up constantly. Attempts to describe the characteristics of his voice, its nature, timbre, transcendent beauty, phenomenal power, seemed invariably to gravitate to one or the other of those two words, or to both.

"Molten gold." "Golden melody." "Gold swathed in velvet." "Clarion of gold." No other noun or adjective seemed adequate to the makers of similes based on Caruso's voice.

Beauty and power. Enrico Caruso's voice combined those two qualities to a degree, in all probability, that no voice ever had before. Certainly no voice has combined them comparably since he ceased to sing. As I think back to the many times I heard the Voice of Gold, I am enraptured in retrospect—now by its beauty, now by its power, now by its matchless blending of both.

Enrico Caruso was endowed by nature with a most extraordinary vocal mechanism. Eventually his natural voice developed into such a marvelous instrument that, I remember, one of the millions who heard him emerged from a veritable coma of enchantment to murmur, "That must be the way they sing in Heaven."

Some experts who examined Caruso's throat and vocal

cords declared that their length and thickness enabled him to emit both extremely high and extremely low notes, which sheds light on why his voice oscillated so long between tenor and baritone, before declaring itself definitely for tenor. They thought that the remarkable softness of his vocal cords was what gave his voice its extraordinary richness and timbre. But the danger of being dogmatic in this world is shown by the fact that other expert laryngologists saw little out of the ordinary in Caruso's vocal cords—they did not think that it was these that gave his voice such superb excellence. Rather, they said, it was the harmonious working of the vocal mechanism as a whole.

But, with all due regard to Caruso's phenomenal natural endowment, there are points about his singing, due primarily to *himself*, not to *nature*, which must not be forgotten for a moment if a just appraisal of his fabulous career on the operatic stage is to be arrived at. Just as too much stress is laid on his love of joking, on his good-humored horseplay, on his refusal for years to watch his diet, on his smoking to excess and doing pretty much as he pleased, so also the exaggerated harping on his congenital vocal endowment has tended to obscure in many minds the fact that, almost from the opening of his brilliant career, he expended on the improvement of his singing, on the utilization of his natural gifts to the utmost limit, an amazing amount of intelligent work.

Salvatore Fucito, during the last six years of Caruso's life his coach, accompanist, and inseparable companion, had unsurpassable opportunities to study, analyze, and appraise the great tenor's gifts and the manner in which he himself supplemented them. In his book about those six years,* Fucito constantly refers to this blending. "It can-

---

* Salvatore Fucito and Barnet J. Beyer, *Caruso and the Art of Singing*, Frederick A. Stokes Co., 1922.

not be doubted, of course," he wrote, "that Caruso had been provided by nature with a remarkable vocal instrument and with a powerful pair of bellows; nevertheless . . . it was his genius for work which made the utmost of his endowment, both as regards the physical organs and those native emotional and mental resources upon which his final artistry drew so heavily. Work does not mean unguided labor: nothing could be more ruinous to the vocal organism. To the genuine artist, work can only mean intelligent direction, painstaking, steady, and infinite patience."

Regarding Caruso's *breathing control*, unquestionably one of his greatest assets, his long-time accompanist and companion points out that the diameter of Caruso's larynx as a vocal organ accorded exactly with the diameter required for its functioning as an organ of respiration. That made possible the amplitude, richness, and power of his singing, by giving him extraordinary respiratory powers.

Caruso gauged early in his phenomenal career the supreme importance to a singer of breathing control. He thought much about it; and, when his artistic conscience had become strong after the heedlessness of his youth, he studied breathing carefully. He strengthened the muscles of his diaphragm to such a remarkable degree that he used to amaze his friends by this trick: he would tell them to press their closed fists with all their strength against his relaxed diaphragm; then, with a sudden spasm of his diaphragm, he would violently fling off the pressure of their fists.

"Caruso," Fucito says, ". . . could inhale slowly and steadily so ample a breath that he was able to exhale at very great length, not merely because the physiological process of expiration is longer than that of inspiration, but also because he had succeeded in adding to his auto-physiological control the *volitional control* which comes from the brain. . . . Caruso governed the expiratory flow of breath with such mastery that not a particle of it escaped without giving up its necessary equivalent in tone. Besides, Caruso emitted for each musical phrase, or even for each note, just enough breath to produce that phrase musically and no more. The remainder of his breath he kept in reserve, which made the enchanted hearer feel that the master was still far from the limit of his resources. . . . The secret of Caruso's priceless gift, his great capacity for respiration, although partly due to the amazing perfection of his vocal apparatus, was also, and perhaps mainly, due to his power of concentration upon the study of himself and of the natural means at his disposal."

When Caruso saw singers who had not solved success- fully the problems of breath control, who gasped for lack of sufficient breath to carry them through a musical phrase, who struggled and clearly showed their hearers that they were struggling, he used to exclaim, "Why, the poor fel- low is violating the first principle of art, the concealment of the artist's effort!"

In a little book * which he wrote when he was singing in London early in his career, Caruso set down briefly some hints on singing, derived from his already consider- able experience as an operatic star. Into this book he put not only much of the fruit of that experience but also much of himself. He remarked there of breath control: "In oper- atic work and with an orchestra to follow . . . it is espe- cially essential to observe a sane respect for the proper tempo. Otherwise one is liable to get into trouble with the conductor [was Caruso thinking of recent clashes with Toscanini at La Scala?]. . . . There are many singers who

* Enrico Caruso, *How to Sing*, John Church Co., 1902.

sing without method and do not fit their breathing, which is really the regulator of vocal performance, to the right period, and, consequently, are never in time. They make all kinds of *rallentandos* when these are not necessary, to gain time to recover the breath that they have not taken when they should. It is not enough to give to notes their full value. The rests, above all, should be carefully observed, in order to have sufficient opportunity to get a good breath and prepare for the next phrase. . . . A singer may make all the efforts he desires and still keep the time —and he *must* keep it."

And he remarked, concerning the importance of emptying the lungs before taking in a new supply of breath, "If this is not done, the effect is like two people trying to get in and out of the same narrow door at the same time."

Like all great artists, in short, Caruso emphasized first and foremost the importance of technique. He would fling out his hands in expressive Italian pantomime, as he asked, "Why don't singers stop to think? Why don't they work intelligently? Why don't they realize that all great art is a product of reserve, of restraint? Imperfect technique means imperfect art."

Caruso's breath control contributed enormously to the extraordinary excellence of his *tone production*. From the beginning he was faced with the problem of turning his breathing into golden tone without injuring *"lo strumento"* ("the instrument"), as he nonchalantly called his voice. In tone production he again succeeded in combining his original vocal equipment with hard-won knowledge of its essential capabilities. He thus described his conception of tone production: "There are two elements to be considered: the first element is *internal*, the other *external*. The internal element concerns the muscles of the throat, the external concerns the position which our body assumes while the tone is being emitted. It is necessary, therefore, through the aid of self-study and the help of a good singing-teacher, to become aware of every physical defect—such as the contraction of the muscles of the throat, of the face, or of the jaw—which can hinder the tone from being emitted in all its fullness and purity. . . . In the second place, one must take into consideration the defects which are external and consequently visible. A discomposed movement of the body, an exaggerated raising of the head while singing, or a too studied position of the chest, will also interfere with the free emission of the tone. . . . The singer should apply himself to his study with great naturalness and relaxation. . . . When he is exercising his voice, he must not disturb the composure of his face, because every contraction of the face is reflected in the throat. A contracted face indicates a lack of composure. . . . Unless he is calm, how can he hope to control his will?

"To have the attack [*i.e.*, the attack on the tone] true and pure, one must consciously try to open the throat not only in front but from behind, as it is the door through which the voice must pass, and, if it is not sufficiently open, it is useless to attempt to get a full round tone.

"In taking high notes the position of the mouth is the position one assumes when smiling.

"It is a good idea to practice opening the throat before a mirror, to try to see the palate—as when you show your throat to a doctor."

Caruso never forced his tone production. Therefore, his tones were harmonious, beautiful—*pure* tones. In singing a series of tones, he strove always to do it with the same ease with which he gave out a single tone. He allowed no part of his breath to "loaf," as it were, when he inhaled or exhaled, to escape between tones without contributing to its share in tone production.

"Caruso secured his brilliancy and resonance," according to Pierre Key, "principally by the resonance supplied by his deep chest [his entire body aided in this respect], but he directed the tone to the front of the face. . . . Many persons will recall that Caruso often frowned when he sang, drawing his eyebrows together. . . . He always said that this seemed to help in concentrating the tone. . . . The base of his nose always expanded sideways during this physiological singing act; it gradually enlarged during his later life, as a comparison of photographs will show."

The famous singer never seemed to be trying when he sang. He heightened the resonant quality of each tone which he emitted, by "letting it filter" to the spots in his throat where it would do the most good. His singing preserved in his maturity the spontaneity which, in his beginnings, was one of its principal characteristics. Unless he was involved in an operatic situation of great dramatic intensity, in which, obviously, naturalness must be sacrificed partially to the violence of the emotions being portrayed, Caruso's singing voice was usually as natural as his ordinary talking voice. "If there was any real secret to the Caruso method," says Pierre Key, "it would seem to lie to a considerable extent in the fact that he 'talked' his tones."

He was enormously helped, too, by the astonishing accuracy of his musical ear, by his keen perception of pitch. "There were times, of course," says Fucito, "when, owing to indisposition, his voice was 'off color,' when his tones failed to come forth with their usual magical beauty of quality, but there was never a time when they were off pitch." He had partly to thank breath control for that. Again, it was the infinite pains taken by him which made him just as much a master of pitch as of other tremen-

dously important phases of vocal art. "We can only specu-
late," wrote Fucito, "as to what another singer—less intelligent, less self-critical, less persevering—might have
made of Caruso's natal equipment; what we *can* know
beyond cavil is Caruso's mastery of this equipment, which
produced tone colors so finely wrought and spread over
so wide a range of delicate nuances that he was unexcelled
and became unique in the world of song. This is the real
reason why his voice continues to survive, as if in the spirit,
within the minds of all who heard it, although his physical
instrument has been silenced forever."

Caruso practiced incessantly. "The talent of an artist,"
he would say, "is revealed in his ability to detect and understand his shortcomings and especially in his courage to
acknowledge their existence."

How did he practice?

First, on rising, coffee. Then what he called *pulire lo
strumento*—cleansing the instrument—for which he used
a steam atomizer. Then, dressing—with the care of a Beau
Brummell. Meanwhile, Fucito, at the piano, played the
score of the opera in which Caruso was next to sing. *The
whole score*. From start to finish. Unlike many singers,
Enrico Caruso refused to confine his practicing to the actual part of an opera comprised within the limits of his
role. He respected the intentions of the composer. He kept
in mind the roles of *all* the singers in each production—of
the relation of each to the others. Above all, he saw each
opera in his repertory *as a whole*—he visualized it in the
spirit of a true artist.

After he was dressed, the raw work of practicing began.
Varying his method constantly, he made his singing accord
with the varied character of the operas in his repertory. If
he was to sing, say, *L'Elisir d'Amore* or *Bohème*, he would

put into his practicing unflagging efforts to impart a *lyrical* quality to his singing—a touch of flexibility, of lightness. If, though, he was practicing for *Samson et Dalila,* or *Pagliacci,* or *La Juive,* which are essentially *dramatic,* he would bring to bear on his practicing the tremendous power of his voice, backed by all the robustness of his splendid physique. And he made the distinction with subtlety—it had no trace of the arbitrary; never was it cast in a conventional mold.

"On the days when I sing," he wrote in his little book on singing, "I take nothing after luncheon, except perhaps a sandwich and a glass of Chianti, until after the performance, when I have supper and whatever I fancy within reasonable bounds. . . . Still I am careful never to indulge to excess in the pleasures of the table, for the condition of our alimentary apparatus and that of the vocal cords are very closely related and the unhealthy state of the one reacts on the other. . . . I am inclined to condemn the use of spirits, whiskey in particular, which is so prevalent in Anglo-Saxon countries, for it is sure to inflame the delicate little ribbons of tissue which produce the singing tone and then—*addio* to a clear ringing high C!"

Although he was not taking proper care of himself in the days when he wrote this book, that did not prevent him from moralizing about others: "Singers who use their voices properly should be at the height of their talents at 45 and keep their voices in full strength and virility up to at least 50."

Caruso wrote that at twenty-nine. At forty-five he was indeed at the height of his powers. On the eve of his forty-eighth birthday he was still singing. By and large, a pretty good peek into the future.

Finally, the great tenor attached enormous importance to vocal *style.* "What made Enrico Caruso a great master of style," wrote Fucito, "was the vitalization of whatever he sang by a great personality. He expressed his musical conceptions in all their intensity and color exactly as he conceived and felt them."

Caruso was well aware of the importance of blending technique with personality. As he grew older in years and in his art, he progressed to an amazing degree as an interpreter of character. Always he impregnated the imaginary persons whom he portrayed on the stage with the hallmark of his strong and vivid personality. But he never did this in violation of their essential selves. This combination of his own individuality with a grasp of the true nature of those whom he depicted was one of the most striking qualities of his varying methods of singing, and of the constantly improving brand of acting with which he supplemented his vocal achievements.

It is indeed odd that this supreme performer, who when he wished could write with lucidity and intelligence on the problems of an operatic singer, was unable to impart his knowledge to others. In his whole career he had only one pupil: a young American tenor, whom, with his customary generosity, he coached free of charge for a short time in New York. It soon became apparent that the gulf between Caruso the singer and Caruso the teacher was of fatal width. No matter what he had in mind when he embarked on a lesson, he failed (partly, no doubt, because of his inadequate command of English) to get it across to his pupil. The lessons were soon given up.

Caruso seldom bothered his head about styles in singing from the historical point of view. When he heard talk from theorists in his entourage about the differences between the singing of his era and that prevalent in the seventeenth and eighteenth centuries, he would inquire, with a little sarcastic smile: "Didn't artists sing with their vocal organs in those good old days?"

He was a believer in giving composers their due—but not too much at the expense of singers.

"The singer," he contended, "must, of course, respect the sentiments of the composer. But, after all, the composer is heard through the temperament of the singer. The singer can only give expression to the ideas and emotions that a musical work arouses in him. Should he attempt to do otherwise, then his interpretation will lack style and conviction."

I have stated before that Caruso's voice had a touch of the baritone in it. That is not the whole story in connection with its extraordinary range—as this anecdote shows:

One night, in Philadelphia, shortly before the curtain was due to go up on the last act of *Bohème*, being performed by the visiting New York Metropolitan Opera company, Andrés de Segurola, the basso singing the part of Colline, confided to Caruso that he was too hoarse to tackle the celebrated Overcoat Song.

"Don't worry," said Caruso cheerfully. "I have an idea. But don't say a word about it to Polacco." (Signor Polacco was the conductor.)

When the time came for the basso's aria, Caruso, with a big hat pulled far down over his face, came on the stage and, to the stupefaction of Polacco, sang the basso aria as if he were accustomed to roam every day among deep, growling low notes.

As soon as possible, Polacco, raging, rushed behind the scenes, but he could get nowhere with Caruso and De Segurola, who were far too elated to mind his scoldings in the least. "To think that nobody in the audience noticed anything wrong!" chuckled Caruso.

Caruso's feat made such a sensation that the company

for which he was regularly making phonograph records got
him to record the Overcoat Aria exactly as he had rendered
it as a pinch-warbler for the ailing De Segurola. When
Edward Johnson, of the Metropolitan managerial staff,
heard the reproduction, he declared in awe: "That is the
most marvelous record ever made! It proves that Caruso's
voice covers three whole octaves!"

Just as audiences en masse all over the world went into
frenzies when they heard Caruso sing, so, too, individuals
who looked on artistic matters with discrimination and
were endowed with true knowledge of music in general and
operatic music in particular grew positively lyrical in their
uninhibited praise of the Voice of Gold.

Giulio Gatti-Casazza, associated with the renowned
tenor from the early years of the latter's career in Italy
until its last phase in the United States, said of him: "I
have heard all the great tenors of my time over and over
again. Many of them were wonderful artists, with exceptional voices, and all sang, I remember, some wonderful
performances. Yet not one in my judgment ever sang an
entire role with the vocal and artistic consistency of Caruso;
and certainly no other tenor I can call to mind remotely
compares with him in having continued to sing—week after
week and season after season—with the same unvarying
achievement and supremacy, almost never disappointing
an audience through inability to appear. . . . He was a
unique artist, with whom no other compared, and I do not
see how we can ever have such another."

After listening to Caruso in Paris in the course of one
of his triumphant seasons there, the great French actor
Coquelin wrote to him: "Nothing in the world equals the
miracle of your voice."

I have already mentioned the prophecy of Jean de
Reszke, king of the Metropolitan's tenors before Caruso's

advent, that the Neapolitan was destined to be his successor—which was putting the case mildly. And Edouard de Reszke, Jean's brother, as famous a basso as Jean was a tenor, told Caruso: "I have never heard a more beautiful voice. You sing like a god. You are an actor and a sincere artist, and, above all, you are modest and without exaggerations. You were able to draw from my eyes many tears. I was very much touched and that happens to me very, very seldom. You have heart, feeling, poetry, truth. . . . With these qualities you will be master of the world."

Arturo Toscanini knew Caruso at the outset of his career, when Caruso was fighting his way to success in Milan. He followed his triumphs from there to the time when Caruso overwhelmed New York. In New York, Toscanini heard him year after year, when the tenor stood on the pinnacle of his fame. And he heard him late in his career, in Rome and Milan. So, if anybody was qualified to judge Caruso's voice it was Arturo Toscanini. Long after Caruso had become world-renowned, Toscanini declared that, around 1901, when the tenor was still in his twenties, when he was first tasting fame, when he was still unknown in London and New York, *his voice was at its best*. Caruso's high-water mark as a singer, according to Toscanini, was that performance of *L'Elisir d'Amore* at La Scala in Milan, when Enrico's superb singing saved the Gatti-Casazza-Toscanini opera season from disaster. "After that," averred Toscanini, "Caruso, as a singer, went downhill." With that judgment few will agree—even though it comes from Arturo Toscanini.

While Caruso was singing in 1915 in Monte Carlo he said to the writer Camillo Antona Traversi, as the two sat chatting in the tenor's dressing room between the acts of an opera:

"Camillo, I am an idiot! I *feel* a role too much! I always

try to give my best in interpreting a part. I know that I am a singer and an actor—yet, in order to give the public the impression that I am neither one nor the other but the *real man* conceived by the author I have to feel and to think as the man the author had in mind.

"The difficulty, the terrible difficulty, does not cease when the artist has reached the pinnacle of perfection— the top of the ladder, as we say. He is haunted when he gets there by the never-ending inner question: 'When shall I go down?' I never step upon a stage without asking myself whether I shall succeed in finishing the opera.

"A conscientious singer is never sure of himself or of anything. He is in the hands of Destiny."

CHAPTER 19

CARICATURIST
AND COLLECTOR

One would think that the goddess of fortune, having bestowed on Enrico Caruso the dual gift of the Voice of Gold and a personality combining the traits of an attractive enjoyer of life, an amusing clown, and a man of honor, would have stopped right there, deeming him sufficiently favored. But she did not. For full measure, she made her gift to him a triple one by equipping him also with marked talent as a caricaturist.

At restaurants he would pick up a menu and start caricaturing on it some diner at a nearby table—with sly glances out of the corner of his eye, to fix in his mind and communicate to his fingers the characteristics in his model which had impressed him—features, apparel, tricks of gesture, expression, anything and everything. If the diner caught him in the act, Caruso, like as not, would hand him, as a souvenir, a delicious, good-humored sketch revealing that diner as a happy, funny artist saw him. To this, Caruso would generously append his signature, with its vigorous lettering and intricate Italian embellishments, thus giving it, in addition to its value as a work of humorous art, considerable financial value as well.

He told his American wife that he would rather draw than sing. Once, when window-shopping with her, he noticed in the show window of an art shop a sketch by him of President Woodrow Wilson. He asked her to go in and inquire the price. She came back with the information that the shopkeeper was charging $75 for it.

"Ah!" exclaimed Caruso, immensely pleased. "Better we stop singing and draw!"

On trains, he drew caricatures despite speed and jolting. On steamships, he liked to seat himself in an inconspicuous nook in the smoking room or lounge, caricaturing some fellow passenger who had caught his fancy. In his dressing room at the Met and in opera houses in many other countries, he made amusing sketches while waiting for his cue— of his fellow singers, his dresser, his valet, of members of the chorus, and stagehands.

His sketches had no malice. He was not concerned with making cruel fun of others but with getting others to laugh good-humoredly with him at themselves. Somebody said of his pictures: "They bite, but never snarl." And there was another striking thing about his caricaturing, which serves better than multitudes of words to show his inborn sense of humor, his utter lack of vanity: he took the greatest delight in caricaturing himself.

It gave him mischievous joy to depict himself in the most ridiculous attitudes, betraying the most absurd quirks of character. His drawings of himself as the bumpkin Nemorino in *L'Elisir d'Amore* reveal, in hilarious completeness, that village swain's lovesickness and awkwardness. When Caruso caricatured himself in one of his impressive roles, that of Rhadamès in *Aïda*, he saw himself not as a military commander of martial grandeur, but as an uncomfortable buffoon of Ancient Egypt, weighed down by his responsibilities and trappings and avoirdupois.

Year after year, when he was at the height of his fame, Caruso sent a caricature every week to *La Follia*, an illustrated Italian weekly published in New York. That Caruso feature was invaluable as a circulation-breeder. *La Follia's* publisher, Marziale Sisca, a close friend of the singer-caricaturist, offered to pay its creator a high price. But Caruso impatiently waved away the offer.

"You are my friend," he told Sisca. "From friends I take no money. My work is singing. For that I accept payment. My caricatures are for my pleasure, to give pleasure to others. Them I draw for nothing."

He saw models everywhere. If he sang a duet with Geraldine Farrar—or any other soprano—he would most probably knock off a comic sketch, depicting admirably her characteristics and his own. While in solemn conference at the Met offices on matters of vast importance with Manager Gatti-Casazza, Caruso, instead of listening, was prone to produce a pencil and do a caricature of his boss—and forestall a scolding by presenting it to its inspirer.

Once, I recall, he drew a picture of the tenor Bonci, who was diminutive, saying something to the basso Chaliapin, who was gigantic. It looked like a tugboat discoursing with the *Lusitania*. And, at a banquet attended by him and his boss, Gatti-Casazza, a man of veritably mournful mien, he dashed off a caricature of Gatti, steeped in gloom worthy of Hamlet himself, and handed it across the table to his victim with this inscription: "The Merriest Guest at Table!"

On another occasion—obviously after a severe dressing-down administered by Manager Gatti-Casazza to the assembled Metropolitan Opera House troupe—Caruso drew the troupe, including himself, as a mass meeting of midgets, all in a state of acute distress, while towering over them stood an enraged Gatti-Casazza, like Gulliver in Lilliput.

True to his propensity for making fun of himself in his caricatures, Caruso made one, still vivid in my memory

Gatti-Casazza addressing his "children"

though five decades have elapsed since I saw it, showing Leo Slezak at the time that that excellent Czech tenor had just joined the Metropolitan's forces. Though Caruso by that time knew perfectly well that neither Slezak nor any other tenor anywhere could hope to compete with him in the field of song, he showed himself in that sketch as grinding his teeth and clenching his fists in apprehensive foreboding, and he wrote under it, "*Ah! La Gelosia!*" ("Ah, jealousy!")

One day, aboard a transatlantic liner, he was busy in the bar making a caricature of himself, when a fellow passenger, a complete stranger, looked over his shoulder. After careful scrutiny of the picture, the seagoing kibitzer exclaimed: "What are you doing?"

"A caricature of Enrico Caruso."

"But that's yourself!"

"No," contradicted Caruso solemnly. "You see, Caruso and I look almost exactly alike. All I have to do, when I want to draw Caruso, is to do a drawing of myself."

The other continued to watch the artist amid exclamations of "Marvelous!" and "Caruso to the life!" The artist finished the sketch, signed it, handed it to the stranger with a polite bow, and walked out on the deck. His fellow passenger looked at the finished product. He read the signature—Enrico Caruso. Suddenly, the truth dawned on him. He rushed to the deck, to thank the distinguished donor. But Caruso had disappeared below.

Perhaps the cleverest of all Caruso's caricatures is the one showing a man's face, in reproducing which the artist did not use pencil or pen or brush, but merely certain keys on a typewriter keyboard—dots, dashes, asterisks, punctuation marks, parentheses, dollar signs, et cetera. Yet the face is unmistakably that of Enrico Caruso.

✦

In the first years of his world-wide success Caruso made his debut as a collector. He loved collecting; and, as the number of his objects of art grew, he loved to take them out and finger them caressingly and tell how he had found them and why he had purchased them.

It all began one day when at last he had plenty of money to spend and bought an ancient gold coin which had caught his fancy in an antique shop in some city visited during his wanderings. To that coin he added many more, some costing a stiff price, others picked up as bargains. Finally, his coin collection had around 2,000 items, ranging in date from 500 B.C. to his own times.

Later, he added the collecting of articles of plastic arts to his original hobby. Often he would stand in silence before a showcase in some museum, gazing regretfully at lovely pieces of pottery not for sale to him or anybody. After he had gathered together some that were purchasable, his delight, when he exhibited them to friends, was like that of a boy.

In New York he was especially attracted to the J. P. Morgan collections at the Metropolitan Museum of Art; and when the Morgan treasures were put on sale he carried away many a piece of high excellence and beauty— and price.

His pottery collection eventually rose to a total of some 300 pieces, some dating back to ancient times, from Egypt, Greece, Rome, Damascus, Rhodes. He knew the history of each, and he was never happier than when he held one of his treasures in his hand, entranced by its beauty. Among his best-loved treasures were a lot of small vases and glass pieces, some iridescent and brightly colored, just the thing for the Neapolitan boy in him.

He also acquired, in the years of his wealth and celebrity, a number of bas-reliefs, small and of fine quality, including a Quattrocento relief which so fascinated him that, after his death, members of his family had it placed on the altar of the chapel erected over his grave in Naples.

One section of his collection especially prized by him was that of enameled gold boxes and gold watches, of which he owned scores. Many were seventeenth century, and, among them, some of the best and most expensive came from the Paris collection of Alfred Rothschild.

Caruso also acquired many paintings and other works of art, as well as old velvets, and embroideries.

All this, of course, cost a lot of money. But, in gratifying his artistic tastes, Caruso showed no reluctance to spend it. However, like the genuine human being that he was, he loved a bargain. He knew that special joy, so typical of collectors, that comes from picking up treasures cheaply. He owned one bronze plaquette by the sixteenth-century Venetian artist Tullio Lombardi, which he delighted to show and talk about—"found it in a London bric-a-brac shop—paid ten shillings for it—it's worth five hundred dollars— *Dio mio,* how happy I was when I learned its true value!"

At his Villa Bellosguardo all the rooms (except one bedroom, which contained original pieces of furniture of the period of Francis I of France) were furnished in the style of sixteenth-century Italy.

His entire collection of objects of art was estimated to be worth around half a million dollars. Perhaps, if it were placed on sale, it would fetch more than that.

He also collected stamps. He had a number of large albums filled with the stamps of many countries. In his hours of leisure he liked to paste new acquisitions on the pages of these albums.

Throughout the years when he collected art objects, he constantly impressed on members of his family and close friends that, when he was no longer alive, there was to be no dispersing of his collections. They must be kept absolutely intact. In deference to his wishes, arrangements were made after his death to have his complete collections go eventually to Gloria Caruso, his daughter by his American wife.

CHAPTER 20

GERALDINE FARRAR
LOOKS BACK

Accompanied by the customary pomp and glitter, Caruso Opening Night began the season of 1915-1916 at the Metropolitan Opera House with the great tenor heading a star cast in Saint-Saëns' *Samson et Dalila* which included Margarete Matzenauer and Pasquale Amato. During that season he added to the list of his bizarre adventures an incident on the stage of the Metropolitan which was grist to the mill of American journalism.

When the season was three months old Enrico Caruso and Geraldine Farrar appeared together in a matinee performance of *Carmen*, he as Don José, she in the title role of the opera. According to the version of the incident that I heard originally, she stalked up to him in the intensely dramatic finale and slapped him across the face with her fan with unprecedented violence.

Front-page stuff!

Next morning the chortles of joy from editors of daily papers could be heard, if one listened attentively, behind the big headlines with which they plastered their sheets. Following up her onslaught, Farrar remarked (according to the generally accepted version of the story) that if Caruso didn't like her vigorous acting he could go find himself another Carmen. And he (again according to that version), forgetting the sugary gallantry for which Latins are noted in their dealings with ladies, retorted that she could go find herself another Don José.

In the course of preparing this book I went one day to Ridgefield, Connecticut, to call on Geraldine Farrar—who has lived in that town ever since her retirement some thirty years ago—and asked her to tell me about Enrico Caruso, long her fellow singer and friend.

Among the questions I put to her, as we sat in her library surrounded by dozens of reminders of long ago, including a caricature of herself by Caruso, was this one: "Is the famous slapping story, as I have heard it, correct?"

"No," said she. "That is, not all of it. I really *did* slap Enrico—hard. But the rest is wrong. Here is what really happened.

"Once, while I was a member of the Metropolitan Opera House company, I went to Hollywood between opera seasons and made a moving picture of *Carmen*.

"I thoroughly enjoyed it—so much so that, when I returned to New York, I decided to put into my acting of the title role of *Carmen* at a Met matinee some of the 'business' I had worked into the movie—which was rather more extreme and violent than the regular sort of operatic stage 'business.' In the last act, at the climax of the big tussle between Don José and Carmen just before he kills her, I brought down my fan, Hollywood style, good and hard on Enrico's cheek. As we came out in front of the curtain to bow to the applauding audience, he was rubbing his cheek and shaking his head at me, implying that I had hurt him— all a joke, of course.

"As soon as I got back to my apartment my telephone started buzzing. One newspaper reporter after another wished to hear all about how I had slapped Caruso. I saw that they wanted a story. So I let them have it. I denied nothing. I never deny anything.

"Another buzz. Caruso on the phone. 'But, Geraldina, what is this? The reporters—the many reporters—they say I am very angry because you slap. I not like. I worry.'

" 'Stop worrying,' I told him. 'Deny nothing. Do you know what's going to happen? Next week, when you and I repeat *Carmen*, everybody will want to see whether I slap you hard again. The house will be packed.'

"That's just the way it was. The next week Enrico and I did *Carmen* again. The house was jammed full."

As the famous prima donna looked back over the years, recollections of Enrico Caruso came readily to her lips, undimmed by the passing of several decades.

"He was a darling," she said. "All those who sang with him liked him. It was impossible not to like him. The stage-hands loved him. He was always trying to help somebody, to do something kind. For instance, John McCormack. John hated to sing in opera; he was essentially a concert singer— quite the reverse of myself and Caruso, who much preferred opera to concerts. When McCormack was having a particularly bad attack of stage fright, before his cue to go on, Enrico would go up to him, as he stood nervously in the wings, and say something funny to him to cheer him up and make him forget his nervousness. He was always doing things like that. He was nice to everyone—he never acted the great tenor.

"And what a worker he was! Always he saw something beyond his best; always he tried to improve his singing and acting, to broaden his repertoire. He worked all the time. And the parts he added to his repertoire became constantly more difficult, especially for acting—John of Leyden, Samson, Eleazar in *La Juive*. He was never satisfied with himself.

"Singing in French was not at all easy for him. Yet he learned to sing in it—especially as Faust—and to sing well. He told me once that he could detect no difference in the

Caruso and Farrar at rehearsal

sound of *des yeux* (of the eyes) and *des cieux* (of the skies). 'But there *is* a difference,' I insisted. He repeated the two phrases slowly. 'There is no difference,' he complained. 'There *is*,' said I. And so it went—over and over again. Yet he *did* learn the difference. And not until his singing showed that he had learned it was he content.

"He loved his two little boys. The younger, Mimmi, was a delightful child, a regular little Murillo, with the most beautiful manners. When I was in Paris one year with my mother, of whom Enrico Caruso was very fond, Enrico had the governess with whom Mimmi lived in London (the little boy was about seven at that time) bring him over to Paris for a visit. One day, turning suddenly to my mother, Enrico said: " 'Mammina' (he always called her by that Neapolitan pet name), 'why don't you adopt Mimmi? You would make a wonderful mother for him.'

"When my mother recovered from her surprise, she shook her head and, pointing at me, remarked: 'Haven't I enough on my hands trying to take care of that young woman?'

"In London Enrico told his little son that he did not want to interfere with his regular life—that he would keep out of the way if he was not wanted.

" 'But I want you to be with me,' said Mimmi. 'I want to show you off to my friends.' One day, when a number of Mimmi's playmates were to come to his home, he asked his father to join them and be introduced to them. So Caruso, after their arrival, knocked on the door of the room where they were all gathered, listening, amid shouts of delighted laughter, to a Harry Lauder record.

" 'You like Harry Lauder records?' Enrico Caruso asked his little son.

" 'Oh, yes!' answered Mimmi, while the heads of his playmates bobbed in unanimous assent. 'We like them much better than Caruso records.'

"One story about Caruso that always pleased me was this: On his return from a successful tour in South America, where he had heard much applause and made a lot of money, he was strolling one day in the Galleria in Milan, wearing a flamboyant, bright-colored waistcoat and a big double gold watch chain, so thick and heavy that it looked like a cable from a big transatlantic liner. As he strolled, a seedy fellow singer rushed up to him with effusive greetings. Then he fingered the first button of Enrico's waistcoat—started to speak—hesitated—and began to finger the second button. Again he tried to speak, hesitated again—and went to work on the third button and the fourth—while Enrico, who was most fastidious and nervous, grew steadily more uncomfortable. The other now started fingering the big gold watch chain, link by link. Finally, he whispered, 'Please lend me five lire'—and, as he spoke, he started to remove a hair from the shoulder of Caruso's coat. Enrico quickly reached into a pocket, fished out a five-lire note, and handed it over. 'Here, take the money,' he said, 'but leave the hair where it is.' "

Like Nellie Melba, Geraldine Farrar met Caruso for the first time at Monte Carlo. That first glimpse of him made a deep impression on her.

"Never shall I forget the apparition as he walked into the first rehearsal, clad in shrieking checks topped by a gray fedora, and yellow gloves. Grasping a gold-headed cane he jauntily walked onto the stage. A happy smile illumined a jolly face, which was punctuated by the two largest black eyes I had ever seen. Fresh from South American triumphs this young phenomenon was affable and pleasant to us all."

They got along well together from the start, Enrico and Geraldine. And the tenor coined for her a personal motto,

"Farrar *farà*" (Farrar will achieve). To get the full savor of that Carusian pun one must be sure to accent the diva's name on the second syllable.

"Of course," Geraldine Farrar told me in Ridgefield, "Enrico Caruso made caricatures of me—as he did of everyone."

"Yes, I know," said I. "I remember particularly one of you and him singing a duet."

"Did it show me with a mouthful of big teeth—tombstone teeth?"

I had to admit that it gave that general impression.

"I knew it! He always drew me like that! And each time I objected he would say: 'But I have never seen you, Geraldina, with your mouth shut. Always you keep it open. Always you smile.'

"He was constantly drawing caricatures. I remember how he used to do it at banquets—which bored him. Once, at a particularly formal banquet, he sat next to me. He whipped a pencil out of his pocket, picked up a menu, and started to sketch somebody at another table. 'Oh, how bored I am!' he would say *sotto voce* to me—and then he would go on with his caricaturing. Then somebody would say something nice to him and immediately he would be all smiles and polite nods—quite charming. Then—back to his picture. A few more deft strokes—and then he would lean toward me once more. 'Geraldina, how bored I am!'

"Once he took me and my mother to his Villa Bellosguardo near Florence. Proudly he showed us all over the place. In one big room, with several doors, I noticed over each door a medallion in the ancient Roman style, each showing Caruso in the costume of one of his favorite roles—Rhadamès, Canio, Cavaradossi, Des Grieux.

"You can hardly say that these date from the times of the Caesars," I commented.

" 'Never mind,' said he, 'I not care. I like.' He never grew up."

"Did he deserve his unique fame?" I inquired.

"He most certainly did. There was nobody like him. He was marvelous. No voice was ever like his."

"Didn't he arouse envy in others?"

"Never. Not a shred."

"Didn't he owe anything to the tremendous advertising he got?"

"Absolutely nothing. He needed no advertising. He himself was his own best advertisement."

Again Geraldine Farrar's eyes seemed to look back to her great days, in which Enrico Caruso played so prominent a part—to his superb singing, to his countless acts of kindness, to his broad smile, his gay neckties, his gaudy waistcoats.

"He was a darling," she repeated.

CHAPTER **21**

THE ONE AND ONLY

In his progress toward unique renown Enrico Caruso was surrounded at the Metropolitan Opera House during all of his seventeen seasons there by other outstanding operatic performers, some of them dangerous rivals in the battle for the favor of New York's operagoing public. Moreover, during several of those seasons, he was also pitted against the squad of stars assembled by Oscar Hammerstein at the Manhattan Opera House down on West Thirty-fourth Street. To think of Caruso during his march to glory as a giant among pygmies is absurd—nothing could be more remote from the truth. In fact, one of the most striking points about his extraordinary record is that he achieved it in competition with the best operatic artists of his day, and held it, once he had achieved it, in the teeth of steady and relentless rivalry from his colleagues, artists whose talent was beyond question.

But even between the best of these stars and Caruso, there was an unbridgeable gap. "I want a seat for the next opera in which Caruso sings." Those words were heard with monotonous regularity at the Met's box office each season. The opera didn't matter. The composer didn't matter. The other singers didn't matter. Nothing mattered except Caruso.

His fame was universal, but it had been bought dearly.

Although throughout his years of celebrity he had remained a boy who wouldn't grow up, and although the wine of his fame had never gone to his head, there were certain inexorable demands which had to be met as he was swept onward and upward, and sometimes he resented their inexorability.

To a reporter, once, during a season of tremendous success, he complained, "I cannot consider my own desires. I have to take care of that delicate watch mechanism in my throat and of the rest of my body, in order that not a grain of sand may get into the intricate wheels and interfere with their workings." This was a far cry from the Enrico Caruso who used to sing for pennies outside Neapolitan bathhouses, pouring out melody with the carelessness and indifference of a nightingale!

But still he went on, season after season, giving everything he had. People were, of course, amazed at how he could do it, and there was no wonder that the rumors that "Caruso's voice is going" were constantly being renewed. This richness and munificence of song were, indeed, hard to believe possible. In 1916, Caruso departed from New York for Europe, as usual. When he arrived in Monte Carlo he heard again the old story: his voice was going—or gone. And, as it always did, this worried him and incited him to an even higher pitch of effort. In his opening, *Aïda*, there were no signs of vocal deterioration.

Again the impresarios were on his trail. Alluring contract forms were laid before him, in the hope that he would sign them. He was pleased, of course, but he was tired. Bellosguardo beckoned.

So when Impresario Mocchi, from Buenos Aires, asked him to agree to sing during another season in South America, Caruso jokingly remarked: "All right—if you agree to pay me 35,000 gold francs ($7,000) per performance." That was an unheard-of fee—and the tenor, of course, pitched his demand at such a fantastic height on the assumption that he would hear no more of the matter and be allowed to get much-needed rest at his villa.

"Fine!" remarked Impresario Mocchi. "You're hired."

Caruso was amazed.

"Please sign here. And be ready to start for South America in a week."

Still wondering whether it was all a dream, the tenor boarded a steamer some days later, and, in due course, appeared before the operagoers of Buenos Aires. He had not been there for years. And his fee on his previous visits had been far, far below what Mocchi had now obligated himself to pay. No singer had ever received such a sum for a few hours of warbling in opera—even the best warbling.

Again the opera selected as the main feature of the opening night was *Aïda,* followed by *Pagliacci*—now one of the main stand-bys of Caruso's repertoire wherever he went. He won a huge success in both. On another evening he appeared in *Lucia* with Amelita Galli-Curci, she of the short reign as queen of the high notes.

When the Buenos Aires series ended, Impresario Mocchi gave the triumphant tenor a gold cigarette case, inscribed:

> *"To Caruso, dearest of all friends—*
> *Least dear of all artists."*

Just before departing from Buenos Aires, Enrico received a cable from Italy, announcing the death of his sister Assunta. Thus, of all the twenty-one children of Marcellino and Anna Caruso, only Enrico and Giovanni, his brother, were left.

Shortly after his return to Europe, the tenor appeared

in Milan. Much certainly had happened since his victories
there in *Fedora* at the Lirico, and in *L'Elisir d'amore* at
La Scala, when the gates of glory had swung wide to admit
him from the everyday world into a sort of Arabian Nights,
Elysian Fields, and Garden of Eden all rolled into one.
On the conductor's podium again was that marvelous
artist, that grim disciplinarian, Arturo Toscanini. Just like
old times!

Twice Caruso sang in *Pagliacci*—and Milan went into
spasms of delight and the Milanese papers printed rhap-
sodies about his voice. It was perhaps more dramatic, they
said, than in his more lyrical days, but it remained the
voice which had turned *Fedora* into gold.

Incidentally, before his return to Milan in 1916, the
Italians had been doing a lot of grumbling because Caruso
would not sing to them any more. The rest of the world
had kept him so busy and paid him so well, more indeed
than any Italian manager could afford, that, for years, if
his fellow countrymen wanted to drink in his golden notes,
they had been forced to go to Paris or London or Berlin
or New York or Buenos Aires. Those two *Pagliaccis* under
Toscanini's dominating baton were the tenor's last appearances in Milan. Shortly after he had thrilled the Milanese
in his pet role—that of love-mad, desperate Canio in
Pagliacci—he was off again to New York. Milan never heard
the Voice of Gold again.

On the opening night in the Met's new season (1916-
1917), Caruso's singing won enthusiastic approval. And
there was much pleased comment on his improved acting.
While rehearsing at his Italian villa he had given the
most careful attention not only to the vocal side of his
coming New York roles but also to the acting of them.

And now his industry and conscientiousness were yielding rich fruit. One of those who had worked with him at his villa to get him into prime condition for New York, was Leopoldo Mugnone, the conductor-composer from whom he had stolen that little ballerina many years before.

In New York, Caruso strutted and warbled in some of his tried old favorites—*Bohème, Tosca, Martha, Aïda, Manon Lescaut, Rigoletto, Carmen*. He missed only one of his scheduled performances. Apparently the man of iron health was himself again.

Having signed up for a tour in Brazil, he got very nervous about his trip southward. German submarines were rampant. They were sending Allied ships to the bottom in alarming numbers. Caruso did not like the situation at all. But he had promised to sing for the Brazilians, and, as always, a promise was, to him, sacrosanct. Before going aboard his steamship, he bought a number of life preservers, also a strange piece of toggery, which, he had been solemnly assured by the vendor, was an unsinkable suit.

No torpedo struck his ship on her voyage. She steamed into the harbor of Rio de Janeiro unscathed. Enrico's collection of life preservers remained in a virgin state. I do not know whether his "unsinkable suit" was such as could be worn out of water. Perhaps he put it in moth balls, in preparation for his homeward journey.

He opened in Rio de Janeiro, the Brazilian capital, as Nemorino in *L'Elisir d'Amore*. The Brazilians were delighted. And when he gave them Canio in *Pagliacci*, the Rio theater was less like an opera house than a madhouse. On this tour, Caruso appeared for the first time in Mascagni's *Lodoletta*, in which that persistent composer had tried yet again to bring back into his life the delicious taste of the frenzied welcome with which the whole world had greeted his *Cavalleria Rusticana*. He tried in vain.

After singing in Montevideo and São Paulo (but not in Buenos Aires this time), Caruso went aboard a steamship bound for New York, placed beside his berth a life preserver, and hung on an easily accessible hook his unsinkable suit. But again he finished the journey without having to scramble into either.

In the United States he found the Americans aflame with patriotism (they had entered World War I the previous April). They were parading and cheering and buying Liberty bonds and looking forward eagerly to the day when Wilhelm II would be no longer German Kaiser. Caruso promptly increased his already considerable stock of Liberty bonds.

At the Met (the 1917-1918 season there opened with *Aïda* and Caruso) he added to his old tested operas two new ones—Mascagni's *Lodoletta* (no more a success with New Yorkers than it had been with Brazilians) and Meyerbeer's *Le Prophète*, in which he played John of Leyden. This role was distinctly on the Rhadamès-Canio side, a heavy one, requiring the voice of a *"tenore robusto."* There were still some carpers who chided Caruso for straying too often from the purely lyrical to the dramatic department of song. But he went straight ahead in his dual capacity of lyric and dramatic tenor.

And now the United States income-tax officials gleefully dug their claws into him. But Enrico was a sport. He forked over the full amount required of him—$59,832.15.

To his usual work as a singer he added now acting in the movies. Yielding to importunate movie magnates, he took the hero's part in two moving pictures built around him. But they were not successes. And he was uncomfortable in this of field of silent films. He did not like himself on the screen: No singing. So he toyed with that phase of dramatic art no more.

He went back to singing at the Met. He went back to concerts. He went back to being the star attraction at Liberty bond drives, at which he sang George M. Cohan's "Over There" in an English so effectively buried under Neapolitan overtones that it drew from audiences roars of delight for the singer and thousands of dollars for the United States Treasury. He went back to voice recordings, which, by now, were making huge contributions toward his financial well-being.

He went back to caricaturing. Always and everywhere— between the acts of operas, at solemn banquets, in pauses at war rallies, while patriotic assistants were handing out Liberty bonds to those whose wallets he had laid waste by his singing—he would take a pencil from his pocket and add to the big total of funny sketches which he had already produced.

At the Metropolitan Opera House the grand opera season of 1917-1918 ended in the spring of the latter year. Caruso's other singing engagements in the United States also ended. Europe beckoned with alluring offers of more engagements. And thoughts of the Villa Bellosguardo must have colored his dreams with pictures of deep, deserved rest.

Yet he stayed on. He bought no return ticket to Europe.

Spring turned to summer. Still he dallied. Uninitiated friends wondered what it was all about. Others chuckled knowingly. Something very important indeed was about to happen in Enrico Caruso's life.

CHAPTER 22

CARUSO THE HUSBAND

"I did not like opera," said a certain young lady of New York. "It seemed to me noisy and unnatural." Yet she became the wife of Enrico Caruso. Her dislike for that which was his lifework, his road to riches and renown, might have been the rock to split their union asunder. Instead, perhaps, it was the rock which endowed that union with a good part of its firm foundation. The marriage of that young lady and the singer with the Voice of Gold, pitifully short in duration, was a success. It brought to each what each lacked and craved: to her, glamour and romance; to him, a goal, an anchorage, and a shrine.

Her name was Dorothy Benjamin. She belonged to an old New York family. Nobody could have guessed from her upbringing and surroundings, from her character and leanings, the kind of marriage that was to be hers, the sort of man who was to be her husband.

Into her book * about how she happened to become the great singer's wife and what manner of life they lived together she put much that is intimate and understanding and revealing about the new Caruso whom she brought into being—Caruso the Husband.

Before her marriage she had known unhappiness at

* Dorothy Caruso, *Enrico Caruso, His Life and Death*, Simon & Schuster, copyright 1945 by Dorothy Caruso.

home. Her mother having been compelled by ill health to live out of New York, Dorothy took charge of her father's household. She didn't like it. Mr. Benjamin, a brilliant and versatile patent lawyer, was, according to her, a tyrant. "I couldn't explain his dislike of me except that I bored him. When he returned from the office at night the sound of his key in the front door made my heart pound. From the hall he would roar out his desires—steak for dinner—and if lamb had been ordered instead he would stamp up the stairs, shouting accusations that I was deliberately trying to starve him."

Soon he invited a cousin's governess to stay in his home. She and he used to go to the opera together. One night, after returning from *Carmen*, he praised the show so eloquently that his daughter, abstracting from his *bibelot* cabinet a little silver windmill, sold it for a dollar and bought standing room for the next performance of *Carmen*.

Caruso sang in it. It was her first glimpse of her future husband. But she was too frightened by what she had done to enjoy his singing or notice him as an individual.

One day the governess told Dorothy that she might go with her, if she wished, to the christening party for the baby of a distinguished singing teacher, where Enrico Caruso was to act as godfather. Miss Benjamin arrived before the other guests and stood waiting at the top of a flight of stairs. Presently the front door opened.

"A man in a big fur-collared coat came in and the 's' in 'Caruso' hissed up at me. He was the first to come up the stairs. He stopped halfway and stood looking at me. In that long instant I knew that I was going to marry him."

The governess introduced them. Having been empowered by Mr. Benjamin to invite guests to his house, she asked Caruso to dine there on a certain night.

He came like a hero from the age of Romance, with a

big cloak flung, Latin fashion, over his shoulder and a big wide-brimmed felt hat, effectively supported by a blue suit with velvet lapels, white silk shirt, flowing tie, silk socks, and patent-leather pumps. This overpowering outfit, he told Miss Benjamin later, was his costume as the hero in Charpentier's opera, *Julien*. "I wore it," he said, "so you would remember me."

After that, he dined often at the Benjamin home. He tried to make himself welcome to the young lady's father by frequently sending him tickets to the opera. Caruso also used to take the daughter of the house and the governess motoring. He sat between them, telling stories about his life. The governess listened with a conscious little smile. Was she not right in believing that the tenor's polite attentions had her as their target?

Once, on returning from their drive, Caruso, having found out that Dorothy was invited out to dinner with some friends nearby, asked her father, after the governess had alighted from the car, to allow him to escort Miss Benjamin to the house where she was dining. Mr. Benjamin gave his permission. Enrico told the driver the address of the house to which Dorothy was bound. The car started. The tenor turned to her.

"Now, Doro," he inquired, "when can we be married?"

Very soon he came to her home to ask her father for her hand. Mr. Benjamin postponed his answer. The daughter and Enrico saw much of each other. All would now be plain sailing for her and Enrico, thought Miss Benjamin. She was mistaken.

Her father abruptly told her that Enrico must never cross his threshold again. A week passed without any explanation from him of his drastic decision. Then, with equal suddenness, he informed her that she might marry Caruso if the tenor settled on her half a million dollars in cash.

That meant, according to Dorothy, not a desire for money, since her father had plenty, but that the governess had informed him that she could not live in his house unless his daughter lived there also, thus driving him to resort to his demand on Caruso as a way to prevent the marriage and enable the governess to continue being a member of Mr. Benjamin's household. Dorothy went in tears to Caruso. He told her that he did not possess half a million dollars in cash and would not sell his Liberty bonds in order to raise it.

Next day they were married. The date was August 20, 1918. A small party assembled on that day at the Caruso apartment in the Hotel Knickerbocker in New York City. It consisted of Enrico Caruso, Miss Benjamin, a friend of hers (Mrs. Keith), and Bruno Zirato, the tenor's secretary. Below, in the street, Caruso's car was waiting. After obtaining a marriage license, the party was driven to the Church of the Transfiguration, much better known as the Little Church Around the Corner, on East Twenty-ninth Street, close to Fifth Avenue. The clergyman there was dubious about performing the marriage ceremony. So Enrico and Dorothy Benjamin were married at the Marble Collegiate Church.

A short time after the wedding Mr. Benjamin adopted the governess as his daughter, which made it perfectly proper for her to go on living in his house. He disinherited his daughter. Meeting her on the street one day he cut her dead. After the death of her mother, he left his entire fortune to the governess.

And now, as Mrs. Enrico Caruso, she entered into a life which, to her, was "like being transported from the nether regions to the stratosphere." For some time she could not believe it real.

When Enrico inaugurated the Central Park open air concerts and she was being whirled to the first of them with an escort of motorcycle police, the thought flashed into her mind "how angry father will be if he sees me." At once everything became unreal. "I heard again the terrifying sound of father's key in the lock of the front door."

After their marriage she and Enrico left for a honeymoon at his Villa Bellosguardo. They walked straight into the disorders which scourged Italy after World War I and resulted eventually in Mussolini's march to supreme power. These disorders were so widespread that they reached even to secluded Bellosguardo.

At the villa, Dorothy and Enrico lived with twenty-one other persons—relatives or guests. Since she spoke no Italian and they no English, this feudal arrangement often engendered complications. In addition to the resident phalanx, the inhabitants of Bellosguardo during part of that summer also included Enrico's two sons and their English governess. Giovanni, the tenor's brother, also spent much time there. And Caruso's stepmother, now an old lady with beautiful white hair, sometimes stayed at the villa. She spoke the dialect of her Southern Italian birthplace in such an undiluted form that even Enrico found her hard to understand.

All ate in a great eighteenth-century banquet hall. For the guests and relatives there were mountains of spaghetti and big caldrons of codfish, for the host and hostess cups of soup and the white meat of chicken. Mario, the tenor's valet, waited on Enrico and Dorothy; the other valet, Martino (he who had met the Kaiser) had been promoted to the post of major-domo at Bellosguardo, of which he took full charge when his master was away.

Mario had remained a bachelor, because Caruso objected

to his marrying. He told Dorothy that he had been engaged for years to a girl called Brunetta and begged her to persuade Enrico to let them marry. "No," objected the singer, when she started persuading, "no man can serve two masters. The wife of my valet would be the head of my house." After a while he relented. Mario and Brunetta were wedded and both accompanied the tenor and his wife on their next trip to the United States.

In New York, Dorothy lived with her husband in his fourteen-room suite at the Hotel Knickerbocker (on the ninth floor, fronting on both Broadway and Forty-second Street). Its other regular occupants were Bruno Zirato, Enrico's secretary; Salvatore Fucito, his accompanist; Mario, his valet; Enrichetta, Dorothy's maid; and an old Neapolitan friend, Punzo, whom Caruso had transformed into a dresser and assistant valet. One room was set aside for the child expected by Dorothy in a few months.

Though Caruso knew that his valet Mario had brought Brunetta his bride with him to New York, he pointedly made no reference to her for some time after their arrival in America. But, one day, in his Hotel Knickerbocker suite, he suddenly asked: "And Brunetta? Where is she?"

His wife told him that she had found a job for the valet's bride in a New York dressmaking establishment.

Caruso was horrified. "What? A member of my household working for somebody else?" He angrily summoned Mario and soundly berated him. "What the devil is this? You let Brunetta work outside? You not know me after all this time?" He ordered Mario to tell Brunetta to give up her job immediately. "Tell her she is to work for the *signora*. Never was anybody stupid like you." Mario stood in silence, stunned by this tempest. As Enrico started out of the room, he turned to the speechless valet: "Take a big room and bath for you both—here in the hotel near to me." Then, as he walked away: "And your salary is now twice."

During his era of fantastic earning power, nothing could check Caruso's generosity and imperial munificence. In her book, his wife gives this description of a shopping tour with him in New York, when he went on a spending rampage:

"As Christmas approached, Enrico began to make a long list of names—people to whom he always gave presents. When he read it to me I was appalled. 'But, Rico, you don't like all these people?' 'No,' he said, 'but they expect.'

"To go Christmas shopping with Enrico was a lovely adventure. He bought what he had planned to buy, never asked the price and chose his presents at only two places —his favorite antique shop and Tiffany's. At Tiffany's he bought gold souvenirs for everyone who didn't like antiques, and at the antiquarian's he bought antiques for everyone who didn't like souvenirs.

"He walked through the aisles of Tiffany's, looking very large in his fur-lined coat, while his good face with its great warm smile expressed the real spirit of Christmas and the happiness he was feeling. He stopped at a counter and peered into the lighted case. 'Look, Doro, nice little boxes for powder and for red.' The salesman dropped his professional boredom and became charged with excitement.

" 'Please, the little boxes,' said Enrico, pointing not with one finger but with his whole hand—a gesture that to me symbolized the limitless generosity of his heart.

" 'We like fifty like this, then thirty like this, ten like this, and one like this.' The clerk stammered that he would find out if so many were available.

"Then we examined the bracelets and neck chains. By this time everyone in Tiffany's knew that Caruso was doing his Christmas shopping and the manager came to greet us.

"'Very much obliged,' said Enrico and shook him warmly by the hand. 'I like now to give you special order.'

"We sat about a table while Enrico made rough sketches of the design he wanted for a gold watch charm—this year's gift to his closest friends. 'You will make twenty like this and send.'

"We shook hands with everyone, left the shop without any idea of how much money we had spent and went on to the antiquarian's. There Enrico chose gifts according to the recipient's taste, not his own. 'This is very ugly and I dislike it very much, but they collect and find interesting.'"

When they were first married, he took his wife to a leading New York fur shop and asked her to choose some furs. As she had become accustomed during her unmarried life to the absence of such luxuries, she decided to keep Enrico's expenses down—on this occasion, at least. So she chose a small fur coat, thinking that its price would be commensurate with its size. He put it on a nearby chair and asked her to choose something else besides, something bigger. One fur led to another, until finally, despite his wife's reluctance, the saleslady had piled around her about a dozen costly fur garments, so that she might make her choice of two or three from among them.

"Thank you," said Caruso to the saleslady. "Very nice. Thank you very much. Very good. We take them all."

Enrico's native Neapolitan explosiveness (at times he seemed to be directly descended from Vesuvius) often made him engulf Zirato or Fucito, Mario or Punzo, in eruptive violence.

"Have you a turnip for a head? Do you think I could sing if I work like you do? Can you stare at the sky and dream and the work do itself? *Per Bacco!* What are these I have around me? Statues?" But soon all was serene as the Bay of Naples in sunshine. His violent fits ended as abruptly as they began.

His suite at the Knickerbocker was filled constantly with knots of self-styled "closest friends." But, in reality, he gave his friendship to very few. The self-appointed retinue of intimates served to make him laugh, or they were useful when he wanted to talk in Neapolitan dialect. They also scoured New York in quest of items for his collections, catered like royal courtiers to his whims, ran errands. As a reward, they sunned themselves in his glory, went free of charge to the Met and some of them did not neglect to levy large amounts on antique dealers as their commission for steering business to them.

A real friend, Antonio Scotti, that excellent and popular Metropolitan baritone, long a favorite with New York operagoers, lived in a suite at the Knickerbocker just below Enrico's. Before the tenor's marriage the two used to lunch together almost daily at a corner table in the hotel's restaurant. That table promptly became famous.

Scotti, handsome and charming, was also a collector— of beautiful women. Once Enrico, returning from a visit to the baritone's suite, poured into Dorothy's lap a cascade of diamond, sapphire, and emerald rings. She started to thank him. But, as she spoke, she noticed something peculiar about his manner. Immediately she guessed what he was up to. "Take those rings back to Scotti," she commanded, "and tell him that, although his latest love affair has had an unhappy ending, he must keep them for the next one."

Sheepishly, Caruso slunk away, loaded with shining rings, to the apartment one flight down.

Enrico took a mischievous delight in looking out of a corner window of his suite on a wintry Broadway or Forty-second Street and watching pedestrians struggling against wind overhead and ice underfoot. "Come quick, Doro," he would call to his wife. "See the windy." And he would call out loudly to some pedestrian, picking his way cautiously amid umbrellas blown inside out and hats suddenly seized with wanderlust: "Take care! You go now on the slip!"

Enrico Caruso lived his own life with such concentration that he had no need to draw on the lives of others to replenish it. "He didn't think of his contemporaries," his wife said, "he greeted them."

In the tenor's apartment, Sergei Rachmaninoff, Fritz Kreisler, John McCormack, and many others of similar prominence would get into furious discussions on subjects related to music and its interpretation, with a violence seemingly endangering both furniture and friendship; and often these whirlwinds ended in the question, asked belligerently by some composer or pianist or violinist: "Is singing a creative art?" Then the storm would rage again, with Caruso listening in silence.

"What do you think, Enrico?" somebody would ask, in a lull while reserves of verbiage were being brought up.

"I don't know," he would reply. Not for him abstract speculation, unpractical theorizing! When he thought of singing, he used to think usually only of what he had to sing that night—or the next.

In general, he disliked social doings. But once he had decided to go to a party, he enjoyed it from the moment he entered the door of the party-giver.

He beamed joyfully at the domestic who opened the

door. He beamed at the one who took his hat and coat. "He passed through events and people as if they were a landscape. They pleased him, he pleased them."

He listened interestedly to the talk of others and, when he talked himself, he never talked too much. "Holding the floor" was outside his ken. Now and then he would indulge in discussion, but he disliked anything acrimonious, preferring silence when he realized that discussions were growing hot. When parties were over "he beamed his way out as he had beamed his way in."

When he himself gave a party, it was worthy of an emperor. Once, to return many social favors, he hired the entire Armenonville restaurant floor at the Hotel Knickerbocker for a huge supper and dance. That floor, in preparation for the party, was literally walled and ceilinged with flowers. One thousand invitations were issued. Three thousand guests turned up.

A band and an orchestra played alternately in two big ballrooms. The three thousand stuffed themselves with food, submerged themselves in champagne, danced themselves into partial—sometimes total—unconsciousness.

For hours, Enrico and Dorothy had nothing to eat or drink. They just stood shaking hands with people (largely total strangers). Finally, since the buffet was invisible and inaccessible behind battalions of enthusiastic free lunch addicts, they fled to their rooms and ordered up some sandwiches. The three thousand, or as many of them as could stand up, danced until three o'clock in the morning.

On days when Caruso was to sing at the opera house down the street there was no music in his suite at the Knickerbocker. He busied himself with solitaire card games (to the end of his life he played exotic ones, learned in Naples), or he pasted newspaper clippings into large books he kept for the purpose, or looked over his collections of coins.

At such times, his wife worked on his stamp collection (he had given it to her soon after their marriage), and kept as silent as he did himself. After a few exercises with Fucito, his accompanist, interspersed with cups of coffee which he held in his hand as he sang the scales, striding up and down the room and gesticulating, he left for the opera house at seven in the evening, with Mario, his valet, and Zirato, his secretary.

Just before singing he was always very nervous and made no attempt to conceal his nervousness—hiding emotion is no part of a Neapolitan's creed. "Of course I am nervous," he used to exclaim. "Each time I sing I feel that there is someone waiting to destroy me, and I must fight like a bull to hold my own. The artist who boasts he is never nervous is not an artist—he is a liar or a fool."

Caruso was in his element at the circus. There, says his wife, "he was not a spectator but a performer. He joined the troupe from the moment he entered the doors of Madison Square Garden. Avid to see everything, he was as unconscious of attracting attention as a child. He played with the clowns from his box, made faces at them and, as they left the arena, leaned out to shake their hands. 'We make funny together,' he whispered. He thought that I and the people around us were laughing at the clowns, never dreaming that it was he who offered us a concentrated three-ring circus. When he visited the freaks it was as if he were calling on friends. 'You like to have so many?' he asked the three-legged man in Italian. 'He is very funny,' he told me, 'he say he like because he can kneel and sit at the same time.' Then he added with pride, 'He is Neapolitan, like me.' "

✦

Bruno Zirato, Caruso's secretary

His wife tells of simple meals which Enrico used to eat with her at a little restaurant in West Forty-seventh Street —boiled chicken or beef, vegetables, fruit, cheese, and coffee—"Enrico didn't drink wine" (did the "foxes of Scotland" cure him once and for all of wine-bibbing?). "The linen was coarse, the silver dull, the plates heavy. Pane, the restaurant keeper, served us and his niece did the cooking." Some years before, "Enrico had helped him when he was in great trouble." After lunch, "Pane brought out a deck of Italian cards and played with Enrico for hours— no strangers to stare or whisper or speak, just two old friends in an old restaurant, playing with an old deck of cards. I sat with them, wrapped in sables, pearls and enchantment."

Just like being back in Naples for Enrico Caruso. And that made everything all right for him. Anything that reminded him of his beloved birthplace, that took him back to it in spirit and set him down in his imagination on the Mergellina, or seated at a table with Zucchi and Vergine and Daspuro at the Caffé dei Fiori, was welcome to him, wherever he was. Nothing could shake his affection for the beautiful city where he had been born, where he had been young and poor and happy.

Nobody could pry out of Enrico Caruso which of his many roles he thought his best. He particularly liked Eleazar in *La Juive* (the last role he ever sang), because it gave him good opportunities both as singer and actor—and, as he grew older, he paid more and more attention to his acting.

On evenings when he sang what was beyond doubt his most famous and popular role—Canio in *Pagliacci*—there was no telling how his rendering of that heart-shaking song of human despair, "*Vesti la giubba*," would affect him.

Sometimes, after it, he sat sobbing in his dressing room. At other times, he would come off the stage, jaunty and smiling, cracking jokes with the chorus and stagehands, whistling happily, just as if he had not committed stage murder and suicide a moment before.

Of Punzo, his assistant valet and dresser, who always awaited him in his dressing room when he came off the stage, Caruso used to tell this story:

He and Punzo both studied singing in early days in Naples under Giuseppe Vergine. Punzo was engaged to Vergine's daughter. Vergine told Punzo: "Some day you will be the greatest tenor in the world." And he gave him the hand of his daughter in marriage.

"Punzo was very proud and very stupid," Enrico used to add, "and still he is very proud and very stupid."

"Then why," inquired his wife, for whom the convolutions of the Latin mind often remained to the end of her marriage a mystery, "do you employ him?"

"Because I will show him how to be a good valet—then he will know something and not be stupid any more."

And that is how Vergine's two pupils, Caruso and Punzo, came together many years after the days of their singing lessons—the pupil who would, the teacher thought, become the greatest tenor in the world, and the other who, in his judgment, sang "like the whistling of the wind through a window."

CHAPTER **23**

CONQUEST OF MEXICO

Early in the autumn of 1919, some weeks
before the opening of New York's 1919-1920 opera season,
Caruso left New York for a tour in Mexico, during which
he was to earn the highest fees ever earned by himself or
any other singer in the whole history of singing. In the
course of his Mexican tour, Caruso wrote constantly to his
wife, sometimes more than one letter a day, couched in
a startlingly Italianate English all his own. He never did
master the language of the country which he adopted, and,
since most of Caruso's quoted remarks were either dressed
up by others or translated from Italian, it is easy to forget
that English was a language he always spoke with difficulty
and which it was even more of a hardship for him to write.

His wife, now an expectant mother, did not accompany
him to the train from New York. He left her in that city
at their Forty-second Street and Broadway apartment. His
first letter was sent to her by messenger from Thirty-third
Street and Seventh Avenue—the Pennsylvania Station. The
second was written on the train between New York and
Philadelphia. I reproduce his brand of English:

"First of all I beg you to forgive me if I will write you
with my little machine because the train go on like a devil
and it is impossible to write with a fauntain pen. Some-
time it seems that the body go away from the legs for the

strong and suddenly rolling of the car. We look like people which have dring a baril of whisky!"

South of Laredo he wrote of his first glimpse of Mexico:

"I am passing a very misery land; a large and immense field with nobody. . . . Now we beguining to see a profile far away of a large chaine of mountins which, with the reflex of a very nice and blu sky, let me remember my beautiful country. . . . Hope to find little culler in two or three hours, as the conductor assure. . . . I will be back soon and I will no more go around the world without you."

He began his letters from Mexico City with this—dated September 22, 1919:

"Finaly there we are after a very long voyage, and what a voyage! . . . The country interesting from the beginning because savage, but at last day very annoying, allways the same.

"In Saltillo . . . the press of the town came to intervistaire me. I said lots good things, and everybody were glad.

". . . At seven we entered in this big house [he had taken a large furnished house for his Mexican singing season]. Was a house of a politicien of the past government, and mounted in French style but no pictures and no little things. Is a little cold but rada comfy.

"Have lots servants and enormous salons, for consequence we have 100 serve us, and lots of space to jomping up and down.

". . . Large movement of veicles, and very large hats and very tait trowsers. . . .

"I thing I talk too much of myself, for consequence, I beguining about you.

". . . I miss you terribly and the day that I will receive a letter from you will be a big joy for me.

"What our dear baby doing? [This refers to a member

of the human race as yet unborn.] She give you any truble? Hope not! . . .

"Excuse me, dear, a newspaper man want see me. . . ."

Later, he suffered from terrible headaches, like those which had tortured him in Germany after the Ada Giachetti trial in Milan. "What day today! Even your two telegrams was not able to let my pain releieve! . . . I am afraid that something will happen to me because I suffre too much!"

In answer to her first letter from New York:

"Eureka! Your first letter arrived! What a joy! . . . Yes, dear, your letter was a balsam for me, and I thank you very, very much. . . .

"You are lost without me? Immagine what is my condition! You have around you many things that talk to you about me, but I, poor me, have nothing with me, only your picture. . . . Never more will I go without you in any place! . . .

"What a pity that I dont know your sweet lenguage because I have many affectuese frases to tell you but I cant put down and sometimes I am afraid to write you, I think you laugh at me . . . and perhaps one day you will leave me! Oh, no! You dont do such a terrible thing! I will kill you in a terrible way! . . . I am terrible on my vengence. Remember that I am geloso . . . I feel sik because I am far away from you."

Describing a performance in Mexico City:

"I was very nervous . . . because before the season beginning many newspaper attaccarono the impresa [attacked the management] and me in telling that I am old and on the decadence, but when I sing my 'largo' in the duet of the first act. . . . What expplosion!! Everybody was creazy. . . . I got my public from this moment. At the end of the act which I put two top notes very strong and beautifully the entusiasm was to the zenit. But my heart! He jomping terrible and nearly I felt down! . . . I never heard such noise after my big aria even in the Metropolitan. . . . Everybody clapped strongly and 'gridavano come dannati' [shrieked like the damned]. . . . The press this morning is simple wonderful and I am glad because I have now everybody in my hand."

To counter his Italianate English his wife wrote him a letter in Anglo-Saxonized Italian. It tickled him. "It is so kiute," he wrote back. "Please dont take any grammatica when you write me because I understand you very much, otherwise you force me to take an inglisch grammere."

Now came the performance of *Carmen* in the great bull ring at Mexico City (fee, $15,000, a world's record):

"After I make all my preparatifs I went to the Plaza. I dress quigly and put some things in my throat and ready for the performance. . . . Before that the first act finished, beginning to reinning and I and Carmen were all wet. We supposed that the public goes away but nobody move. . . . Thousand of umbrellas was open and covered all the aera of the Plaza. We dont see any head and dont hear the orchestra. . . . I begin to sing my romanza and at the midle I dont now if it was effect of the rein on my condition, I think that was the reason, one note come out broken. Quigly I tought, 'Now come the revolution,' but nobody say enyting . . . and the public mak me a big ovation. But there the rein that come down strongly. We finished the act and had five callings. It was very funny to see one enormous bleek [black] spot all around the Plaza with some color reed and bleu, there were all umbrellas."

He did extraordinarily well in a performance of *Martha*:

"Ah, dearie, I don't know where I found such a voice! I never sing that aria [*M'apparì*] so beautifully and there was a demonstration delirante. Twenty minutes of callings and the people were crazy. . . . my dressing room were assalted from all the friends whom I meet here. I saw one trembling so hard that we were obliged to help him. Everybody had tiers in the eyes and all kiss my hands.

"At moment wich I went in the auto there were a crowd and everybody shake hand with me and some lady kiss me."

As the time drew near for his wife to have her baby her husband grew more and more concerned about her: "What about our baby Puschina." He always called her by that pet name before and after her birth. "Are she good? She trouble you? Do you find the name? What you think about Fiora, Flora, or Florinda? Do you like Erminlinda? Or Floriana?" It is noticeable that Enrico thought only of a girl child; and his wife, after learning that he wanted a daughter, also refrained from thinking of a boy.

He returned from Mexico shortly before the beginning of the 1919-1920 season at the Met. During the season a daughter was born to his wife—on December 18, 1919— at the Knickerbocker Hotel in New York. The night before her birth the right name for her came to Enrico—Gloria. "Because," he said, "she will be my crowning glory."

But, true to his Neapolitan exuberance, he felt that one little name, all alone without any little playmates, was not right at all. So he surrounded it with a whole cluster of other names: Grazianna, a compound meaning "gratitude to Anna," in token of his deep affection for his mother; Ameriga, because the baby was born in New York; Vittoria, because the Allies had won World War I; and Maria, for the Virgin Mary.

When the baby appeared in the world he ordered champagne for the entire staff of the Knickerbocker and gave Gloria Grazianna Ameriga Vittoria Maria a drop from the end of his little finger. That night he sang *L'Elisir d'Amore* at the Met and there were loud shouts from the gallery of "*Viva Papa!*"

In April 1920, he went to Cuba, again for an enormous fee per performance. It was another triumphal tour. Turning from descriptions of ovations to him, he complained to Dorothy about his entourage.

"They are so stupid and at the same time noughty. More I do, more they serve me bad. Punzo is the limit! He try to put Mario in bad light with me and there is fight every moment between everybody, included myself.

". . . The only moment which I am quite [quiet] is when I am here to write to you, or when I am enclosed in the bath.

"Nevermaind! We born for working and for suffrence, and we must took the life as God send to us."

Returning to his singing, he wrote: "I win another battle with my second performance of 'Martha.' I took the public by the—what you call the lower part of the mouth, 'il mento,' [chin] and shake terribly until he come down at my feet."

At one of his Havana appearances somebody threw a bomb during the second act of *Aïda*. Caruso was knocked down by the explosion. As soon as he had picked himself up, he rushed out to cable his wife that he was all right. Whether it had been intended for the tenor or the audience was not quite clear. About thirty persons were injured. "Fortunately," wrote Caruso, "the public went out slowly and nothing happened."

A few days later he was back in New York, with a fine diamond watch and a lump of gold bigger than an egg for his wife.

CHAPTER **24**

SHOWERS OF GOLD

Date: 1891; *Scene:* The church at the village of Maiori, near Naples; *Occasion:* A festival of church music; *Singer:* Enrico Caruso; *Attendance:* 200 (at a guess); *Audience reaction:* Unknown; nobody bothered to record it; *Singer's fee:* $2.00.

Date: 1920; *Scene:* Bull ring, Mexico City; *Occasion:* Outdoor operatic concert; *Singer:* Enrico Caruso; *Attendance:* 25,000; *Audience reaction:* Delirious enthusiasm; *Singer's fee:* $15,000.

That second figure of remuneration, please note, is 7,500 times as large as the first. The two figures together, I think, give a rough idea of the Arabian Nights success achieved, within the span of a single generation, by Caruso the Great.

For each of several appearances in Mexico City, Caruso received that record total of $15,000. A little later, he was paid $10,000 per performance for a short season in Havana. When he appeared in Buenos Aires at the pinnacle of his glory after his New York debut, the Argentines paid him as much as $7,000 an evening for sending them into hysterics. All those fees were far larger than any he ever earned at the Metropolitan Opera House in New York, though he reigned there in unapproached splendor through a round dozen of golden seasons.

Why the discrepancy? It was his own doing. And the reason for it was typical of the man.

His success was so extraordinary that he became the core and pivot of the New York opera season. The Met operatic programs for months ahead were built around him by the management. His rate of payment per performance stood at $2,000. The time came for him to sign a new contract. The management laid a contract form before the tenor, with the fee per performance left blank, and asked him to fill in what he thought a fair price for his services. It was delicately suggested to him that his demands should not exceed $4,000 per night.

At that moment, America looked pretty good to Enrico Caruso. At its leading opera house he was being engaged regularly for months in each season. New York was showering dollars on him in undreamed-of abundance. It had crowned him King Enrico the First and Only, monarch of song, supreme overlord of the brilliant realm of opera.

So it is not surprising that, when that blank contract form was placed before him at the Metropolitan offices, he was feeling grateful toward those who had made it possible for him to return year after year to such a nice place.

Picking up a pen he wrote in the blank space on the contract form "two thousand five hundred dollars." And from that day until his last appearance in New York he never asked the Metropolitan Opera management for a raise.

From the start of his Met career Caruso sang also in concerts, with highly lucrative results. At first he had to turn over to the Metropolitan Opera bosses his total concert earnings, receiving a percentage for himself. Later, as his fame grew, he made arrangements for the managing of his concerts separately from his opera performances. This made his yearly earnings shoot upward at sensational speed. And it must always be borne in mind that it was not New York and the United States alone which were contributing to lining his purse with gold—in proportion as his voice improved and his renown solidified, South America and Europe clamored for him with increasing persistence.

For single concerts in the United States and in other countries he often got as much as he did for regular appearances in operas at the Metropolitan—and, in a number of cases, much more. Once Mr. and Mrs. Perry Belmont paid him $2,500 to sing for them and their guests at a big evening party given by them in Washington; and they also staked him to a ride in a private Pullman from New York to Washington and back.

In proportion as his renown swelled, during the last years of his life, he received, more or less regularly, $3,000 for a single concert in New York and other American cities. Occasionally, in the United States, he received $7,000; and for one concert, at Springfield, Massachusetts, he was paid $8,000.

Despite their highly lucrative consequences to him, Caruso rather disliked concerts. He was not really at home on a platform, in tail coat and white tie. He felt uncomfortable; he undoubtedly missed the trappings of his operatic roles—of martial Rhadamès and elegant Des Grieux and heartbroken Canio. He was essentially a stage singer, born to wear brilliant stage finery and make brilliant stage love to brilliant divas and die (or inflict) brilliant stage deaths. And you could not do any of those things at Mrs. Astor's or Mr. Otto Kahn's or Mrs. Perry Belmont's!

Another shower of gold fell on him in the shape of earnings from reproductions of his voice on phonograph recordings. From 1904, the year after his New York debut, he earned a fortune from records of his voice made in the United States. This income totaled $1,825,000 between

1904 and 1920, or more than $115,000 a year. In the year of the tenor's death, 1921, the income accruing to his estate on account of recordings of his voice leaped to an all-time high of $400,000. Thus, in a period of eighteen years, he (or his estate) received a grand total from voice reproductions of $2,225,000, or close to $125,000 a year.

However, even before 1904, records of the great tenor's singing were made in Europe, before he signed up for exclusive recordings with the Victor Company. Those early European records, primitive even in comparison with the 1904 product, earned a lot of money for Caruso. F. W. Gaisberg, pioneer record-maker for the Gramophone Company of London, estimated that they netted Caruso something like $1,000,000 in addition to his United States records proceeds.

"I made the first Caruso records," wrote Mr. Gaisberg * proudly, many years after he produced them. "They were made when the singer was in the prime of life, on the threshold of his brilliant career." He describes the reproduction method used in those pioneering days as follows: "The singer sang into a small trumpet that collected the sound and directed the waves onto a small diaphragm, which in turn activated the cutting stylus. . . . Caruso's . . . effortless and even production, helped the recording."

Since Caruso was a born singer with a phenomenally accurate sense of pitch, he was, according to Mr. Gaisberg, "the answer to a recording man's dreams."

Gaisberg, accompanied by several assistant gramophone experts, went from England to Milan hoping to interest Enrico Caruso in having his voice recorded for the first time. They secured a grand tier box at La Scala for the opening night (the opera was Baron Franchetti's *Germania*) —and securing it was an extremely difficult feat, since there

* F. W. Gaisberg, "Enrico Caruso," *The Gramophone*, Jan. 1944, pp. 117-119.

was immense interest in the production and seats for it were well-nigh unobtainable. Gaisberg and his associates had been solemnly assured by the providers of the box that the rightful owner, a Milanese nobleman (who would not have dreamed for a moment of allowing outsiders to sit in it) was away from town and sure not to reappear for days.

Unfortunately, he stalked into the box while the overture to the opera was being played, and, in high aristocratic dudgeon, told Gaisberg and the other interlopers to clear out. They objected. Voices grew loud and bellicose. The audience shouted for silence. The conductor and orchestra looked pained and ruffled. And the noble owner of the box, working himself up into still higher dudgeon, challenged one of the gramophonists to a duel. Arrangements for it were made then and there (Mr. Gaisberg's brother volunteered to act as second for his challenged gramophonist comrade). When, between the acts, Gaisberg and his staff went behind the scenes to meet Enrico Caruso and persuade him to have his voice recorded, the duel was definitely scheduled for a very early future date. But it never came off—an old dueling custom.

Gaisberg, filled with enthusiasm for Caruso's voice, which had burst on his ears shortly after the rumpus in connection with the projected duel had subsided, signed him up tentatively for ten recordings for a total of one hundred pounds sterling (a little less than $500 at the prevailing exchange rate). Feeling that he had brought off a big coup, he wired his London head office what he had done. "Forget it," London wired back. His employers were not going to risk one hundred pounds on Enrico Caruso, an unknown warbler. Confident that London would change its mind as soon as it heard the Caruso records, Gaisberg boldly went ahead with his arrangements.

So, a few days later, Caruso appeared at the gramophone recording room followed by an entourage (for even at that early stage of his career Enrico felt that without a dozen-odd followers at his heels he was practically naked). Gaisberg promptly barred the entourage from entering the recording headquarters, since recording processes had to be kept secret from competitors, and, for all he knew to the contrary, the Caruso entourage might be composed entirely of spies working for recording rivals.

So the entourage-less tenor started his recordings with *"Questa o quella"* from *Rigoletto*. "The fame of these records," declares Gaisberg, "spread like a prairie fire"; and, within a few months, when Caruso appeared in London for the first time, his name was already a big box-office draw.

Convincing proof of the extraordinary persistence of Caruso's fame since his death has been provided by the continuing steady sale of Caruso records; and by the fact that, in an effort to preserve his voice unimpaired, there have been re-recordings.

Caruso always had an amusing detached attitude toward his voice. (As I have already stated, his pet name for it was *lo strumento*, the instrument.) It was, to him, something outside of himself. Of course, he approved of it highly, because it brought him streams of wealth, but he acted and talked as if it were no part of the real Enrico Caruso—just something that had been presented to him by a well-meaning but incomprehensible fate.

At first, when enormous earnings poured in, there was no American income tax for the singer to bother about. Toward the end of his career, however, Federal and New York State authorities reached out to take a large slice of his emoluments. Shortly before his death he paid something like $159,000 for one year's income tax, the penalty levied on him because of his princely earnings in this country.

Then, on top of that, there was his Italian tax, charged because he owned that fine villa outside Florence, as well as other Italian property. And Mussolini, after he had come to power in Italy in the early 1920's, saw to it that, after the great singer's death, the Fascist treasury got its full share of the income of the Caruso estate.

All through the years of his glory, members of Caruso's family in Italy profited from his generosity. He gave much money to Assunta, his sister, until her death, and also to his stepmother and his brother Giovanni, who survived him. And he lavished money on his two sons by Ada Giachetti. To them and to his daughter Gloria, the issue of his marriage, and to his brother Giovanni, he left the bulk of his fortune.

What was Caruso's "take" in the years of his highest earning power?

It is difficult to make anything like an accurate estimate of it. But one can make a guess.

Adding together all his sources of income—sixty performances of grand opera yearly in New York (at $2,500 a performance for an annual total of about $150,000); engagements, for about six months out of the year at foreign opera houses, the profits from which probably totaled another $150,000; some $125,000 a year from recordings sold in the United States and another $25,000 from European sales; and about $50,000 yearly from concert appearances—adding all these together, it seems reasonable to estimate the famous tenor's total income, in each of the most golden of his golden years, at, say, half a million dollars. That is the equivalent of 5 per cent on a capital of $10,000,000. Three cheers for *lo strumento!*

CHAPTER 25

SHADOWS

On his Mexican tour the middle-aged Caruso had been buoyant in discomfort, taking the hardships of travel with a laugh. And his letters to his wife often had been the love letters of a young lover singing of his love.

But, on a later tour (his last), in the autumn of 1920, in Canada and the western part of the United States, there was a change. A cold wind seemed to sweep over him. Love still glowed in his letters to Dorothy, but the young lover seemed to have faded from most of them—also, as a matter of fact, the middle-aged Caruso. In the place of both there now seemed to be a tired old man, beset with foreboding, even with fear.

Somehow he had developed a cough and he could not get rid of it and that depressed him. He sang well in Montreal at the outset of his tour; but, later, instead of thinking of his success in that city, he got to worrying about the possibility of failure—a situation typical of the mood which was supplanting more and more his Neapolitan gaiety of heart.

At the concert in Montreal he sang an aria from that veteran old stand-by of his, Puccini's *Bohème*, and, at the end, he declared (again tripped up by the English language) that "a tremendous applause broke down." His confidence having been restored for the time being, the tenor made this cryptic remark to Mr. Coppicus, his manager—probably he was trying to translate into English a Neapolitan proverb: "Who well begin is half of his work."

Things which before he had considered trifles and made into jokes he now found annoying. All the Montreal critics praised him, except one—and, true to his new mood, he let the dispraise of that lone scribe eclipse the encomiums of the others.

Reporters in the past had often tickled his sense of humor and created an atmosphere of lightness and good humor, with the great tenor doing caricatures of his journalistic visitors and himself, and bandying quips with them. But now he was prone to irritation at the absurdity of some of their questions.

One asked: "Will you make an acrobat out of Gloria?" which so incensed her father that he sputtered to Gloria's mother: "I tell you, if was not for such big amount of money which I gat, many time I can send this people to Hell!"

In Houston, Texas, he became enraged at Manager Coppicus because chairs had been placed on the platform of the hall where he was to sing, to accommodate privileged auditors. ". . . I dont want people back to me when I sing. . . . I jomp on him. . . . Coppicus decided to take away all the chaires from the stage. You see, if I dont say anything he will put people even between my legs when I walk."

Having learned of the death of Pane, the old restaurant-keeper in New York, his friend of other days in Naples, Enrico wrote: ". . . Too bad. . . . That is the life. Work, work and after six foot of ground and goodbye!"

When he arrived back in New York he was exhausted. His cold had gone from his head to his chest. He was

plagued anew by those old-time torturers, headaches. True
to the iron in him, he hardly ever mentioned his health;
but that alone told volumes to his anxious wife, who knew
well that only when something trivial was the matter with
him did he fume and complain.

He returned from his tour late in October 1920. On the
15th of November there was to be still another of the
Metropolitan's Caruso Opening Nights. The opera selected
for it was Halévy's *La Juive*. He had not sung in it since
Havana. It behooved him to restudy it.

He was not himself. His cold robbed him of sleep. At
last he called in a doctor, a man whom his wife disliked.
She had not been impressed favorably by his handling of
Enrico's headaches. But Enrico insisted on consulting him
again.

On his opening night Caruso sang well. He appeared in
more performances after that, without serious consequences. But, while driving with his wife one day in Central Park, he caught a chill, followed by a pain in his side.
It persisted day after day. As he left the Vanderbilt Hotel
one evening to sing, he said to his wife, "Pray for me."

The opera that night was *Pagliacci*. In *"Vesti la giubba"*
his voice broke. He finished the aria somehow, then he
staggered toward the wings, almost fell before reaching
them. Fortunately, Zirato, his secretary, having sensed
something wrong, was on the spot, and caught the almost
unconscious tenor in his arms. "My voice . . . I thought
it was gone!" he gasped. The curtain came down.

Three days later, he was billed to appear at the Academy
of Music in Brooklyn as Nemorino in *L'Elisir d'Amore*,
his vehicle to glory at Milan's La Scala. His doctor (Dorothy's bête noire) insisted that he was well enough to sing.

In his dressing room that night, when he rinsed his

throat and spat out the water, he noticed that the wash basin was pink. He gargled again, again he spat; this time the water was red. Undaunted, he told his wife to go back to her front-row seat. She obeyed, terribly worried, for she remembered what he had often said to her: "Tenors die sometimes on the stage after big note, from hemorrhage."

What ensued is best told in her own words:

"Enrico came running out over the little rustic bridge, laughing. . . . The audience applauded wildly. Standing close to the footlights, he began at once to sing. When he had finished he turned his back and reached for his hand-kerchief. . . . When he faced the audience I saw that the front of his smock was scarlet. . . . This time it was an aria and he couldn't turn his back. From the wings Zirato's hand held out a towel. Enrico took it, wiped his lips and went on singing. Towel after towel was passed to him and still he sang on. All about him on the stage lay crimson towels. At last he finished the aria and ran off. The act was ended and the curtain came down. . . .

"Then, as if a signal had been given, a thunder of sound and movement shook the audience. I heard shouts and screams, voices crying, 'Stop him!' 'Don't let him go on!' "

In the dressing room, Enrico lay stretched out on a sofa, deadly white. A doctor was beside him. Around him stood a little group of worried friends. Gatti-Casazza, notified over the telephone of the crisis, had ordered the perform-ance stopped. Caruso's friends—among them Ziegler, the Metropolitan's assistant manager, and Bill Guard—begged Caruso to acquiesce in Gatti-Casazza's ruling, to recognize the justice and affection underlying it.

Caruso, whose will of steel had enabled him to weather so many crises, who had always had a horror of letting down the public which had paid to hear him, weakly nodded his head. Like Canio, the heartbroken clown of *Pagliacci*, whose agony he had so often portrayed in thrilling fashion, he seemed to say, *"La commedia è finita!"*

Bill Guard went out before the curtain and announced that Caruso could sing no more that night. In silence, the audience filed into the aisles and out of the doors. What the singer's decision had meant to him was perfectly well known to the friends gathered around him—there was not one among them who did not realize the significance of the bowing of that gallant head in reluctant surrender.

As he drove from Brooklyn to Manhattan, Caruso was silent about the blow which had felled him. He talked about other matters, trifles; he insisted that the doctor and Zirato come up to his suite for supper—he wanted everything exactly the same as usual, the regular after-the-show routine must be followed as if nothing out of the way had happened. After his guests had gone, he went to bed and soon was fast asleep.

But the shock which had come to him was not to be overcome so easily. At three the next morning his wife awoke to see him getting out of bed. "I must have air," he gasped, half asleep. He went over to the open window, high above Thirty-fourth Street and Park Avenue, and for a moment stared, unseeing, at the street far below. Then he began to climb over the sill. By this time his wife was close beside him. "I do not know how I reached him in time. I put my arms around him and dragged him back. Without a word he lay down on his bed and slept again. Perhaps he had had a dream. We did not speak of it, and I think he never remembered."

Next day he was up and about, refusing to stay in bed. Preparations were under way for little Gloria's Christmas, a few days off, and, chuckling as if he were a playmate of her own age, he joined in getting ready her celebration of the day. The doctor came—again the one on whom Dorothy looked askance. "Just intercostal neuralgia—nothing to worry about." Gatti-Casazza oscillated, like a portly pendulum, between the Metropolitan Opera House and the Vanderbilt.

But acting normally could not make things normal. It soon became clear that Caruso could not sing in *L'Elisir d'Amore*, billed for December 21st. All those around him urged him to rest for three days, to concentrate on getting well enough to sing on Christmas Eve. Again Caruso—a weakened, apprehensive Caruso—nodded his head.

Early on the day before Christmas, with his appearance in *La Juive* only a few hours away, Gatti-Casazza, his manager and friend, said to him, referring to whether or not he should sing that night: "Caruso, this is a matter for you alone. I don't want to make any suggestion. You have always decided everything concerning your performances."

And Caruso answered: "*Padrone* [boss], I will sing."

At the performance, it soon became evident that he was in difficulties. Bodanzky, the conductor, hurried, between the acts, to the tenor's dressing room, to urge him to allow certain cuts to be made in the score, in order to shorten his ordeal. Caruso flatly refused to have this done.

Somehow, drawing once more on the steel which had never failed to sustain him, he sang his role in *La Juive* to the end. That steel propped him up when he faltered, stiffened him when pain stabbed into his side. On his return to his hotel, his wife, whom Christmas preparations had prevented from going to the opera, asked him anxiously how he had fared. "They liked," he answered, "but my side hurt—not strong, but much." He dropped wearily into a chair—that new Caruso, Caruso the old man.

He did not know it—or did he guess, perhaps?—that the performance of *La Juive* in which he had just taken part was the last in which he was ever to appear, that the applause of the Metropolitan's audience that evening—the audience of whom he had said "they liked"—was the last applause he was ever to reap from the world's public, which he had dazzled and delighted for so long, which had rewarded him with such unstinted admiration, which had given him riches, and, above all, solid and sincere affection.

Christmas Day, 1920, dawned with bright sunshine; the Caruso suite at the Vanderbilt was flooded with it, the Christmas tree glistened in its Christmas finery, gift followed gift in a long procession, Gloria squealed with joy at the noise and happiness around her, at the array of new toys being steadily augmented as still more packages were opened.

Enrico handed a big box to Dorothy. "Hope you will like this—it took two years to find." It was a wonderful South American chinchilla coat; it had cost thousands and thousands of dollars.

On the table in the living room was a fat little bag filled with gold pieces, for distribution to all those who worked behind the scenes at the opera house. Enrico poured out a handful of the shining coins before Gloria. "Play with them," he told her. Then he left the room, to prepare for going to the theater and distributing largesse—like the goodhearted monarch that he was, a monarch of song and friendliness.

Gloria played with the gold pieces. Dorothy wrapped some of them up in little boxes—one hundred dollars for the old property man, fifty for the wig-maker. . . .

Suddenly, from somewhere inside the apartment, Enrico screamed. Instantly his wife and Zirato and Mario, his devoted valet, rushed to him. He was in the bathtub, and from it came more agonized screams. Mario, finding somewhere what seemed like superhuman strength, lifted his master from the tub to a couch. Sweat was streaming down Enrico's face.

The hotel doctor came, gave him an injection, went away. The screams began again. For some time neither that doctor nor any other could be found. In despair, Dorothy herself soaked a handkerchief in ether, held it to his face. The screams stopped "but his moans were so frightening that I put my fingers in my ears."

At last a doctor arrived, a good one, one who inspired confidence and hope. After a swift examination, he announced that Caruso had acute pleurisy, which would probably develop into pneumonia.

After that, doctors appeared one after another, nurses were installed by the sick man's bedside, the situation was brought under control. Life for Dorothy and Enrico's friends became the alternation of hope and fear which hovers over those attending sufferers from a desperately serious illness. Three days after he had been stricken, Caruso almost died—only prompt recourse to oxygen saved him—his wife, as his face gradually lost the awful pallor which had covered it, realized that she "had seen death approach a human being, and turn away."

The doctors, in conference, decided that an operation was necessary to forestall another similar crisis. It was performed by a prominent New York surgeon, Dr. John Erdman. Fortunately, there was no need to remove part of a rib—which might have ended then and there the singer's chance of ever singing again.

Hope and fear, fear and hope. Dorothy Caruso practically never left her husband's bedside. And she became less and less satisfied with the doctor, who, ever since Enrico had first summoned him, had incurred her dislike. Now he considered himself the leading physician among those treating the patient; he seemed to think that he outranked them.

At last, when Dorothy learned that he had administered a treatment to her husband without consultation with anybody, she confronted him as he was moving toward the door of Caruso's room, and said, in a shaking voice: "I do not want you to come here again. Please leave now and never come back."

As if he had not heard her, he moved nearer to the door of the sickroom. She blocked his way. "If you take one more step I'll drop you out of that window." He turned, fled down the corridor. She never saw him again.

The weeks dragged on. A few blocks away, the Metropolitan's season went on its way without Caruso, without him who, season after season, had been the shining superstar among its singers.

In February the situation worsened. It became necessary for Dr. Erdman to operate again. He reopened the incision made by him before. In the cavity he found a quantity of poison; only prompt and decisive action could save Caruso's life. That action was taken. And this time it became absolutely imperative to remove four inches of one of the tenor's ribs. Nobody said a word to him about it—they knew only too well what the reaction would be from one whose whole life was song.

Gloria was brought to her father's bedside every day. His son, Enrico, Jr., was sent for from school.

During these months of agony, letters poured in by the hundred; flowers, elaborate bouquets and humble little nosegays, streamed to the suite. Fellow Italians wrote suggesting old, tried home remedies of Italy—massage with onions, wilted lettuce hung around the neck—they sent him amulets and holy pictures, they told him that they were praying for him in their churches.

One morning, half a dozen Italian laborers, engaged in digging up East Thirty-fourth Street in front of the Vanderbilt, filed, with their rough clothes and muddy boots, into the hotel's ornate and immaculate lobby. They stood before the desk.

"What can I do for you?" asked an astonished, supercilious clerk.

"How did Caruso sleep last night?"

They were told, they bowed, they tramped back through the lobby. A few minutes later they were busy again in the street outside with their picks and shovels.

Just as if the most eminent man in the United States were lying between life and death, a room in the hotel was turned into a press headquarters. There, the reporters from all the papers in town gathered, and the frequent bulletins issued by the doctors were snatched from their hands and telephoned to newspaper offices.

One day a madman forced his way into the suite, declaring that he was Jesus Christ and must see Caruso. This made the watchers by the tenor's side realize that the door of the suite must be guarded. The guardian chosen was "Old Schol," a little German Jew, who made umbrellas by day and led the Metropolitan claque by night, who was absolutely devoted to Enrico Caruso. For years he had waited every night outside the opera house to hold open the door of Enrico's car, asking no further reward than a smile and a "Thank you, Schol." Now he was installed at a little table in the corridor outside the Caruso suite, with a book before him, in which visitors—who came by the hundreds—might write their names.

Little by little the patient's condition improved. But X rays showed that his left lung had contracted—this was kept a secret from the singer as was the removal of part of one rib—and his right hand, as he put it, felt "like the foot when asleep."

He spoke constantly of returning to Italy, to Naples. His thoughts turned more and more to the beloved city of his birth. He kept recalling incidents of his early days there, remembering trifles which brought vividly into his New York life the flavor of Naples, of the little things which, together, blended into the irresistible charm of the place.

To offset his appalling weakness, a blood transfusion was given him, volunteered by a young man from Meriden, Connecticut, who, after it, remarked: "I wouldn't change places today with the King of England!" Enrico's reaction was one of apprehensive patriotism and pride of race: "I have no more my pure Italian blood—what now am I?"

And now the return to Italy was definitely decided upon and the mere decision did things to Enrico Caruso beyond the scope of medicines and operations. In May, Mario and Punzo began packing.

Seated at a table nearby, Caruso painfully wrote out check after check—bills, particularly doctors' bills, were dropping around him like leaves from autumn trees. He complained to his wife that he could not find a certain bill—from the doctor who had attended him at the beginning of his illness, the one whom his wife had ordered out of the hotel. She told him what had happened. "But he *did* try to be kind," said Enrico gently.

When he went out for the first time since he had become ill, he chose at a jeweler's shop a gold-mesh bag costing several thousands of dollars, for the wife of the discharged doctor. While he was busy making his choice, his wife saw a platinum chain exactly suited for use with a watch which he had brought her from Havana.

"May I have it?" she asked. "It costs one hundred dollars."

He became very serious indeed. "You know that I have not sung all winter," he said. "I have many expenses—I must pay the doctors." At once she forgot the platinum chain. How could she have been so thoughtless?

He suggested that they drive in Central Park. As the car started, he handed her a little box. My platinum chain, she thought with delight. She opened the box and from it drew a long string of diamonds.

"I give you this," he said, "because it is the first time you ask me for something." Then he handed her another little box, in which was a ring with one perfect black pearl. "And I give you this because you ask with such sweetness."

Among the friends who called on him in his convalescence was Luisa Tetrazzini, the famous soprano, whose friendship with Caruso went back to the days they had both spent in Russia in the early part of their careers. "You are looking happy," she told him.

"Of course," said Enrico. And, after waltzing with her about the room, he pointed to a lot of trunks being packed. "I am going to Italy," he cried. "To Naples!"

Geraldine Farrar, however, who also paid a farewell call at the Hotel Vanderbilt, was shocked by his appearance. "His eyes were pools of sadness," she told me. " 'I cannot sing,' he said, pointing to his throat. 'Geraldina, do you think I'll ever sing again?' And I, God forgive me, lied. 'Of course you will sing again.' "

The day before the date set for sailing they took another drive, in the course of which Caruso stopped the car before a place where he wished to pay a bill for X rays.

The young man who received the check remarked: "By

the way, Mr. Caruso, your rib has already grown half an inch."

"My *rib?*" inquired the tenor, puzzled.

And out came the dark secret of the Hotel Vanderbilt!

When he reached his apartment there, Enrico found Fucito, his accompanist, packing away heaps of musical scores. The singer motioned him to stop.

"I have decided not to take with me my music," he said. Then he walked quietly over to the piano and closed the lid.

They left New York in the early summer of 1921, on the Italian steamship *Presidente Wilson*—Enrico, Dorothy, Gloria, Gloria's nurse, the valet Mario, Brunetta, his wife, Dorothy's maid, Enrichetta, her other maid, and old Punzo, assistant valet. Punzo, like his employer, was returning to the city where he had been born—the city which one of them was destined never to leave again.

CHAPTER 26

"SEE NAPLES AND DIE"

Soon there came a day when Naples, shining in the sunlight, rose out of the sea before Enrico Caruso's moistened eyes, and her loveliness must have seemed to him a caress and a kiss and a song of welcome. What a rich treasure of memories she enshrined for him!—memories of bright days when he had been young and happy—darkly contrasting memories of want and sorrow—memories of his mother, sitting in silence in her poverty-stricken home, thinking of eighteen little coffins, strengthening with her tears the depth and sincerity of his love for her.

Naples! He must have felt, as he gazed on the beloved city from the deck of his steamer, that she would bring back health to his wasted and pain-racked limbs, that she would, by folding him in her arms, plant hope anew in him and send him forth, restored and rejuvenated, to reconquer the world. *Napoli, mia bella Napoli!* If there was a cure for him anywhere, Naples would hold it out to him. For that he had returned to her. Forgotten was his glory, forgotten the thundering applause of enraptured audiences, the taste of fame ever-renewed. What were all of these compared with seeing Naples again? As he looked on the enchanting curve of her water front, nestling under Vesuvius, he must have thanked God for heeding his agonized prayers and allowing him to come back once more to the city of his heart.

A few days after landing in Naples, the Caruso party crossed the bay to Sorrento, that beautiful town of which Enrico had sung the praises so often in *"Torna a Surriento,"* the song which, in the local dialect, describes Sorrento's loveliness and the love which those who live there feel for it. The tenor took a whole floor at Sorrento's Hotel Victoria, overlooking the sparkling waters of the Mediterranean. From the windows, he could see Naples smiling at him—he could see Posilipo, where, with Salvatore Cortesi beside him, he had sung to the crowd which had followed his triumphal progress through the city, and charmed them with the magic of his singing, and lured even the cook from his kitchen.

After some days of rest, he went into Sorrento for the first time and the people made way for him and bowed to him and smiled at him, and little children ran up to him, put nosegays of wild flowers into his hand, refused the pennies which he held out to them in payment. People did not stare at him. They asked no questions. They did not even try to shake hands with him. They understood.

At first, only a few friends visited him. But, after a while, as he felt better, more came. There were excursions—one, a most fatiguing one, particularly deplorable in the circumstances, to Pompeii.

The day was hot and dusty. At the restaurant where they lunched, flies swarmed. But Enrico, filled with some of his old-time zest, refused to cut the excursion short.

Among the ruins of Pompeii, he found a distinguished visitor, the Japanese Crown Prince Hirohito, now Emperor of Japan. While the prince was strolling about, workmen cried out suddenly that they had at that very moment dug up an ancient statue and bronze bowl. Hirohito got quite excited. But Caruso, his sense of humor bubbling up in him again, chuckled to his wife: "The workmen just buried those things!"

He walked for hours under the hot sun, among the ruins, refusing the sedan chairs beloved by tourists. His wife's protests were in vain. But at last his illness again clutched at him, broke into his enjoyment. He suddenly stood still. His face was red. "I think now we send for chairs," he gasped.

Back at his Sorrento hotel, he went right to bed. He was exhausted.

Next day, a young man, who fancied himself as a tenor and had asked to be allowed to sing before the most famous tenor in the world, shyly appeared. He had brought along some music. It included *"M'apparì"* from *Martha,* one of Caruso's favorite and most applauded arias. The youth started to sing it. He was no singer. The notes came out— faltering, wrongly produced.

"No!" exclaimed Caruso. "Not like that. . . ."

"And then," wrote his wife, "I heard a voice! I ran to the salon. There stood Enrico, singing as he had never sung before. His voice was like a shower of stars, more beautiful than it had ever been. As he finished the song he flung out his arms. His face was transfigured. 'Doro, I can sing! I can sing! I have not lost my voice! I can sing!'"

Next day, one of his visitors was Giuseppe De Luca, that much-esteemed friend, he with whom Enrico had lived the Bohemian life in Genoa. Long they talked and laughed about the good old days. A short time after he had left, Mario, the valet, much agitated, told Dorothy that Enrico had another visitor. She hurried to her husband's room. An old man was with him, bending over him, holding a probe in his hand, a dirty hand.

"This is the doctor who took care of my dear mother," Enrico explained.

Before she could stop him, the old man plunged his probe—unsterilized—into the incision in Caruso's side. Much gratified, he announced that the wound was almost healed.

Next morning, Enrico awoke with a fever. And he was frightened. Giuseppe De Luca, hastily summoned, realized that a crisis had come. The Bastinelli brothers, he said, the best doctors in Italy, must be brought at once from Rome.

Next day they arrived. After a short examination they announced that the patient must have a kidney removed— at their clinic in Rome. They fixed a date for it, more than a week away.

That night—Saturday, July 30, 1921—Enrico tossed in delirium. His wife decided to wait no longer for the operation. She got in touch with his brother Giovanni in Naples. Giovanni arrived in Sorrento next morning.

Sunday, July 31, 1921. The journey to Rome, desperately decided upon, was about to begin. Enrico Caruso was seated at a table in the living room of his Sorrento suite, with the glorious panorama of the Bay of Naples sparkling before his eyes.

He was writing a letter. It was for Giulio Gatti-Casazza, for long years his trusted manager, counselor, and friend.

A short time before, Gatti-Casazza had written to him, inquiring diplomatically about the tenor's plans for the next New York season. After all, that season was to open in less than four months—there were singers to engage, operas to be selected for production, casts to be announced. Would Caruso say something about the prospects of his heading some of those casts, as he had so often headed them before?

In his reply—kept by its recipient to the end of his life—
Caruso wrote: "I cannot say anything. I am not yet in good
health. Dear friend, as I write I see my wife sitting in a
corner, weeping. That upsets me. . . . The Good Lord
will do as he wishes. I embrace you affectionately."

At noon the little group of unhappy, terrified men and
women around Caruso crossed the bay to Naples. The sick
man was so weak that it had been decided to break the
journey to Rome by staying overnight at the Hotel Vesuvius, on the Neapolitan water front.

Monday, August 1st. Enrico asked to have little Gloria
brought to him. He played with her for a few minutes,
kissed her. Preparations were going forward for resumption
of the journey to Rome. Suddenly, without warning, Enrico
screamed. Mario rushed out for a doctor. His wife held
Enrico in her arms. He "sounded like a tortured animal—
his voice was no longer human. His screams became long
howls. . . ."

Mario, Giovanni Caruso, the hotel manager—nobody
could find a doctor. Dorothy begged them to bring a
dentist, a nurse, a veterinary—anybody who had access to
morphine and a needle. Through four hours of agony
Enrico screamed. Then, finally, a doctor came to him.
But he had no morphine. When, at last, he obtained
some, his hand shook so badly that Dorothy snatched the
needle from him and herself applied the morphine. The
screams stopped. Enrico sank into a stupor.

Then doctor after doctor arrived. And hope arrived with
them. But, after examining the patient, they shook their
heads. Confirming the verdict of the Bastinelli brothers
they said that a kidney must be removed—that very night—
that the operation must be performed with partial anesthe-

sia, since the condition of the patient's heart was such that total anesthesia might bring death under the knife.

They said: "If we operate he will live two weeks in terrible pain, and, at the end of that time, his chance of living longer will be one in a thousand. If we do not operate, he will die before dawn."

It was decided to operate.

But Enrico's wife begged the doctors to open an incision in the patient's side before the operation.

"Go in four inches," she implored them, "and with your fingers feel for an abscess the size of a walnut. Break it and insert a drain—in twenty-four hours he will be out of danger. I will take all the responsibility. If you don't find the abscess, then you can operate on the kidney."

They refused to do as she wished. Then she begged them to give a blood transfusion. Again they refused. That same day they operated.

Tuesday, August 2, 1921. Dawn came, cold and gray. Enrico's wife was at his bedside—had been, for hours. Nine o'clock struck. The patient groaned—stirred—looked up at her.

"Doro—they hurt me again."

He gasped.

"Doro—I—can't—get—my—breath . . ."

A few more struggles to speak, the pitiful struggles of the dying, and then, at last, the look of suffering left his face. At last he lay in stillness and peace. Silent forever was the Voice of Gold.

All Naples went into mourning. Black tokens of mourning covered the fronts of houses, hid their windows. "*Lutto per Caruso*" (Mourning for Caruso)—those words, in enormous black letters, hung over the city's streets, testifying to the sorrow of hundreds of thousands of the dead man's fellow citizens, a sorrow shared by millions of people all over the world.

On the day of the funeral immense crowds packed the streets along which the coffin was borne from the Hotel Vesuvius to the funeral church; and other crowds of Caruso's fellow Neapolitans, massed outside and inside the church, wept unrestrainedly; and many among them went down on their knees and murmured prayers for the repose of his soul, as he lay before the altar, shrouded in the silent majesty of death.

For the funeral services, King Victor Emmanuel of Italy had offered the royal basilica of the Church of San Francisco di Paola, reserved until then for members of the royal family.

After the services, the body was taken to a cemetery outside Naples. There, half hidden by the flowers banked around it, it was placed in a temporary chapel awaiting the permanent one which the dead man's widow and his brother and his stepmother planned to build as a shrine to Enrico Caruso's memory and a place of pilgrimage for the multitudes in many countries who had thrilled to him as a singer and loved him as a man.

Shortly before the funeral Caruso's widow received a telegram. It was from old Schol, the Metropolitan's claque leader, Enrico's devoted admirer and friend, who had retired to Germany some time before with his life's savings, five thousand dollars. "I am coming," was all it said.

The old man arrived—after the funeral. Not knowing that it was forbidden for Germans to take money out of Germany in those days following World War I, he had been arrested at the frontier of his country, he had been subjected to maddening delay, his money had been taken from him—and now he stood, penniless and robbed of the man whom he had adored, in Enrico Caruso's native land.

He was one of the very first of the pilgrims to the temporary chapel at the Naples cemetery. He stood silent before the body of the man whom he had worshiped in life. He leaned over and whispered to Enrico Caruso, dead among the flowers: "Don't you know poor old Schol?"

There was no answer.

After Caruso's death, thousands of messages of condolence poured into Sorrento. They came from all over the world—an overwhelming testimonial to the admiration and affection inspired by him in millions of people of all kinds in many lands.

After some weeks, his widow returned to her native United States. Old Punzo, Enrico's assistant valet, remained in Naples.

On the last day aboard the steamer which had brought his employer and himself to Naples, Enrico, angered at the old fellow about something, had upbraided him with typical Carusian vehemence, as Punzo stood gazing at his home city.

"You are enjoying to be lazy as usual? Have you no head? Do you forget you have work to do? Go and pack!"

After Punzo had shuffled away, Enrico, turning to his wife, said: "Poor Punzo. I tell you something, Doro. . . . I bought for him a nice house in Naples and put money in the bank for him and his wife. He will have big surprise. We will tell no one in Naples that he was my servant—we say he is my assistant. Punzo is a proud man, and here is his home."

As for Mario, Caruso's valet, Dorothy Caruso bought a

shop for him and Brunetta, his wife, in Florence, and set them up in the dressmaking business.

Old Schol, by her express wish, accompanied her and little Gloria back to the United States.

She turned over Villa Bellosguardo, with the big acreage around it, dotted with farms tilled by Enrico's tenant-farmers, to members of his family. Martino, the old valet, whose fidelity had been rewarded by Caruso with promotion to the post of manager of the Bellosguardo estate, now became also the custodian of Caruso's art collections.

King Victor Emmanuel of Italy, an ardent collector like Caruso, acquired the tenor's collection of ancient coins.

After the new chapel was completed at the Naples cemetery, Enrico Caruso's body was transferred to it from the temporary chapel where it had lain since the day of his funeral. For some time the body remained visible, behind a covering of glass, in accordance with the custom of the Italians in honoring their distinguished dead. Some time later, Caruso's widow obtained permission from the Italian government to have her husband's body concealed from public view, in accordance with the custom of her native United States.

She was lavish in giving presents from among his possessions to many who had known and loved him, that they might treasure them in remembrance of the days when he had laughed with them and sung to them. But one thing which had belonged to him she refused to give away—the white clown's costume which he had worn as Canio in *Pagliacci*.

In New York, she went over his papers. Among these she found a list of 120 persons in Italy, whom he had supported. They did not include members of his family, nor close friends, whom, year after year, he had aided without

Caruso's last self-caricature

stint. Most of them were men and women who had been kind to him in his years of hunger and struggle, when kindness was precious. His wife had never heard of any of them. Enrico Caruso could not see why such matters should be talked about.

FINALE

Did he deserve his unique fame?

I shut my eyes. I see him again, striding along Broadway or Fifth Avenue, laughing, gesticulating, flooding his sedulous entourage of friends and sycophants with the intoxicating wine of his personality.

I shut my eyes. He stands on the Metropolitan's stage, hailed with tempests of frantic applause, after an aria. Among those shouting and stamping and clapping are many who are weeping.

Then—silence falls on all of us. He is singing again.

He is the Duke of Mantua—cynical, heartless, predatory, wicked. He gives us *"La donna è mobile."* Amorous, passionate, he brings to *"Bella figlia dell' amore"* his golden share.

He is Rhadamès. He overwhelms us all with the clarion tones of *"Io son' disonorato."* He makes us feel, in the death duet in the tomb, the celestial loveliness of the music.

He is Turiddu. He is Faust. He is Des Grieux. He is Manrico. He is Rodolfo.

Then, abruptly, all of them grow dim. They disappear into the past whence they came.

Suddenly, he stands out of the darkness of time—alone, racked, deadly pale. He wears a long white smock, with big pompons down its front. His head is crowned with a high, pointed, white clown's cap. He is Canio.

He strides to the footlights. Hundreds and hundreds, sitting in long, silent rows, breathless, chained by enchantment, watch and listen. He opens his mouth. From the lives of those hundreds reality vanishes.

> *"Vesti la giubba,*
> *La faccia infarina . . ."*

Will any other singer ever put into those words the same hopelessness and despair and agony?—and melody?

> *"Ridi, Pagliaccio . . ."*

I leave to others who, like myself, have heard him sing that phrase, the task of describing the impact, the ringing splendor, the shattering thrill of it. As for me, I am content to remember—and to thank God that I shall never forget.

> *"Ridi, Pagliaccio . . ."*

I sit again, among hundreds of other speechless listeners, stunned and shaken by the Voice of Gold. Did he who had it deserve his unique fame? Yes, yes, yes, a thousand times yes.

In the grand main lobby of the Metropolitan Opera House in New York there is one bust. Only one.

APPENDIX

		OPERA	COMPOSER
1903	Nov. 23	Rigoletto	Verdi
	Nov. 30	Aïda	Verdi
	Dec. 2	Tosca	Puccini
	Dec. 5	Bohème	Puccini
	Dec. 9	Pagliacci.	Leoncavallo
	Dec. 23	Traviata	Verdi
1904	Jan. 8	Lucia	Donizetti
	Jan. 23	L'Elisir d'Amore	Donizetti
	Nov. 28	Gioconda	Ponchielli
	Dec. 5	Lucrezia Borgia	Donizetti
1905	Jan. 27	Ballo in Maschera	Verdi
	Feb. 3	Huguenots	Meyerbeer
	Nov. 29	Favorita	Donizetti
	Dec. 15	Sonnambula	Bellini
1906	Jan. 3	Faust	Gounod
	Feb. 9	Marta	Flotow
	Feb. 20	Carmen	Bizet
	Dec. 25	Fedora	Giordano
1907	Jan. 11	Africaine	Meyerbeer
	Jan. 18	Manon Lescaut	Puccini
	Feb. 11	Madame Butterfly	Puccini
	Nov. 28	Adriana Lecouvreur	Cilèa
	Dec. 6	Iris	Mascagni

			OPERA	COMPOSER
1908	Feb.	16	*Trovatore*	Verdi
	Dec.	17	*Cavalleria Rusticana*	Mascagni
1910	Jan.	22	*Germania*	Franchetti
	Nov.	19	*Armide*	Gluck
	Dec.	10	*Fanciulla del West*	Puccini
1913	Jan.	22	*Manon*	Massenet
1914	Feb.	26	*Julien*	Charpentier
1915	Nov.	15	*Samson et Dalila*	Saint-Saëns
1916	Nov.	3	*Pêcheurs de Perles*	Bizet
1918	Jan.	12	*Lodoletta*	Mascagni
	Feb.	7	*Prophète*	Meyerbeer
	Mar.	19	*Amore dei Tre Re*	Montemezzi
1919	Mar.	25	*Forza del Destino*	Verdi
1920	Nov.	22	*La Juive*	Halévy

BIBLIOGRAPHY

BOOKS

Alda, Frances, *Men, Women and Tenors*, Houghton Mifflin, Boston, 1937.

Burke, Thomas, *Nights in London*, Henry Holt, New York, 1918.

Carelli, Augusto, *Emma Carelli: Trent' Anni di Vita del Teatro Lirico*, Prof. P. Maglioni, Rome, 1932.

Caruso, Dorothy, *Enrico Caruso, His Life and Death*, Simon and Schuster, New York, 1945.

Caruso, Enrico, *How to Sing: Some Practical Hints*, John Church Co., London, 1902.

Cortesi, Salvatore, *My Thirty Years of Friendships*, Harper and Bros., New York, 1927.

Daspuro, Nicola, *Enrico Caruso*, tr. by Arrigo Coen Anitua, Ediciones Coli, Mexico, 1943.

De Lara, Isidore, *Many Tales of Many Cities*, Hutchinson and Co., London, 1928.

Farrar, Geraldine, *The Autobiography of Geraldine Farrar: Such Sweet Compulsion*, Greystone Press, New York, 1938.

Flint, Mary H., *Impressions of Caruso and His Art as Portrayed at the Metropolitan Opera House*, Privately printed by J. P. Paret and Co., 1917.

Fucito, Salvatore, and Beyer, Barnet J., *Caruso and the Art of Singing*, Frederick A. Stokes, New York, 1922.

Gara, Eugenio, *Caruso, Storia di un Emigrante*, Ruzzoli, Milan, 1947.

Gatti-Casazza, Giulio, *Memories of the Opera*, Charles Scribner's Sons, New York, 1941.

Huneker, James, *Bedouins*, Charles Scribner's Sons, New York, 1920.

Key, Pierre van Renssalaer, and Zirato, Bruno, *Enrico Caruso*, Little, Brown, Boston, 1922.

Kolodin, Irving, *The Metropolitan Opera 1883-1939*, Oxford University Press, New York, 1940.

Krehbiel, H. E., *Chapters of Opera*, Henry Holt, New York, 1908.

Krehbiel, H. E., *More Chapters of Opera*, Henry Holt, New York, 1919.

Ledner, Emil, *Erinnerungen an Caruso*, P. Steegemann, Hanover, 1922.

Lehmann, Lotte, *Midway in My Song*, Bobbs-Merrill Co., Indianapolis and New York, 1938.

Marek, George R., *Puccini: A Biography*, Simon and Schuster, New York, 1951.

Melba, Dame Nellie, *Melodies and Memories*, T. Butterworth, London, 1925.

Morazzoni, Giuseppe and others, *La Scala 1778-May 11, 1946*, Consorzio Editoriale Saturnia, Milan, 1950.

Peltz, Mary Ellis (Opdycke), *Spotlights on the Stars*, Metropolitan Opera Guild, New York, 1943.

Seltsam, William H., compiler, *Metropolitan Opera Annals*, H. W. Wilson Co. in association with the Metropolitan Opera Guild, New York, 1949.

Sisca, Marziale, ed., *Caricatures by Enrico Caruso, La Follia di New York*, New York, 1922, 1951.

Taubman, Howard, *The Maestro*, Simon and Schuster, New York, 1951.

MAGAZINE ARTICLES

Gaisberg, F. W., "Enrico Caruso," *The Gramophone*, London, January 1944, pp. 117-119.

"Italy, the Home of Grand Opera," an interview with Enrico Caruso in *Etude*, vol. 30, January 1912, p. 112.

Kobbé, Gustav, "Enrico Caruso," *The Musician*, vol. 10, No. 1, January 1905, Boston, pp. 9-10.

Lancellotti, Arturo, "Enrico Caruso," *Musica d'Oggi*, Milan, Anno V, December 1923, pp. 350-355.

Monaldi, Gino, "Enrico Caruso," *Nuova Antologia*, Rome, vol. 213, ser. 6, July-August, 1921, pp. 369-372.

Vernon, Grenville, "Caruso and the Newspaper Man," *Bookman*, New York, 1922.